S.A.C.
Great
YEARS

MSGT. THOMAS KAYE RET.

Order this book online at www.trafford.com
or email orders@trafford.com

Most Trafford titles are also available at major online book retailers.

Print information available on the last page.

ISBN: 978-1-4251-0702-4 (sc)
ISBN: 978-1-4251-9341-6 (e)

Trafford rev. 02/26/2019

Trafford
PUBLISHING® www.trafford.com

North America & international
toll-free: 1 888 232 4444 (USA & Canada)
fax: 812 355 4082

"WARNING"

BOOK IS NOT POLITICALLY CORRECT

Book is written about times when men were men and women were damn glad of it. Our adventures took place all over the world. We lived it. Nowadays young people seldom venture further than a hundred miles from home. As a matter of fact just about everyone in my graduation class served in the Army-Navy and Air Force. Many of the girls in my class also served in the service. In closing, this book relates to bare facts. If you are shy and faint of heart this book is not for you. This is the service before political correctness and women were integrated into the flight crews. However, I must say, they are doing a fine job but they ruined the service for a "man-only kingdom."

M/SGT Thomas Kaye, Ret.

Dedication

This is to thank all the officers and men whose years in SAC and their unswerving dedication to duty and their job allowed the free world to triumph over the Russian Colossus. Their unswerving bravery cannot be minimized. The only ones who understand are us old-timers who were there.

M/Sgt Thomas Kaye (USAF Ret.)

Author

The Blue Sky is a symbol of Air Force Operations. The Gauntlet is a symbol of Bomb - Nav. guiding the airplane from second station. The three bolts of lightning represent the three numbered Air Forces 2nd, 8th, 15th. The olive branch is a symbol of peace thru the power of the Strategic Air Command.

ACKNOWLEDGEMENTS

I would like to thank the following people. Without their help I would have never completed this work. First and foremost, Ms. Nancy Boyer, who edited, typed, and counseled me. She was the wife of M/Sgt. Kermit Boyer, deceased, who was one of the finest; SMS Bruce Reichenbach; Big Bad Billy Bocz; M/Sgt. Leroy Engle, deceased; T/Sgt. J. J. Kallas and M/Sgt. J. J. Motley, who revived my failing memory of some of the things we did.

For: M/Sgt. Leroy Engle   who passed 26 Feb. 2006
       M/Sgt. Kermit Boyer   who passed 7 Aug. 1989
       T/Sgt. Armand Scalzi   who passed in 2003

This page is for my old comrades.

Well, you all have caught the last launch and gone to our final destination. I hope to meet you all there. Perhaps there is a special little bar outside of the Main Gate. It will have a great air conditioner (rewarding us for the years on the hot flight line), good 50's music, and a lot of cold beers. We can talk about launching and recovering F105's, F4's, B47's, B52's, C130's and C141's. The girls there will be young and will hang on and listen to our war stories. We will be youthful again. We will also see our old mentor's at the end of the bar. They will give us the high sign, welcoming us back to the fold.

M/Sgt. Thomas Kaye, USAF Ret.
Author

BOOKS TO READ

Boeing B47 Strato-Jet - Mark Natola

Pilato – Henry Cervantes

Little Toy Dog – William White

Flying the RB47 – Bruce Bailey

Spy Flights of Cold War – Paul Lashmar

Operation Over flight – Frances Gary Powers

As the Crow Flies – Bruce Bailey

B47 Strato-Jet – Tegler

Recommended Viewing

S.A.C.

Bomber B52

Gathering of Eagles

I have put the Glossary of Terms in the front of the book for a few reasons. One, nothing irritated me more than having to go to back of book to find an explanation. I have put it in front and tried to explain it more or less in a story form. If read first, it will remain in your mind throughout the book.

For clarity, I only mentioned Russia and China as an enemy. There were a lot more, missions were flown against Korea, Cuba, Egypt, Iraq, Iran, Somalia and all the soviet satellites such as Albania, Yugoslavia, Hungary, Romania and many more. Outside of Great Britain we had few friends we could count on thru thick and thin times. France was never helpful. I remember when in 1957, I believe, DeGaulle came back into power; he told us to leave immediately. No over flights were to be tolerated whether accidentally or on purpose. This was evidenced by FB111 missions from England to Libya. They had to fly around France and Spain down to Gibraltar to go into the Mediterranean Sea. This caused about three more aerial refuelings than necessary.

There will probably be some mistakes in the book. "Sorry about that," will do better on second book.

THE AUTHOR

GLOSSARY

A/C – Aircraft Commander, senior pilot in charge of pilot, navigator/bombardier and Ravens (Crows, EWOs) on B47 type aircraft.

Alert – A period of time when possibility of war with Russia was increased, i.e.: shooting down of Francis Gary Power's U-2 over Russia and the shoot down of Maj. Willard Palm's RB47H over Barents Sea.

Alert Force – at one time we had 1/3 of all B47s on alert and ready to strike. This was around 700 aircraft located all around the world: in Morocco, Spain, England, Greenland, Guam, Philippines, Alaska and all our bases in the ZI.

Alert Strip – a portion (usually in remote area) of aircraft parking area heavily guarded by Air Police and sentry dogs. Entry limited to only authorized technicians (with special restricted area badges/line badges) and aircrew.

Aircraft:

B-47 – first swept wing jet bomber, designed in late '40s. With six J47 axial flow turbojet engines, flew at up to 600 mph. Restricted to .87 Mach and built by Boeing. Produced in many different models for different missions.

B47B-E: standard bombing platform, armed with up to four 22-megaton nuclear bombs.

RB47E: reconnaissance version for photo mapping which carried up to eleven cameras. Much cleaner version than the bomber model but still restricted to .87 Mach.

RB47H: electronic recon aircraft had three Ravens (Crows, EWOs) located in specially built belly section. It became a very 'dirty' aircraft aerodynamically with many bumps, pods and electronic equipment hanging out all over the wings, fuselage and fin. Consequently, it burned more fuel at the same speeds than other B47s.

EB47E(TT): called Tell Two (or Iron Works) was a special version for listening to radio communications and telemetry data transmissions (**TELINT**). Only three made. Used in Adana, Turkey to monitor Soviet missile launches.

KC135 – a refueling version of the Boeing 707. Used to refuel RB47s and later replaced them on the reconnaissance missions when the RB47s went to the bone yard. It had four axial flow dual spool turbo-jet engines, later replaced with larger fan-jet engines.

KC97 – another fine aircraft built by Boeing, based on the Stratocruiser. Essentially it was a double-bellied B29/B50. Full of auxiliary fuel tanks plumbed to a flying boom operated by a Boom Operator who would insert the boom into a receptacle on the forward fuselage of the B47, amidships on the B45 and on top of the B52 fuselage. It would transfer fuel into the bomber, doubling its range. Later versions had two auxiliary jet engines to help the four R4360 twenty eight cylinder piston engines. That increased their speed about 50 knots, which greatly aided the B47s, which flew just above stall speed, even with partial flap deployment.

ASAP – as soon as possible.

Coffin Corner – max speed flown by B47. To go any faster you would experience extreme buffeting, any slower you would stall from lack of airflow. This changed with altitude and air density. Max altitude with light fuel load was about 45,000 feet.

Blue Cradle – a special group of B47Es from Lockbourne AFB, which had a unique pressurized ECM, pod with two men (one officer and one enlisted) in it, equipped with specialized jamming equipment. They reflexed to Brize Norton, England and were tasked to fly lead with the nuclear bombers to saturate enemy radar defenses. Another thirty of these aircraft were located at home base.

ATO – assisted takeoff. On the B47, eighteen special rocket bottles, located in the aft fuselage, were ignited for boost on heavy weight takeoffs. These were internal bottles that had to be carried throughout the mission – a waste. They were replaced with horse-collars attached under the aft fuselage containing thirty-three bottles, doubling the thrust and increasing takeoff weights to 220,000 pounds. These were jettisoned shortly after burnout.

Bordello – for those that are P.C. or faint of heart, do not read on. For men (GI's, sailors, Marines) read on. All over the world before, during and after WWII and Korea there were 'bordellos' – cat houses, houses of ill repute. They are still in place in foreign countries and pray tell, still in the U.S. Here men went to satisfy sexual desires at a set price (no haggling or room to pay for) and government run in many countries and therefore free from sexual disease. During my day these were usually staffed by women who came to the city after leaving the farm. Perhaps 50-60% of their men had been killed or maimed. Most of the world at that time was farmland, so women came to the cities to work. Jobs were not plentiful so they resorted to selling their bodies either on the street or in the bars and bordellos. Most of the women were DPs and in some countries were thrown into debtor prisons such as Turkey (with their 'compounds'), Morocco, Algeria and Libya (with its walled-in compounds known as 'Medinas'). The beauty and knowledge of some of those women was unbelievable. Some were articulate in five, six or seven languages. The street prostitutes, or "good time girls," were content to be with a GI for a 72-hour pass or a week's leave. They would service us, clean our clothes, show us points of interest in big cities and take care of us. Many of these girls wound up marrying GI's and becoming good wives, being quite happy to have a home, etc. The beauty of the women of London was unbelievable. Greatest legs in the world. After dark, Bayswater Rd, Queensway, Picadilly Circus, Oxford, Cheltenham,

Birmingham, AYR and Glasgow, Scotland were some great places to pick up women.

Commands:
　　MAC – Military Airlift Command, previously known at MATS (Military Air Transport Service, or jokingly as May Arrive Sometime Tomorrow). Once it became MAC in 1966 under the command of General Catton, it became a first rate organization, equipped with top of the line C141s, C130s and C133s.
　　SAC – Strategic Air Command. Portion of the Air Force which had all the strategic nuclear bombers and commanded by General Curtis Emerson LeMay – the greatest general of all time, by my standards.
　　TAC – Tactical Air Command. Contained all the short-range, or tactical, strike aircraft. They were tasked to open lanes for the nuclear bombers by nuking defenses along coasts and borders. They encircled Russia with F84Fs, F100s and F105s.

Crawlway – a small tunnel between entrance ladder and bomb bay on B47s, used for access to arm nuke weapons or for Ravens to crawl back to ECM compartment after takeoff.

Dallas Hut – small houses erected in North Africa for troops to live in. Made from 4x8 plywood with screen from four feet up. It had plywood awnings that folded down to cover the screens in case of a Sirocco (sand storm). The roof was plywood and in the center of the floor was a four-foot square of sand in which an M43 potbellied stove sat. It was fed by kerosene or diesel fuel and was rally comfy in winter.

DDT – a lot of sickness was caused by body infestation of lice and bugs, with no facilities for water or soap. People were constantly trying to find work and sleeping in fields, etc. DDT powders were found to kill infestation so people in mass went through dusting in one year. This eradicated Typhus, Typhoid, Malaria, etc. and DDT was also used to protect crops by spraying.

DP – Displaced Person. During WWII people all over Europe fled the oncoming Germans and went into France, Italy and Morocco to catch ships and immigrate to England, USA, Palestine and all over the world. After the war ended all manufacturing industries had been destroyed, so there were no jobs. The DPs were constantly on the move looking for some kind of work.

Some work was found in the fields and farmers would take in an entire family. There was no mechanization in farming; it was all done by hand. Italy had farming, wineries and a few factories. Life was hard for the DPs. Some women gravitated to seaports and became ladies of the evening, working their trade on sailors. At this time the U.S. was building many (hundreds) of new bases, which put DPs to work. The Marshall Plan, started by Harry S. Truman, started rebuilding roads, infrastructures and factories in order to put everyone back to work. In the long run it hurt the U.S. as they built modern types of electric steel mills using fewer people. When they got up to full production they became stiff competition, beating U.S. steel prices because we had not modernized.

ECM – electronic countermeasures. ECM compartments on "H" models housed three Ravens (Crows, EWOs) and two Ravens on TT models. Compartment had its own air conditioning and pressurization systems. The refrigeration unit turbine screamed at 100,000 rpm and was right inside with the Ravens. The other unit for AC/pilot/nav was on top of the crawlway and usually dug into Crows backs as they crawled aft or forward. Electronic countermeasure equipment broadcast a signal that blanked out enemy radar.

GI – an abbreviation for Government Issue. However, in WWII it became the title of anyone in the military. I loved it and took great pride in being called a GI. It made me feel closer to my country.

Latrine – Usually 150 feet away from Dallas Huts, as it would have to serve two or three squadrons. It consisted of large open showers and many washbasins and toilets.

LOX – Liquid Oxygen. Converters store oxygen in a liquid form. This took very little space compared to oxygen bottles all over the place. It stored ten times the oxygen, which allowed the aircraft to fly 27,000 miles and still have oxygen left.

MD3 – a power unit with a six-cylinder Lycoming engine and several generators supplying DC and AC power to aircraft. The unit was pulled out to the aircraft on its four wheels. The sound of the engine starting up at 0400 in the morning and idling was music to a technician's ears. It was a sound of power with its two straight exhaust pipes. It plugged in just forward of the bomb bay doors and allowed testing of all electronic components without running the engines.

MITO – Minimum Interval Takeoff. During a USCM, aircraft on alert strip would take off at fifteen-second intervals. At times, four or five aircraft would be rolling on the runway at the same time.

ORI – Operational Readiness Inspection. A no-notice arrival of the SAC Inspection Team meant going in the EWP (Emergency War Plan) and launching all aircraft. No failures were tolerated. It caused immediate dismissal of the Wing Commander if they failed. Besides flying, operations, maintenance, fire fighters and security police, everyone was checked and tested – a very grueling three or four days.

Reconnaissance Missions:

Comint (Communications Intelligence) Mission – RB47 equipped with listening devices has ability to vary frequencies to pick up radio or radiotelephone conversations.

Elint (Electronic Intelligence) Mission – RB47H which flew perimeter of Russia and China to locate radar stations and radar frequencies, so in war the strike planes would know which areas to avoid and which jamming devices to use. This started in 1946 with modified B29 aircraft.

Sigint (Signals Intelligence) Mission – early missions flown by RAF and USAF with special people fluent in target language to monitor radio communications. Later, with the advent of tape recorders, everything was brought back for special technicians to interpret.

Photo Mapping – This was done with standard cameras, starting with RB45 and then RB47. Special adapter was used to photograph radar scope for use by bomber crews for use in event of war.

Reflex – In the beginning, once all the B47 aircraft were combat ready, all of them were concentrated in the states. General LeMay decided to increase the number of specialists on all the bases surrounding Russia. Then we would, at a minutes notice, pack clothes and pre-positioned spares in flyaway kits and the complete wing would move to Africa, England, etc., where we would operate our missions close to Russian borders. We would also maintain an alert strip of 15 out of 45 aircraft loaded and ready to go. LeMay determined, after a few years, that sending complete units of 4,300 personnel was not very efficient. He decided to maintain just the strip alert and change three planes weekly. It was more cost effective and morale was better. There is a picture of Sgt. M. Cherim, my friend of forty-seven years, at Sidi Slimane alert guard shack. He sits on a scooter he brought on an airplane, to help him function better and quicker. Also in the picture you see a Dallas Hut that I described and a weapons carrier that the sleeping crew used to go swiftly in case the klaxon blared. This continued until about 1967.

TAD – Navy term for Temporary Additional Duty, i.e.: six months at sea or overseas to Port Lyautey, Morocco, Sigonella, Italy, Black Bushe, England to name a few.

TDY – three letters indicating that you are going from your home base to another location for temporary duty for a period of three to six months. Single men in shops and flight line usually snapped these up. It was an extra $30 a month and the possibility of adventure in foreign countries. You would work hard and play hard between missions. Some of us got to fly in bombers and others in KC97s or KC135s.

USCM – Unit Simulated Combat Mission. This was done periodically and also during ORIs (operational readiness inspections). Aircraft were uploaded with inert weapons and launched in minimum time to fly a mission with air refueling and a city to practice bomb. Pictures were taken of the radarscopes.

WAI – Water Alcohol injection. Special tanks in wings of B47s held 600 gallons of demineralized water, methanol alcohol and fish oil for water pump lubrication. The mixture was critical, had to be within 1% of what T.O. called for. I mixed it on Midway for a C133, which required 72% water, 28% alcohol. I had to take a sample and test it with a hydrometer before servicing. It gave the T34 turboprop an additional 1000shp per engine. The reciprocating engines (4360 and 3350) used a 60-40 mix. This was inadvertently given to a 55SRW RB47H at Bermuda during the Cuban crisis and caused the aircraft to crash.

I want to describe this magnificent country of ours as it was in 1950 and in that era. First of all, you must remember that with all the families that were over here in the United States, there was no such thing as birth control. So everybody had 8, 9, 10 or 11 children. They had them during the depression, so consequently they all hit 15, 16, 17 or 18 years old right around 1950. So everywhere you looked, there were young people, not all these old farts like we have now because we're the young people from that day. The city of Jacksonville, or anywhere you went was just filled with lovely, slender girls and they all dressed so lovely and they had little tiny waists because food was hard to get during World War II and prior to that. All the girls had 19 or 20-inch waists and all the boys were tall and slender. There were no fat people and we had a tremendous amount of pride in ourselves and a tremendous amount of pride in our country. It's just unbelievable when you hear the people talk nowadays. They have no pride and when you look at most of the young people, they look like unmade beds, smell like billy goats and have 15 or 20 assorted earrings through their noses, ears, eyebrows, belly buttons, etc. They don't know how to dress, they don't know how to act, and they have absolutely no manners. When we rode the buses in our days, if I didn't get up and give a lady my seat my mother would have smacked me upside the head and embarrassed me in front of everybody. So if any woman came on the bus, I would automatically get up. You traveled around Jacksonville by bus in those days. Now let me describe Jacksonville. It was a city of lights. At 4:00 a.m., Main Street had cars going up and down it and it was full of light. We had all the stores downtown and their fronts were well lit. Instead of these stupid sodium vapor lights whose blue lights don't put out any light compared to the plain old light bulbs of old, which were aimed downward. The stupid city of Jacksonville spent $5,000 a piece to put up these beautiful lights and then positioned them to shine up in the air. A good example of this is on Forsyth Street. They have eleven of these lights on one block and if you're walking down the other side of the street, it is pitch black. It's pretty damn good if an airplane wants to land there, but we were looking for safety for people. Now there are no lights downtown so consequently, downtown is dead. Saturday and Sunday all the girls would be dressed with beautiful clothes, beautiful skirts, and they would have their little ballerina slippers on with their little purses and gloves. We had about six or seven movies on Forsyth Street and they would all be going to the movies. It was just a magnificent city, the greatest city in the world. That's when I decided I would never leave here. I might ship out and go elsewhere, but I would never leave here. So I bought a home down here when I was 19 years old.

The city was just full of life and of course out on US1 there were a lot of bordellos out there and there were a lot of bars in Nassau County where you could walk in and get your hair parted with a beer bottle with no strain because you went in where the bubbas were. They had bubbas in those days too, but they were proud bubbas. They didn't wear bib overalls and have snuff hanging out the side of their mouths like these pigs do now. At lease they were all dressed well. Most of them carried a knife or a straight razor and if you got in a fight, the best thing for you to do was to run like hell. If you got cut, you just got cut in the ass.

THE COLD WAR

What I'm going to endeavor to do is to try to explain to most people what the Cold War was about. I realize that this is some 50 years later and you're probably not taught this in History. After World War II we were allies with the French, who never won a war on their own and the English and the Russians and us were against all of Germany, Japan and Italy. Well, we triumphed and immediately Russia and Joseph Stalin wanted to become the greatest power in the world. Now, the only thing that was stopping them from being the greatest power in the world was that we had the atomic bombs and we had proved that we weren't afraid to use them. So what they did in essence was to draw a line from the top of the Swedish peninsula all the way through Europe half way through Germany and encompassing Austria, Hungary, Rumania, Yugoslavia, Ukraine and all of Russia and they dropped what was called the Iron Curtain. It was actually a barbed wire fence that prevented people from coming back over to our side. Well, at this time we knew that eventually we were going to probably have to fight a war with them. Now, Harry Truman was in charge of the United States during the beginning of the Cold War and said that if we could just keep from fighting them until they all see television and they all see cars, and they all see plenty in the stores and everything, they will never want to fight a war. So, what it was up to us to do – the United States Air Force, Strategic Air Command and my General Curtis Emerson LeMay, was to protect all of Europe by being able to strike deep within the heart of Russia, where all their manufacturing capabilities were. Now, during the war, as Hitler was coming toward Moscow and Stalingrad, they took all of the steel mills and all the manufacturing facilities and they moved them by train behind the

Ural Mountains. Now, we had never been in Russia at all, so we had no concept of where these factories or buildings or bases were. There was no such thing as running a spy in there. The dreamers of today will say you can just run a spy in there and find out all this information. You couldn't, they tried and the Russians killed every one of them that went on through. It was up to the Strategic Air Command to find some way to find where the targets were and take radar pictures of the targets so we could prepare our bombing crews and our strategic air command to fight their way in, drop the bombs and wipe out these cities and perhaps, if they were lucky, struggle their way out, land back in England, refuel and go back to the states. About 99% of it was a one-way ticket. All the men in the Strategic Air Command who were pilots of the B-47''s and later the B-52's knew it was a one-way ticket. Once we were on the way, the Russians would be trying to strike us and everybody had no way of coming back out a) because the fuel would be depleted and b) because we didn't know what they had for radar and guns or anything else. The Strategic Air Command went to Eisenhower who had replaced Harry S. Truman, and told him, "Look, if we're going to be the protectors of the World, we've got to be able to fly incursion missions and fly over Russia to take radar pictures of all of these places where we don't know where they are at. You cannot send 1,000 bombers merrily on their way and not have a target for them. They must have a target and they must have dummy runs on simulated targets of the same style so they will be able to do this in the middle of the night." Now, you'd not be bombing in the middle of the day, you'd be doing all of this at night which gives you a better chance of survival. General LeMay talked to Eisenhower. Eisenhower said no, we're not going to do it that way; we can't do it that way because that wouldn't be fair and it wouldn't be playing according to the rules. Any flight that we would make trying to take radar pictures, or standard photos, we would be encroachment upon enemy territory and would be an act of war. Really, Eisenhower being a great General during World War II was a little bit chicken in my personal estimation. Because the line was drawn in order for us to do anything we had to have these radar pictures. So we had RB-45's, fifteen of them, stationed in Sculthorpe, England and they had the large radar set with a 17" or 18" radar scope. They had units that would bolt on the top of them and they were able to go over these targets and find them; they could take a radar picture of the target. This could later be brought back to the States. The RB-45's at Sculthorpe had the ideal equipment to penetrate the USSR and bring back radar pictures of all targets for comparison by our Bomb/Nav's. This would also let us find similar cities in the US on which to make practice runs. We were stymied by Eisenhower so we had to find an alternate way to do this. At this time Churchill had been voted back into power and this was what was needed, a strong man who could see into the future and the need for preparedness. The RAF went to him saying our Canberra's cannot do the mission, why not train four (4) RAF crews on B-45's and let them do the mission. He said yes so LeMay and the RAF trained four (4) crews for a spy mission. The mission would cover every major city in Russia. After training, when the time came, all US insignia painted on our aircraft was removed and RAF was painted in its place.

The aircraft took off and went north of Sweden and Norway into the Berent Sea and were in-flight refueled at dusk; they then headed inland. The entire nation was virtually black as very little power was available to the countryside. The planes flew in and there was no opposition, no radar, no guns, no fighter, nothing. The RAF flew all over Russia for 10 hours taking the necessary radar pictures and then flew back to Sculthorpe. Upon arrival the aircraft were pulled directly into the hangar, and all RAF insignia was removed and replaced with the US Stars and markings. The film was downloaded, developed, and sent to Offut, Nebraska to be studied for targeting and setting up training courses. The Russians had no idea that we had been there. LeMay and SAC, after seeing no radar, guns, or fighters at night went back with 30 RB-47E's. They photographed all of the Russian bases in one 12-hour period.

Schools on target and bomb runs were set up and Bomb/Nav's trained and final targets assigned to each crew. The training was endless. USCM's were flown at every ORI and there were constant TDY's so they would become familiar with all countries surrounding the USSR. This constant training went on until SAC was disbanded after the USSR broke up. This was for about 30 years.

After the initial flight by RB-45C's and RB-47E's, the USSR radar and aircraft improved. Therefore, SAC started using U2's at 90,000 feet and special RB-57D's at 103,000 feet. The B57's were English Canberras with larger engines, specially built J57 engines with 10,000 lbs of thrust, and the wings were stretched to approximately 104 feet. These 21 aircraft usually flew out of Brize Norton with U2's flying out of Adana, Turkey.

At the same time SAC was flying RB-47H's out of Adana, Brize, Bodo and other places. The aircraft had a specially built fuselage with three crows (Ravens) sitting in the belly of the aircraft monitoring ECM equipment and recording radar signal strength and location and how to jam them. These were exceptionally brave men. In reality they had no way out. If attacked, in theory, the seats would be blasted out of an opening with knives in the bottom. I don't believe it ever worked.

The Navy had a similar function with VQ1 squadron. They flew the P4M-1 Mercator aircraft. They were powered by 4360 propeller engines with a J33 Jet engine in the same nacelle. This was for dash speed in case of attack. There were only 19 made and the loss rate was high as incursion missions were flown into China, Korea and Russia. When only six were left they did away with the squadron and started using P2V-7's.

To truly understand these incursion missions one needs to read, "Flying the RB-47" by Colonel Bruce Bailey. It tells the complete story of many missions.

Another good book to read is called "The Little Toy Dog" by William L. White for the two survivors of the aircraft shot down on the Berent Sea. The survivors were Captain McKone and Captain Olmstead.

During the beginning of 1955 thru 1960 I went into Adana, Libya, French Morocco, Spain and Norway to train personnel on the B47 aircraft. It was wonderful to be part of the missions flown by these people.

I cannot say enough about the bravery of the B47 crews. In case of war it was a one way ticket very few would survive, however, not a one ever gave up his wings and quit flying.

The recon crews were doubly in jeopardy because on just about every mission they were chased by the Russians. It was unbelievable and they would go right back to get more radar signal and info. The 55 SRW, the wing of RB-47H's, could not give any recognition on missions flown as all was classified.

As I said, my hat is off to these valiant Americans.

Author

This is the story of the life of Master Sergeant Thomas Kaye, U.S.A.F. retired, and his many adventures in foreign places and in the United States. To start I would like to dedicate this book to my mother Mrs. Elizabeth Paulus and I would like to thank God for looking after me in my many adventures. I would like to thank the United States of America for giving me a wonderful education and a wonderful chance to enjoy and reach my aspirations and goals.

The schooling I received was outstanding and my schooling mainly came during the depression era. The schooling I first received was in Millwood, Pennsylvania. I was five years old when I started the first grade. I was in a two-room schoolhouse. Grades one through six were on one side of the building and grades seven through nine were on the other side of the building. I had one teacher, Mrs. Olive Ackerman, who gave us all a fantastic education. She was a very devoted teacher. As I was growing up I was living with my aunt and uncle and their son and daughter. Everyone had come from overseas, so consequently they spoke very little English except for their son Danny.

At a very young age, three or so, I was trying to learn to read. I would get Danny to read me his comic books, and then I would turn around and try to read them myself. Danny would get disgusted with my reading ability. He told me that I was going to have to learn how to read, so he started to teach me how to read. I learned at a very rapid pace. At the age of about five or six there was a comic strip called "Smiling Jack" written by Zack Moseley and it was all about airplanes. This was my favorite comic strip to read.

During that era, you would only see an airplane once in a while. Occasionally, a bi-plane would fly over the valley where I lived. Between looking at that aircraft flying overhead and reading "Smiling Jack" and "Tailspin Tommy," I said to myself that someday I was going to be up there. I will be working and flying in those airplanes. "Smiling Jack" and "Tailspin Tommy" had a lot of adventures overseas and in South America. I said to myself that when I grew up to be a big boy I was going to go overseas and see everything that they saw. Later on in my life, I did try to contact Zack to thank him for setting me on the path of aviation. Unfortunately, he had passed away two years before, but I did meet his daughter Jill, and talked to her many times for many hours.

At this period of time in my life, my mother was working as a housekeeper in Pittsburgh, Pennsylvania. She worked for a wonderful Jewish family named Drucker. She would come and visit me once a month. She would ride the train, and spend the weekend with me. Every three months or so, my Aunt and Uncle would put a tag on my little collar and put me on a train. I would make the trip to Pittsburgh to see my Mom by myself. I made this trip from the ages of five to eight. Nowadays it's unimaginable to think of putting a small child on a train and letting him go on a journey of a hundred miles or so by himself.

The Jewish family had two children named Carla and Melvin. They were a year older and a year younger than I was. The Drucker's said to my mother, "why don't you bring Thomas here to live with us? He will gain an excellent education and will be living right here with you." This would allow me to be closer to my mother. It would be more like a family. Besides, they thought that I was a good little kid that didn't eat a lot. The Drucker's treated me as if I were one of their own. My mother loved this idea, so I went back to Millwood and packed up the few belongings that I had. Then my Aunt and Uncle put me on a train and I went to live with my mother and the Drucker's in Pittsburgh. I immediately went to school and started learning. I learned to have a great amount of pride in what I did and what I learned. I strove to be the best that I could be. I wanted to be first in my class and held that notion throughout my whole life. I never was less than first in any of my classes. Living with the Drucker's, I learned that you must reach for the highest goals that you can and that there was nothing in America that cannot be accomplished.

CHAPTER 1
U. S. NAVY

Between 1949 and 1950, when I was seventeen, it was required that everybody had to go into the military. This was no problem as I had already made up my mind that I was going into the military. I made arrangements in Pittsburgh, took my physical, and joined the United States Navy. From Pittsburgh I went to Great Lakes for sixteen weeks of boot camp. About three or four days after getting there the Korean War started. I went through boot camp and thoroughly enjoyed it. I learned a tremendous amount of things that these young lads don't learn nowadays. During our boot camp we had one hour a day, five days a week, of naval history and the history of the United States. As I meet the sailors of today I find that they don't even know who John Paul Jones was. He was our greatest naval hero during the War of 1812 and was really termed the Father of the United States Navy.

At the end of our sixteen weeks we got no leave time and were pressed into our next assignments. Since my grade were so high for knowledge level testing exams, I qualified to go to school in Bainbridge, Maryland to prepare me to go to Annapolis. I decided that I did not want to go. I went on and decided to become an aircraft mechanic (structural mechanic). I immediately got my orders and went to Memphis, Tennessee to airman preparatory school. Airman preparatory school was nine weeks long. While there I learned the theory of flight, the theory of navigation, the theory of structures, and the theory of everything upon an airplane. This I just absorbed like a sponge. While in there I decided to become an aircraft structural mechanic, which was everything outside of the firewall of the engine. The only things that I couldn't work on were the engine and the instruments. Structural mechanics was a course that I think lasted seventeen weeks and encompassed sheet metal work, fabric work, plastic work, rigging, painting, welding, erection and tearing down and reassembling of an aircraft. When I came out of there I could actually do the work, instead of just being an observer. This was up my alley since I was already very handy with tools before I even joined the service.

During my time stationed in Memphis, Tennessee I occasionally worked extra duty as a gate guard. I guarded the commissary in the middle of the winter, the 10th of December. It was about four degrees above zero and I was in my P-coat trying to stay warm huddled against a smokestack outside this one great building. This was a great motivational factor in my schooling because they told us that at the end of the schooling, the people who scored the highest in the classes would get to pick the billets for their next assignments. A billet is where there is an existing vacancy. They would place billets on the board and the highest sailors in the class could pick where they wanted to go. I think I ended up second or third in my class and I was going to go where it was warm. I was sick of being cold; I lived in the cold all my life. So, I picked Jacksonville, Florida.

I got my orders and off to Jacksonville, Florida I went, giving the cold north the bird. Once I reported in at Jacksonville, I went into an overhaul and repair facility. This was an outstanding place, again, to learn, because they had what was called rotational training. You would go and work in each different shop for two weeks. At the end of two weeks you could pretty well do a fair job on whatever was called upon. You could emulate the civilians who were teaching you. I believe that this was the greatest and the best way for young sailors to learn how to work on aircraft. These systems and these ways no longer exist in the service today. They simply channelize you so much, they fit you in a little slot and they train you in that little slot and that's it. This way, with the rotational training you got to do everything on the aircraft.

The aircraft that I was working on was the F4U1, FG1D and F4U4 and F4U5 Corsair. They were a reciprocating engine, they were called the bent wing bird and the Japanese used to call them the "whistling death." They had an R2800 engine of 2,000 horsepower, an inverted gull wing, and the single seat fighter with six 50-caliber machine guns. It was great for a young lad to be able to work on those aircraft because they were the prime aircraft in World War II. So, I worked on them and as I switched from shop to shop, I ended up working on an R4D, which is a C47 or a DC3. I got a good background in the DC3 termed the Gooney Bird. I stayed there for a period of about one year. Then I had a chance to go to the crash crew. This, to me, was going to be exciting and I would learn even more. As I joined the crash crew, I was trained as a crash crewman and I was sent Temporary Additional Duty (TAD) to be on the crash crew in Green Cove Springs, Florida. (Check out the picture in the book of Green Cove Springs.)

At that time, there were about five hundred ships all sealed, ready, and waiting. There were destroyers, tankers, escorts, everything we needed in case they had to be opened up and go back to war. We were prepared. I was assigned to a ground control approach unit (GCA) that brought the aircraft in simulated conditions where they couldn't see. This same type of unit is still used nowadays. Anyhow, while becoming friends with the people in the GCA outfit, since we were all one unit, they let me sit in and observe. Being that I was nosey, eventually I learned how to be the Asmith Operator and talk to the pilot as he was coming down and bringing the aircraft back in. It was truly thrilling for a 19-year-old to be in on the bottom of that. So, I was there for about three or four months.

This was the time when I started becoming involved in motorcycles. Now, I didn't have a driver's license because I didn't know how to drive a car at the time. But I did have a motorcycle. So, I would ride up to Jacksonville and have a good time. Then I would go back to Green Cove Springs, which is down Route 17 about 30 miles. We had a small town in Green Cove Springs with one policeman. He was a typical snuff-dipping cop just waiting to get some sailor and throw him in jail. So, when you came into town, you came in about 20 miles per hour and you just putt, putt, putted through the town and went out the other side of town heading down for Route 16 and on up to the base. I came through about two or three o'clock one morning and I didn't see the cop sitting in town. So I just eased on down through town and a pair of lights came behind me very quickly and hit the brakes. After three or four times, I naturally thought it was just somebody wanting to race. So I backed down a few gears and then ran up through the gears. He started chasing me. The next thing I knew he turned on his red light. He had captured me. I pulled over and he got his book out and said, "Let me see your driver's license." I said, "I don't have a driver's license." He said, "What do you mean you don't have a driver's license?" I said, "I don't know how to drive a car." He said, "Well, you've got to have a driver's license." I said, "No I don't. I have driven to Pennsylvania twice on this motorcycle without a driver's license. I don't have a car." This totally devastated his mind and he couldn't figure out what to do. I guess his ticket book did not have a space to check mark for 'no driver's license' in those days, remember that this was 1951. So, he took me up to the base and turned me in to the station police and said, "This sailor doesn't have a driver's license and I don't want him driving this motorcycle in town without one. What I suggest you do is teach this dumb sailor how to drive something and get a Navy driver's license and thereby take the navy driver's license downtown and get a Florida license." So, when I got back to the squadron the Commander had heard about it. He restricted me to the base for two weeks. In the meantime, my motorcycle was taken and put in a compound right next to the hangar in which I slept.

I slept on the second floor of the hangar, which is circled in the drawing. It was heart wrenching to be lying in my bunk, looking out, and seeing my motorcycle. I missed not being able to drive it. My Commander took the head of the fire division aside and said, "teach him how to drive a fire truck and we'll get him a driver's license for the fire truck and it will be a Navy driver's license, and then we'll get him a regular license." Therefore, I learned how to drive on an FFN-5 fire truck. After about a week of driving the fire truck up and down the runways and throughout the base, I took my test and got a Navy driver's license. Then I went to town to get my Florida driver's license. It was the only driver's test that I have ever taken in 55 years.

When my TAD was over I returned from Green Cove Springs to the Jacksonville Naval Air Station. Once back, I was then attached to a VA-15, which is an attack squadron of AD4L sky raiders. They could carry the same thing as the broad side of a destroyer. They could carry a torpedo, 12 rockets, 2,000-pound bombs, and 4 twenty-millimeter cannons. What a load it carried. It was not all work. I was able to get into mischief with my motorcycle.

Of course, when I went into the Navy a great to do was made about VD and how we didn't want to get any VD and it was going to kill you and you were going to go blind, etc., etc., etc. So they showed us some movies, the most horrible movies you've ever seen of VD and syphilis, cankers and all of that stuff. In fact, it was so bad when you saw a girl across the street you would look for a brick to throw at her because she would have the potential to give you VD. Even when I would go home on the weekend I would look at my mother out of the corner of my eye and be suspicious of my poor little mother. Well, anyhow one weekend in Jacksonville we were up at 8th and Walnut and this one girl came into the bar while we were in there drinking, dancing, screaming and hollering. She says, "Tommy Kaye, would you take me for a ride out on Hexler Drive on your BSA motorcycle?" I said, "Well honey, I don't have any money for gas." So she said, "I'll put fifty cents worth of gas in your motorcycle and I'll buy you a half pint of whiskey." I said, "Okay, okay, I'm not hard to get along with." She got on my motorcycle (she was a little bit fat) and we went on down to the corner. She bought a half pint of whiskey and some PM (I always thought it meant Post Mortem because it was the most god-awful drink that I have ever drank in my life). We went up to the gas station and put fifty cents worth of gas, that was 2 gallons of gas in the old days, and away we went out to Hexler Drive. It was a beautiful drive; it was winding roads and everything. We turned around and went all the way to Fort George. We had a bridge out there that was being built and if you wanted to go across to Hexler Drive, it had a floating bridge; it was a barge that pivoted. You would get on the barge and go across it and it would pivot to open up to let any boats through. It was a very unique bridge. So, we went out and came on back and I dropped her off at her house and she said, "Why don't you come up with me?" I said, "Okay." Me being known for having round heels and being an easy pushover, I didn't hesitate at all. So we snuck up the back way into her apartment and she says, "I have a boyfriend." I said, "Where's he at?" She said, "Well, he's working 3:00 p.m. to 11:00 p.m. shift and he won't be home until about 12:00 a.m." I said, "Well, it's 10:00 p.m. already." She said, "Well, let's get it on." So we leaped into bed with no further ado, stripped down for action and I attacked her with a great ferocity. In those days, it was two or three climaxes on one erection….Oh, for the old days. Well, anyhow, while we were getting it on for the second or the third time she heard the door open downstairs and said, "He's home, he's home early." I said, "Oh my God, I'm dead." So, I put my pants on and my boots and she says go out this window here, there's a downstairs roof. So I let myself out the window down on the roof and slid off to the end of the roof and then got on my motorcycle and hauled ass, never to venture forth with that girl again. The next night I was in there drinking, dancing and carrying on at the same place and I met my old flame Birdie Marie White. She was a tall, slender girl and she only gave it to her friends and she didn't have an enemy south of North Carolina. So, she says, "Let's go to the beach." I said okay and she put a little bit of gas in the tank and we went to the beach. We came on back and she said, "Do you want a little bit?" I said, "Yeah, where can we go?" She said, "Well, I'm living with my parents now, we can go on the living room floor and get some because they're probably sleeping because they probably went out and got drunk tonight." I said, "No, no, no, no, no, let's go to the bathroom. I'll sit on the toilet and you can straddle me." She said, "No, let's get it standing up in the bathtub." I said, "Lord have mercy, I've never done that before." She was a nice tall girl. The next thing you know, we strip for action and I got her up against a wall and we're playing hide the wienie, or hide the bologna and everything is going good, not changing strokes or anything and I started getting excited and I reached back for a handle. There was no handle, but a shower curtain, so about the time I climaxed I grabbed a hold of the shower curtain, fell back, pulled the shower curtain down, the curtain rod, the whole works came down and I hit the deck and fortunately didn't wake everybody up. We were laughing. We got dressed and she took me out and put me on my motorcycle. I was so exhausted from this action that I had and all the laughing that I did, that I couldn't even get my motorcycle started. She had to start my motorcycle and push it off and I just got on it and rode it and wobbled all the way back to the base. The next night I came in, we had gone to the beach, it was Sunday night, and I met this girl named Beverly who lived in Jacksonville. She was about 16; all of these girls were just about 16, 17, 18 or 19 years old. We were dancing at the sandbar having a good time and when they closed up the sandbar we discussed where to go next. I said, "Let's go down on the beach and we'll walk down the beach." So she and I walked down the beach and I had my leather jacket on and we got way on down the beach where there were no lights or anything and I threw my jacket on the ground and said, "Let's get a little." Being a nice girl she said, "Okay." We got down and I laid her butt on the jacket and then I did the beast with two backs and we were really getting with it. I tended to look back and I and I looked back on the beach and where we had been, there was a groove cut in where I was going with my knees and elbows. They had made indentations in the beach and looked like a giant sea turtle had gone down there. Thank God they didn't have the turtle watchers in those days because they would have thought the turtle flew in and then crawled down the beach and then flew back out again. So anyhow, that was the weekend. I came back to the base and about Wednesday I got up in the morning and realized there was something wrong "downstairs." So I went to the bathroom and when I went to urinate, good God, it was like a logging chain coming out. I said, "I've got the VD, I've got the VD, oh my God, I'm gonna die, my dork is gonna fall off." So anyhow, I got dressed and put my clothes on and went across to the medics, which just happened to be across the street from my barracks. I went in there and they said, "What's your problem?" I said, "I think I got it" (whispering). So they said, "You think you got the clap, big boy?" I said, "Shh." He said, "Look here, we're medics, we know what's going on." So they took me in the back and they took a smear and they milked it down and said, "It looks like you got it. So, this is the way we're gonna do it" Now, you've got to remember this was the old days. He said, "You're gonna eat your meals for the next week in the ward, all the way in the back where all the VD carriers go to eat." We were quite ostracized you know, as we would walk by they would clap their hands. We had to get our three meals a day back there because we were unclean. Then they would give us one shot every day of 250,000 units of penicillin and then in a week everything was gone and we didn't worry about it anymore.

Another funny thing happened after I caught the clap with the three girls in that one weekend. In those days the city would follow up and find the girls that gave it to you and see that they received shots in order to keep the VD rate down. Of course, you can't do that now because of the ACLU, which is why AIDS and those other terrible diseases such as herpes and hepatitis are so widespread. Because you can't trace down anyone anymore, you would be invading his or her privacy. Those who were infected could go on and infect ten more people. Anyhow, a guy from the city came out to see me and interview me. He asked me what happened and I told him about the first girl then I told him about the second girl and about the third girl. He said, "Damn, how do you get all these girls? Do you get girls like that all the time?" I said, "Yeah, all the time. We've got motorcycles and these girls just fall all over you to get on these motorcycles." He said, "Where did you buy your motorcycle?" I said, "Over at the BSA shop on Old Kings Road South." The following week I was in there at the shop on a Friday night and who comes in looking to buy a motorcycle but the guy who took my statement. He bought himself a motorcycle because he figured if we were getting it all he was gonna get some too.

This next story takes place in 1954. They had a big road race, the only one they ever had in New Smyrna Beach, Florida. These were the days when guys hung together and we didn't have to have a lot of money to go anyplace, as long as we had gas money and a couple of quarters to rub together, we could get along. Anyhow, we all decided we were going to see the road races down in New Smyrna from Jacksonville. So, we got on our motorcycles. It was me, my best buddy Hang Belly Hawkins, who I just laid to rest, and then there was Douglas Barnes, who died. He was run over by a drunken judge in Miami. There was Little Irwin and Hazen Willerton and one other guy. So we got on our motorcycles, filled up our gas tanks and we hauled butt down there to New Smyrna. You'll see one picture where we're walking down the main street during the racing weekend. We had a good time. We did very little drinking. We just raced around town and met other motorcycle riders and just generally had a good time. Well, while we were running around we kept running into these guys that had these little plaid hats on who were riding 55 cubic inch Harley KHK's. One would say Pucket of Orlando; one would say Pucket of St. Petersburg, one said Pucket of Daytona, another said Pucket of Miami and another said Pucket of West

Palm Beach. Evidently this one family had branched out and they owned most of the Harley Davidson motorcycle shops in Southern Florida at the time. They put on quite a show, like they were really big and bad like Alan Ladd. I figured it was time to clean their clock so I kept asking them, "How fast will those motorcycles go?" They said, "They're the fastest motorcycles in the State of Florida." I said, "Well, that's very nice. Are you going to be over at the trials this afternoon?" The trials are where they made obstacles and you would have to ride slow and go around the obstacles and in between garbage cans, up hills, etc. etc. They had a nice big two-lane road right in front and I said, "What time are you guys gonna be over there?" They said, "Why?" I said, "Well, I thing my motorcycle will chow down on you and just eat you a new butt." They said, "Well, we'll meet you over there by 1:00 p.m." We were over there about 12:30 p.m. checking my motorcycle over making sure everything was right, ready and waiting. We were sitting there waiting and they came in there with a real entourage of about 30 motorcycles. I said, "Well, which one is the fastest?" This one guy came out and said his was the fastest. I said, "I'm not going to race all 50 of you but I'll race the fastest guy three times; one time from a dead stop and two times from a rolling stop. I'm gonna tell you when I drop the clutch on this BSA; this thing will jump all over the place." Then I said, "Let's get with it and get lined up. Get the place cleared off for about ½ mile." Well, luckily where this road was there was water on both sides of the road, so it wasn't very difficult to clear it. We got people to flag us off, and people at the dead end. Needless to say, I burned them a new ass three times in a row. When I came back the third time he said, "Well, you did it, you did it good." I said, "I just wanted to prove it to myself." We then went on back into town. It was time to get something to eat and I want you to just imagine what six or seven motorcycles looked like. One guy bought a couple of cantaloupes, another guy bought a watermelon and stuck it in his saddlebags and we bought a bunch of bread and bologna and cheese, some mayonnaise, mustard and a couple of cokes – one for each of us and then we hauled ass out of New Smyrna and went out and found a place in the field. We got underneath a tree and had a big picnic. We could have good times without hurting anybody or bothering anybody. It was just a wonderful life.

Another quick vignette occurred one Friday evening about 5:00 p.m. We looked at the curve down by where the shipyards were and here comes this guy around that curve on a Harley Davidson. He had on a leather helmet, his goggles were down and his face was all burned. He saw our motorcycles and pulled up in front of the shop on the sidewalk. He had a chopped Harley, bobbed back fender, small solo seat and a small gas tank, flanders and risers. He had taken his big Harley front wheel off and put a Matchless front wheel and brake on it. He had a set of Chattanooga over and under stacks, which were twin stacks. It sounded good and we looked at his license plate and it said California. I said, "Man, you rode that 'chine all the way from California?" He said, "Sure enough." I said, "Well, we've never seen a California machine, it looks pretty good. Are they fast out there?" He said, "They are the fastest motorcycles in the United States." I said, "Is yours fast?" He said, "Yeah." I said, "Well that's great. My motorcycle is the fastest motorcycle in Jacksonville. Would you like to have a drag race? We have a street about three blocks behind here. We've got a quarter of a mile marked off with paint and the street is deserted now because they're building stuff down the road and there's nobody down in that area. They're building a power plant down there." He said, "Yeah, I'll tell you what, the loser buys a gallon of wine and we'll have a little party here." So, immediately everybody fired up their engines and we drove back there and had three quick races. One from a standing start and two rolling starts. I chowed down on him something fierce. I really cleaned his clock. He went across the street and got a gallon of wine and I went and got some ice and plastic cups to drink out of. We were drinking some purple Jesus; it's cheap wine and made your head hurt so bad the next morning you'd say Jesus, what did I do that for, drinking that purple shit? Anyhow, he was saying, "I've driven 3,000 miles to come home and have my ass beat by a little English motorcycle." Well, Milton Ricks was the shop owner at the time. Milton was in the prime of life; he was about 27 years old at the time and had a magnificent build. He lifted weights and everything. He said, "Shit, sonny, you came 3,000 miles to be beat by that little English motorcycle. I'll tell you what I'll do. I'll outrun you from telephone pole to telephone pole. Me on my bare feet and you on that big 80 cubic inch Harley." Well the guy's eyes lit up and he said, "I can outrun the guy on his bare feet." He was never thinking that a man built like a horse hits the ground going full speed and that stupid Harley is spinning rubber. So, the guy said, "We'll go for $30.00." Milton said, "No, Tommy Kaye's already beat your ass. I'll only take $10.00 off of you." We got out there and Milton took his shoes and socks off and got in a three-point position like a lineman and the guy on the Harley got ready and was winding up his engine. Milton told him, "The minute I hear your tires spinning I'm gone." So, that's exactly what happened, the tires started spinning and Milton ran and he was down at the second telephone pole, leaning against the pole when the guy went by. He said, "My God, 3,000 miles to be outrun by a little BSA motorcycle and then be outrun by a guy on foot. Here's your $10.00. I'm going on home to Fort Pierce." He drove on down the road, just shaking his head. Those were wonderful times.

During this time, of course, I spent plenty of time getting into mischief with the motorcycle in the evenings. I turned around and began racing over the Main Street Bridge. On December 13th Chandler (whose birthday was the same day) and I were racing on the bridge. While we were racing, Chandler fell and slid 450 feet down the street. He ended up with just a broken thumb. Later in life, he ended up becoming a Baptist Minister. I wonder if that had anything to do with it, but I don't know if it did. We also hung out at 5th and Main at Van's Pub and at 8th and Walnut at Van's Tavern. We had some wonderful, wonderful times.

In 1953 I went to the Daytona races. Buck Brigance was one of the star racers at this time. He was riding in the street one day, while I was riding my BSA Super Flash; you can guess what that led to. We ended up drag racing several times down the main drag of Daytona. I beat him three out of three times. Now we get to the girls. One weekend I was riding up over the Main Street Bridge going to Daytona Beach. My friend David Matthew Snyder was riding his Triumph Tiger and I was riding my BSA Star Twin. As we started up the bridge to Daytona Beach I spied a beautiful girl, I looked ahead and there was a beautiful girl, well shaped, like an hourglass, in a peach one-piece bathing suit with white sandals on. What a swing she had on her back porch. She walked like Marilyn Monroe before MM was discovered. I raced up to her and screeched to a stop. DMS went past me as I had a 7" front brake and he had a 6" brake. To this day he says I would never had got her if he had better brakes. I said to her my name is Tommy Kaye and I ride a BSA, do you want a ride? She squealed with delight and climbed on my little pillion seat. DMS said her butt was the most gorgeous he had ever seen. Always thinking of my friend I asked "Do you have a friend for DMS?" She replied, "yes, turn here and go down a few blocks and see if she is home or already at the beach." While waiting for her little fat (isn't it always) friend to get into a bathing suit, I found out her name was Ginger Cos_____. She was 15 years old. Oh hell, I was 20 but so what. We drove to the beach and raced down to where the Daytona races were held in the old days. Half on the beach and half on AIA, we were on a secluded part of the beach and started locking tongues and swabbing tonsils and she was getting hot. I asked if she wanted to go skinny-dipping. She said yes, so we stripped down and hit the water. DMS and his girl were down the beach a ways. We played a while and I said let's go to the bushes. We could take our clothes and lie on them and get some. Yes!!! In about 25 minutes I had scored and it was good. I never worried about statutory rape, hell, I couldn't even spell it. We all stayed together the rest of the day and went to Steak & Shake for supper. I told her I would come down every weekend that I could, and I would bring a sleeping bag in one of my saddle bags and a pup tent in the other bag. We kept this up for about two months – she was insatiable. Then the world fell in. I had to go to sea on a Mediterranean cruise.

During the week I was getting more cooter. They were all 15 or 16 years old. I picked one up walking on Kings Ave. and we went to the old Boy Scout camp and went skinny dipping and got some on the picnic table. I really had a line in those days.

CHAPTER 2
I GO TO SEA. A CRUISE TO THE MEDITERRANIAN

The name of the ship I went aboard was the "Franklin Delano Roosevelt", CVA-42. Captain John Thatch was the skipper of the ship. He was quite a famous fighter pilot in World War II. He designed the Thatch Weave, which was the only way to protect from zeros in the beginning of the war. He was an immaculate looking leader and very fastidious and his ship reflected this. We loaded up the ship, which was not done the way ships are loaded today. Nowadays the ship is brought up to the dock for loading and unloading. In those times, there were no docks in Jacksonville. So what we had to do was anchor out at sea. Then we put everything on a barge and drug it out to the ship. Then everything had to be transferred from the barge to the ship. Once on the ship, we had to put everything away in its proper location. Then we proceeded from Jacksonville to Norfolk, Virginia. Then we went from Norfolk straight across the Atlantic Ocean to Gibraltar.

During this time I was a third class petty officer. I was given the responsibility for five sky raiders and a five-man crew. Two out of the five boys were named Starke, which I will never forget. The first place we went was to Gibraltar. This was our welcome to the Mediterranean. It was pretty crowded in the local bars in Gibraltar, since the whole fleet, six ships, was there too. Then to top it off, there were a tremendous amount of English sailors there. This led to some minor scuffles here and there. Well, my two Starke boys were about 6'3" and they were as mean as wolverines. They started arguing with these two little English sailors as to who was the toughest and the roughest. What the Starke boys did not know was that these two English sailors were on a coal-fired tug that went back and forth between London and Gibraltar. They had muscles that had never been used. So, in the ensuing battle in the alley, my two boys came out on the bitter end and their teeth looked like finger rakes. The English sailors had knocked several of their teeth out.

While pulling Shore Patrol in Algercias, Spain I was scouting for girls bars and where to go on liberty. I noticed a sailor who looked familiar; it was Leo, my old pool-shooting friend. Leo said he was on the USS Monrovia and his brother Stitch and brother Dan were in the fleet also. Leo had spent a lot of his life growing up in the seminary; however, when he found out girls were different, softer, prettier and smelled good, he gave up the priesthood. I still see him at class reunions and he's like me, still working.

After that episode we found that there was a severe lack of girls in Gibraltar, unless you wanted to stand in line. I was elected to take the double-ended motorboat and scout out the little town called Algeciras. It was right across the bay. Now, Algercias was part of Spain and we had to be very careful because at this time General Francisco Franco was starting to get friendly with the Americans. I came over the first time on shore patrol, to scan out where all the girls were. So, when I came back the following night on liberty, I knew exactly where to go. I headed up the street and up the hill. At the top of the hill there was a little bordello with a three-piece band. The best I can remember the band was made up of drums, a clarinet and a trumpet. But more importantly there were several ladies of dubious virtue who could be acquired for a few pesetas. Needless to say, I invested about $5.00 worth of that money in the stuff that the big boys were getting. If you're an older person like me you can probably remember the song "Anna" that was made from the movie with "Silvano Manjano." It was a hauntingly beautiful song and it stuck with me all my like. To think that the first time I heard it was in a bordello in Spain.

After having our fun ashore, we proceeded back to the ship. We went out to sea and did our first complete NATO operation. This was about 1953 and NATO was just coming into being. This was one of the first times NATO ships were working together. It was called Operation Black Wave. We operated like that for about ten days, flying aircraft round the clock. Captain Thatch had been in World War II when his carrier had received a hole in the front of the deck. The Captain had the whole fleet back down to about 11 knots. We flew our Corsairs and Sky Raiders off the fantail to prove that it could be done if we were hit up front, since the world would not cease and we would not stop fighting.

After working on Black Wave for quite a while, we turned around and went to Cannes, France. This was the most beautiful place that I had ever seen in my life. The French language sounded so beautiful that I would sit at a coffee bar drinking that mud all day long just to listen to them speak. Then I had to go invest my money in lots and houses, which meant lots of booze and cathouses. So, I invested a few dollars there and had a lot of fun. After our short stay, we went out to sea and operated for about twelve days. Then we went to Barcelona, Spain.

We were the first ships to dock in Barcelona. Since we had never docked there before, we had to watch our P's and Q's. Franco told the Spaniards not to beat, rob, or mess with the sailors. He had what was called the LaGuardia De Nationale for policemen. They carried German machine guns, we were told. When the LaGuardia ordered you to "halt" they meant it. You had better stop and not say a word because they would shoot you down like a dog. It is still that way 50 years later. Now, Barcelona was a beautiful place. While we were there I took a bus ride up into the mountains of Monserrat. I must describe the bus to you. It was old and falling apart. It was probably a 1938 bus with the engine out in front, like an old car. There was much clashing and grinding of gears going up. It was a little better than a crawl. What was unnerving was that there were no safety posts or metal to keep you from going over the side. We could have ridden a cog railway up, but we thought this was faster and safer. Upon getting to the church there was a restaurant so we went in and ate many sandwiches. We then went inside of the monastery. It was definitely something to see, especially as it was built on the side of the mountain a couple of thousand feet up (see picture on back page). They had what was called the Black Virgin statue. The Virgin Mary had turned black from soot from candles. You will see pictures of this later on in the book. Soon it was time to go down. Well, going down was very frightening. Remember, there were no safety posts. The driver was having trouble slowing the bus. He got stopped and got some wrenches to add to the brakes. The bus was so old it had mechanical brakes. He had to add length of brake rods. Once he was done and we started back down, it was very quiet. You could hear everyone's heart beating. We made it OK, but what a ride. After we operated in Barcelona for another ten or fifteen days we went into Genoa, Italy.

Genoa was a lovely place with a lot of good music and singers. They had a Madam Rinas there. Madam Rinas was a cathouse on the top of a building. You had to ride an elevator to the sixth floor. This was pretty high class for us sailors. When you walked into this place it was full of pillars. Against each pillar there was a beautiful girl dressed in nothing but gauze. For 1,000 lira, which was about $1.25 at the time, you could have one of these girls. Now, you must remember that this was after World War II. There were tens of thousands of displaced people and very little work. So women naturally turned to selling their bodies in order to make ends meet. And of course, as sailors, we did our part in order to give them plenty of money for food and everything else. It was our way of helping the world get better.

I was going repeatedly on shore patrol and regular liberty. While on liberty, I fell desperately in love with another little redhead named Aurora, in the Black Cat nightclub. Of course, we indulged and I donated money to the cause, because they didn't have enough money and they needed food. The women in those days were like the women at home. Everyone was slender; there were very few fat people in the world at the time, not like it is now. In the 30's, 40's and early 50's money was not plentiful so you just had enough money to get along on. Consequently, all the girls at home in the States and all the girls in Europe were slender and vivacious looking with beautiful skin. They weren't big fat porkers like they are now.

From there we went to Naples, again I pulled shore patrol duty. One night while in the Trocidero Club I saw a big round table inside a round booth and I saw a Chief leaning back like he was passed out. So I told the boys at the table, "Look, you're gonna have to get rid of the Chief, because if the Shore Patrol Officer comes around and he sees that he's passed out, I'll get in trouble." They argued saying there's nothing the matter with him, "he's all right, he's all right." Anyhow, I came back in about five minutes and I said, "Okay, get him out" and they told me, "Just look under the table."

As I looked under the table, there was a girl under there giving him a hum job. The chief was all right and his eyes opened up about five minutes later.

We also had the opportunity to go to Rome at this time, so my buddy Kelly and I plus another five or six hundred sailors took a tour. We rode the train complete with wine bottles flying out the window, all over Italy as we made our way to Rome. We stayed in a hotel at Nova Norda Roma and God; I bet they were disgusted from seeing us. Of course, we didn't do any destruction. It was those damn Marines. They were up on the top floor and boy-oh-boy those boys could party and fight. So, we went out and we went swimming in Mussolini's pool and we rented motorcycles. We rode around the coliseum and saw all of the sites during the day. At night, we came back and went to this giant outside nightclub. People were sitting in tiers on old-fashioned gliders with the tales in front of them. Us stupid sailors were spending money like water thinking we were going to police up on these young ladies of dubious virtue. Once one o'clock rolled around, all we got was a "high ho" as they hauled butt out of there. We ended up walking home, because we had blown all of our money. But, it was fun anyhow.

We then rode the train back to Naples, got on the ship and went to operate for a couple of days. During this time one of our sky raiders went down inland at Toronto. It had an engine failure, so we had to do an engine change. Of course, anytime anything came up where I could go; I volunteered to go along with it to do a lot of the accessory section work on the engine. So we had to load an engine on an L-frame, and then load the L-frame on the six-by truck and the six-by truck on a landing craft. Then we turned around and loaded all of our toolboxes where we could on the truck and everybody got in the six-by and away we went. We landed on the beach, drove out very carefully and went to Toronto airport. It took us three days to change the engine. There was very little to work with. Nothing in the way of food to eat we ate nothing but eggs and tomatoes for three days because they didn't have anything. They were flying Curtiss Helldivers SB2C4's. They had no tools at all to work on them. So, when we finished our engine change and did our slow time on the run up and got ready to leave, we gave all the Italians our tools and I shall never forget their faces when we gave them our toolboxes. We were loved in those days, it's not like it is now.

From here, we went back to sea again for another ten to fifteen days of flights and daily bombing runs and everything. I got to fly in the back end of a sky raider in order to get my $25 flight skins, which was big money in those days. We had another operation with NATO that lasted about five days this time. Everything was beginning to gel and come together and everybody was beginning to work pretty well. Our ship was a fantastic ship again with our Commander, Captain Thatch. He was just fascinating. I read many books on him and the things he did in World War II with next to nothing; it was really unbelievable.

We had a liberty port in LaSpezia, Italy. We were warned it was a hot bed of communist activity. We were to hang together because if a fight would start you would likely get stabbed. They told us to be careful in bars and that agitators were everywhere. I was careful. I pulled S.P. duty and found a nice clean bordello with an escape route out the back door through the alley. As I was on liberty, investing my money in lots and houses (cathouses), I happened to be on the second floor when S.P.'s and SP officers raided the house. I grabbed my pants, slipped my Johnson boots on and climbed out the 2nd floor window on to garbage drums and hauled ass. I stopped two blocks away and put on my pants. I then went shopping for souvenirs like a good boy. A friend asked me to sneak a Beretta (25 cal.) he bought onto the ship. I said how, they search us. He said "under your hat. They never search there." He was correct. I stood close to the railing so if it got dicey I would throw it in the ocean. No problem, never looked under my hat.

From there we landed at Marsaille, France and that's where I had several, several good adventures. In Marsaille, of course, I went on shore patrol to get the lay of the land and I found where we weren't supposed to go and that's exactly where I would go the next day and I would be the first off of the liberty launch. So, I went into these areas and they said there were very evil people there. These guys had their necks tattooed with a dotted line and in French it said, "Cut on the dotted line." But these were mighty fine fellows; there were no problems with them. We were in there and of course we met the girls. I stayed most of the time in the Black Horse Café with a girl named Delorez and I just fell in love with that name. She was a wonderful girl and we did the beast with two backs, and 341/2 and 69 and all the good things that young sailors do to learn what's going on.

From there I went back on shore patrol again and I went with a buddy named Karen who was a French Canadian. We were on shore patrol; some of his friends came up and he said, "see if you can arrange an exhibition."

This was where two girls play 69 and we can watch them and then get a shot of leg afterwards. This was going to be for a couple of thousand francs so he talked it up with a couple of girls. I remember one's name was Vivian. They said they were gonna go up to the second floor here on this square and I said to Karen, "Ask the girls if we can come along to observe that they don't get too rowdy." So, we came along free for nothing in order to observe all these antics. By the time the girls got done, the two young sailors didn't want to indulge, so I had Karen ask the girls if I could indulge in their place and they said "yes." So, here I am with my shore patrol brassard on, my ammo belt, my club hanging down and I stripped down out of my britches. I then made the beast with two backs with both of the girls; ahh, for youth again. So when we got done, I went up and they were washing me off in the sink. They had the louvered windows and they turned around and pushed the windows open to get more fresh air in there. There I stood with my schlong in the sink getting it washed by two girls. Everybody on City Square was up there looking at me. Needless to say, I got my drawers on and we evacuated the area quite swiftly.

We then proceeded onto operations and were flying night and day again. It was a wonderful life; it was exciting and you were on the flight deck working on the airplanes. If you were working on the airplanes at night, you worked with a little bitty red light so it couldn't be seen very far away. It was thrilling to be part of such a big team effort.

From there we went into Athens, Greece. In Athens they told us not to drink any of their milk because it had not been pasteurized and we'd probably get sick as a dog and probably get dysentery. Well, we had a great time chasing girls and indulging a little bit. We got in this one nightclub and there everybody got into a fight and everything was flying; tables, chairs, etc. I was laying down on the floor, a couple of guys walking all over and I was saying, "Damn, this is just like the movies, this is just like big John Wayne" and then I got kicked in the head. Anyhow, we survived that fight and we went on. We got cleaned up and came back the next time and as I was sitting in the restaurant they also told us not to eat any of the meat or anything. The only thing we could eat was eggs and chips. So, while I'm sitting in there trying to eat my eggs and chips, I look at the table next to me and here's some guy getting a hand job while I'm trying to eat. So, of course I counseled him severely that you don't do things like that to get off, you go around the corner or something.

Well, we had not had any ice cream for a long time and very stupidly, and didn't figure that the ice cream was made from milk. A bunch of us had eaten two or three ice cream cones or sundaes and needless to say, when we got back to the ship we had diarrhea. We had it in the worse way. We were getting to the point where we were on a steady run to the bathroom and we were getting jaundice looking. Finally they gave us some stuff to clear it up and then they gave us each a clove of garlic. The garlic did more than the other stuff. When everything else fails, just eat a couple of cloves of garlic and that will kill anything in your stomach when you have the runs.

We went back out to sea and we were not out to sea very long when we had heard that there had been a big earthquake in Argistole, Greece. Argistole is the same place that the movie was made about four or five years ago about Argistole and the Germans in World War II. This was where they killed all the Greeks and all the Italian soldiers. Anyhow, as we approached Argistole, all we saw was a mountain. So the skipper said to us that we were gonna have these bags made which contained groceries and we were to put them over our shoulder, climb the mountain, and when we reached the other side we were to give the food away in the little city located there. Well, the food was Sea and K rations and apples, bananas and oranges. We had great delusions of swapping it for wooly booger. But when we got over the top of the mountain and were coming down we found out that the United States Air Force had already been there. They saturated them with food and we could barely get rid of the food that we had. Damn the Air Force, I'm going to have to get in there and get some of that good stuff.

About this time my hitch was nearly up. I was on what you call a diaper cruise at the time. I signed up when I was 17, so by Federal law they had to let me out of the service the day before I turned 21. My birthday was probably a month or two away. So, they said, "From here we're going to go through the Suez Canal and go on to the Far East. If you want to re-enlist, you could stay on with us." I should have done it, but I didn't. I said, "No, I will go on back home." So, they put me on the AD sky raider and flew me from the ship to Port Lyauty in French Morocco. Now, at this time anyone who was coming through like I was was on the lowest priority in the World. So they had to get some work out of me. So I had to do river patrol there. That was called the Sabu river patrol and we would go out with the boats during take offs and landings of the aircraft. We would be out there to rescue anybody if they crashed. Also, we didn't stay in the standard barracks, we stayed in the Quonset huts all the way back towards the river, probably a mile or two from the regular base. During this time was when Jomo Keynatta of Kenya organized the Mau Mau's. They started chopping off all the white people's heads. On the outside of the Navy barracks where we slept there was a place where you could wash your clothes and hang them up. There was also a rack where we put all the mops and the brooms. Shance, one of the cooks down there with us, came back from the club to the barracks. He was drunk and had a brilliant idea. He thought he would take two of the mop sticks and run them over the corrugated side of our Quonset hut, which was made of corrugated metal. He ran up and down the sides of the building and it sounded like a machine gun going off and he kept hollering, "The Mau Mau's are coming, the Mau Mau's are coming." We ran, I mean we really took off. We went through the screen door right on out and back into the desert. We hid out there for a couple of hours until we finally figured out what was going on. Then we went back and beat the hell out of him.

After staying there for about a month they decided it was time to send me back. I was really enjoying myself because they had P2V aircraft there, the Neptune patrol bombers. They had P4M-1's. There were only 19 of those made. They were P4M Mercator's. They were very swift aircraft made by Martin. They had two 4360 engines and two jet engines behind in the same nacelle. These were spy planes. They had five guys in the back end of the aircraft plus all the gunners. Guns were hanging out all over, making it look like a porcupine. They would fly up and swoop into Russia and agitate the radar. They did lose a couple of them over there. In fact, out of the 19 original ones that went world wide, only six of them were remaining in the space of about three years. It was a pretty deadly job. They also had A2J Savages, which were made by North America. They had two 4360 engines and a jet engine built in the back of the fuselage. The reason they had a two engine aircraft with a third engine in there was because they were designed for the first atomic bombs. Now, you must remember that the first atomic bombs were about seven megatons, but they were one gigantic piece of equipment. They were probably every bit of 5 foot in diameter and 10 to 12 feet long and weighed about 11,000 pounds. It took a pretty big bird to haul them. They were on alert and ready to go at a moments notice. Of course the bombs were not loaded at that time, they were in the big holes in the ground. But they were on alert in case we went back to war with Russia.

After this I went home. I took my discharge and went home and was going to find a job, make a million dollars and enjoy life. When I got out, I went to work for U.S. Gypsum in the laboratory. I proceeded up the ladder of success until I couldn't go any higher, until I became foreman. The current foreman was only 27 years old and unless I snuffed him out I would never go any higher. One day in the lab with all this dust I realized I hated my job. I realized that I was missing my airplanes. I started to think about going back into the Navy. During this time, a friend of mine named James showed up at home every weekend. I asked him, "James, where do you work?" He said, "I'm in the service, but I'm in the Air Force." I said, "But James, you're home every weekend." He said, "Well, we're in the Air Force. I'm in the Strategic Air Command (SAC) and we don't work weekends. One weekend a month we have to stand up and have a parade like you have captain's inspections in the Navy. But we work three shifts around the clock and we have a wonderful time down there." He said, "Furthermore, when you were in the Navy, you had to leave your motorcycle out of the gates and walk all the way into the barracks, two or three miles." At two or three o'clock in the morning that was pretty hard to do if you were three sheets to the wind. I asked him, "What's it like in there?" He said, "You don't eat off of trays, you eat off of plates because we're in SAC. You're treated much better. You don't have any additional duties because you're a specialist." I said, "Oh, that sounds nice." He said, "Oh, Thomas, I forgot to tell you that you can take your motorcycle onto the base." I said, "Onto the base, right inside the gate?" He said, "No, you can drive your motorcycle right to the barracks." Now, the gates of heaven, the pearly gates were opening to me and I said, "Right to the barracks?" He said, "When you get up in the morning, Thomas, you can ride your motorcycle to the chow hall and eat and then get on your motorcycle and ride it right down to the flight line and park it under your airplane." I said, "Say no more, the pearly gates have opened. I'm gonna join the Air Force."

The next day I went to 12th and Liberty, to the Post Office. I told the guy up there, some young Lieutenant that "I want to join the Air Force and I want to go to Mac Dill." He thought I was a smart-ass and I probably was. But he said I would have to show him my discharge from the Navy to figure out what my rank would be. I showed him my discharge papers from the Navy and he said, "Wow, we're gonna give you two stripes, we are going to make you a Corporal." I said, "That's a loss of one, but now I have a dependent because I 'm taking care of my mother." He said, "We'll take care of that. Don't worry about her. Let's take this test." So, I took the test.

It was called the AQE test. The highest you could get was nine. Now, he was sitting right in front of me when I took the test. I was the only one there and I got a 9-9-8-9, which was the mathematics, mechanics, clerical and something else having to do with the military. He said, "You must have cheated." I said, "I couldn't have cheated, I'm sitting here right in front of you. There's nobody else in the room." He said, "Somehow you cheated." I said, "Think about it Lieutenant, there's nobody here but you and me." He said, "Well, nobody has ever gotten a score like that. You're in the Air Force." The Lieutenant swore me in and asked where I wanted to go. I said, "I want to go to Mac Dill Air Force Base in Tampa, Florida."

CHAPTER 3
USAF AT MACDILL

After I was sworn in I went on home and told my mother I was leaving again. I packed my bag, tied it on the back of my motorcycle and as I was leaving town my generator died and I lost my headlight. It was twilight now and I had 200 miles to go to Tampa. I had to be there by 0800 in the morning or start off my Air Force career by going to jail for being AWOL. I tied a flashlight on the side of my headlight with masking tape. Then I fell in behind a car going down Highway 301. That's how I made it all the way to Tampa. I got into the base about 7:30 a.m. and I checked in with my First Sergeant. The First Sergeant said, "Well, the first thing we've got to do is get you some uniforms." He took me over to where you get the uniforms and filled out the necessary paperwork. Then they took me back to the squadron and into the barracks. He showed me where my bunk was, where the footlockers were, and how we hang up the uniforms in a certain sequence. We didn't have any wall lockers. He showed me how to make the bunk and where the latrine was. Then he said, "Go back and get your uniforms, they'll have your stripes and everything on them. Bring them back here, hang them up and get in your fatigues with your fatigue hat and report back to me." So, I went and picked up the clothes and tried on the Blues. The Blues fit great and I tried the khakis on and they fit well. But when I put the one-piece fatigues on and with me weighing 135 pounds, they were made for a guy that weighed 235. But I cinched up the belt and put my hat on and went back to see the First Sergeant. He said, "My God, you look pitiful." I said, "Well, Sir, this is what they gave me." He said, "Follow me and let's go get you more suitable fatigues." I got the other pairs of fatigues and went back there. He was the roughest guy you have ever seen. He went through that clothing sale like a dose of salts. He ripped every one of them a new butt. He said, "Look at that, that poor airman looks pitiful. Now you take where that fold over is and you put big darts in there all the way down. I want it done right now, before he leaves." They turned around and tailored the one-piece fatigues for me and I looked pretty good. I really did. He said, "Okay, let's get back to the office."

Once at the office the Sergeant said, "Well, what do you want to do, what jobs do you want to do on the aircraft?" I said, "Well, I told them what I did in the Navy." He said, "Well, we're specialized, we don't operate like that. So you go take a coffee break and come on back and then we'll figure out what field we're going to put you in." I went on a coffee break. I was sitting there looking at the most beautiful airplane in the World. It was a B-47 Bomber and it was brand new. It had the most beautiful lines even to this very day. It was a six-engine jet bomber. It was the first one to exceed 600 miles and hour. It had in-flight refueling, ejection seats, and could carry the atomic bomb in the belly. I asked one airman who was working on it what made the landing gear go up and down and he said, "Electric motors." I said, "Ooh good, that's one less thing I have to worry about." Then I asked, "What makes the flaps go up and down?" He said, "Electric motors." I thought that was good, there couldn't be much left except steering and brakes. I would get me a racket job and get into hydraulics. I went back to Sergeant Rudner and I told him that I wanted to be a hydraulic man. He said, "Here, take this test and we'll see if you're qualified to be a three-level." I took the test and I qualified as a three-level, which is an apprentice. Sergeant said, "Just for drill, take the journeyman test." This was a five-level and I took it and passed it too. So, now I was coming in as a pre-service man, as a Corporal with a five-level, which means I didn't have to go to school. This actually put me short, since I did not know the aircraft and this was a very complicated aircraft.

I checked into the hydraulic shop and met the shop chief named Bicknell. As I was looking around, everybody in there had a vise and was working on a square object with an eyebolt on one end and a fork on the other end. I said, "What are they all repacking there, Bicknell?" He said, "Those are power control units. There are two aileron power control units and two flaperon power control units. There's the elevator power control unit and the rudder power control unit. They all leak like hell. We have to pull them out and repack them." I said, "Uh oh, I've done stepped into doo

doo now." So then I looked in the back of this shop and here are these big brakes that they were rebuilding. They were off of a KC97 and you had to drill out the rivets, and then put new pads on them with new rivets. It was all done with leg power pushing down on the lever to crush the rivets in there. Consequently, that was the first job I got on and my right leg ended up being as big as a Green Bay Packer's.

After that episode, there for weeks I was allowed to go out on the flight line with Robert, who became my leader for the next couple of years, and my mentor. We went out and I said, "Just explain it to me one time." Robert took me through the whole airplane. Then I said, "Okay, now let me take you through the airplane." I had very good retentive capabilities, so then I took him through the airplane. He was amazed. He said, "Have you ever been to school on this?" I said, "No, I've never been to school on anything like this. But I love airplanes." He then took me back to the shop and showed be how to take the Power Control Unit (PCU) apart, replace the seals in it, and then showed me how to do an operational test on it. Then he took me out on the aircraft and we changed one on the aircraft. Then he showed me how to repair the bomb door actuators and do several other jobs. Then he said, "Well, you're on your own." I said, "My God, don't I need to go to school or something?" He said, "No, you're already an ex-sailor and you've already been to school in the Navy and we can't afford to waste time because we're just learning the aircraft now, so we'll all learn it together." I said, "Fine." Everything was going good and I was quite happy. I was in the barracks and I could ride my motorcycle to the barracks, I could ride it to the chow hall and ride it down to the flight line. Hell, life couldn't get and better than that.

After I got settled in I decided to go to town to try and find out where all the motorcycle riders hung out. Now, we had over 600 motorcycles on the base. This was good for the Air Force because when we went TDY we had special racks for taking our motorcycle with us. All we had to do was drain the gas and tie them down to the rack. Then we put them in a bomb bay where the AIO racks usually went. When you got there, you had transportation. You didn't have to worry about trucks or any other form of transportation. Everything was accelerated and became better for the SAC, which I was a part of now. I was a part of the mighty mailed fist of SAC. The mailed fist was the bombardier's hand controlling the aircraft from the second station, which was up forward and called the bombardier position. The other thing is there were three bolts of lightning, which stood for the three numbered air forces, the 2nd, the 8th and the 15th. Then there was the olive branch, or peace, because the only reason the Russian's hadn't attacked us for 20 years was because we had all these bombers ready and waiting to go bomb the hell out of them if they looked at us cross-eyed. It was time to go to town and find out where all the motorcycles hung out.

As I drove around the base I would wave to other motorcycle riders going by and they wouldn't acknowledge me. Now, my motorcycle had a small tank, small seat, pillion seat, upswept megaphones, flanders, and risers for handlebars. It was different from the majority of what the others had. I was more or less looked down upon. Back in Jacksonville, I had the fastest motorcycle. I was fixing to show these people that I had the fastest one in Tampa. Well, I kept riding up and down Dale Mabry and riding around town, but nobody would even look at me. As I was coming off the base one evening, this guy named Ernie pulled up next to me and said, "Hey there." I said, "Hey, where are you going?" He said, "I'm going to town, do you want to come with me?" I said, "Okay." Ernie and I went down to town to the El Moro club; this was where all the motorcycle riders hung out; strictly motorcycles, no cars or trucks. The El Moro Club was located on Grand Central right where it made an abrupt right turn. It was an old white two-story building. There was a porch on the right side with four steps up. Once into the front door the bar ran straight for about 25' to 30'. There was a divider wall from the floor and up 5' between the bar & a large room full of booths. It had a large dance floor with a jukebox at the far end. The booths had no leather or vinyl, just wood – we were tough, none of that soft shit for us. Out front at the abrupt 90° turn to the left was a big oak tree. Buried in the tree, still actually sticking out, was the femur bone of a cycle rider who was racing another guy and wouldn't shut off and ran into the tree at about 100 mph. It tore him to pieces. However, it was something to show the girls and talk about. So we were sitting there having a nice cool beer. We had a choice of two beers, tropical ale or silver bar ale; both left you with a terrible hangover. They were both cheap beers. I kept asking him, "Well, what's going on?" He said, "This is where most of the guys hang out but they ain't gonna talk to you because they don't know you. They don't know what status you're on; where you are going to fit in." I said, "Well, who's got the fastest motorcycle in town?" He said, "Leroy, he's got a T-110 and he works up at the Simmons Texaco station." As Ernie and I were finishing out beers I got to thinking about what he had told me.

I decided to get on my motorcycle and go see Leroy. As I pulled in and Leroy looked at my motorcycle, which was a BSA, and he was riding a Triumph, he put his thumbs down. He thought that my motorcycle was no good. I said, "Is your motorcycle pretty fast?" He said, "Yeah." I said, "I'll tell you what, I'll come back tomorrow about 2200 since you get off at 2300, and we'll go down Dale Mabry to Hillsborough. There is nothing between Hillsborough and Olds Mar but white road. Then we will have three races; one from a standing start and two from a rolling start, and we'll see who has the fastest machine." Then I said, "Now the other thing is we're going to drag for a beer and I'm not gonna have any money to buy a beer so you already know you're going to lose." He looked at me and must have said to himself, "This guy is pretty cocky or he's crazy." Afterwards, I went back to the base for the night.

The next day I took a half a day off to lube my chain and adjusted everything so my motorcycle was just purring like a kitten, a very loud kitten with the megaphones. I eased downtown and I pulled into where he was working and he said, "I don't get off until 11:00." I said, "Well, I'll sit here and wait." As I sat on my motorcycle on a center stand and watched him as he was selling gas and doing everything else, he said, "Do you want to tune up your motorcycle?" I said, "No, it's running pretty good." He pulled the plugs out of his megaphones, cleaned his carburetors, checked his points, and had everything ready to go. When 11:00 arrived, Leroy shut up the place and we got ready to go on down Hillsborough Avenue. Before we left, I told him, "Now, this is the way it's going to be, after I win, which I'm going to do, we won't tell anybody that I beat you. I don't want to race everybody in this city and wear my motorcycle out. So you can still be the top dog in the city with the fastest motorcycle. Just you and I will know that I'm faster than you." Leroy said, "Okay." Then we shook on it. We rode down to Hillsborough out to the city limits. We stopped, lined up and saw there was nothing on the road. That road was so straight you could see down there 'til the day after tomorrow. I said, "Okay, you call it. We're going from a standing start for about two miles down the road." Well, I beat the hell out of him going on down there. We came back and were going to try a rolling start because he said, "Well, my clutch is sticking a little bit." I said, "Okay, let's go again." I beat him the second time. He said, "Well, one more time. I'll get you this time." Then I beat him the third time. As we were coming back to tow3n slowly and we were talking back and forth, I said, "Now, remember the deal, you don't say anything about me beating you." We went back to the El Moro club. We went inside and again I was a stranger to everybody. They all were looking at my motorcycle and me. We went in and Leroy said, "Two beers over here." He bought the beer because he lost and Dixon looked at him and said, "That BSA chowed down on your ass and beat you, didn't it?" Leroy didn't say anything but everybody knew that I had the fastest motorcycle in town. We had great times down there; we hung out at three or four bars.

ALTERCATION WITH MACDILL'S SPOTTERS
(Officers who could say you were speeding and get you thrown off base)

As I was driving on base for the first time I noticed three white crosses. I asked what was with the crosses. They said that three airman were killed in car accidents last year. I said, "Shit, in the USN we would lose six in a car and thing nothing of it." The guy enlightened me; speeding on base or off would get your vehicle thrown off base, no trial, just turn in your sticker. To promote safety any Officer who saw anyone speeding simply turned in the tag number, and you were thrown off. Thus, I was pretty careful.

At this time, we got a new squadron commander who replaced Major Atkension, of Flying Tiger fame. This officer was called "Boom Boom Bust Him" Utley, also of WWII fame. I only had two stripes ($140.00 a month), so I would keep out of trouble.

J. D. Rio, who got me to join the USAF, introduced me to two of his friends, J.O. and W.J. Wright. We became fast friends and they both rode Triumphs.

One day while working on a 364th Bomb Squadron airplane, I met an airman named Lee Bobo. He rode a Triumph bike. One afternoon while leaving the base we were riding down MacDill Avenue and were caught in a crowd of cars. I did not notice a car with two officers following us. After several blocks of slow riding I said let's pass them. So we went swiftly around 4 cars and cut back in. The spotters pulled up behind us and honked the horn and told us to pull over. We raced away to Interbay St., made a right turn and accelerated away. The street made a wide sweeping 180° turn. I made the turn but Bobo ended up in someone's bushes and the officers captured him. They turned him over to local police.

I raced away to see W.J., who said "you were with us since 1630 hours. I had lost my tag and had an old scooter tag on my bike. I removed my tag, we got our stories straight and after dark I went back to base and parked my bike and threw my shirt away. I went to see Lee Bobo. He said if I would pay half of his ticket he would swear he didn't know me. This I did.

A week went by, and then I was told to put on a Class A uniform and report to the CO's office. As I walked in the door I saluted, looking splendid in my Class A's with 2 rows of ribbons (for service in Europe). I reported and he immediately said, "I'm going to bust your ass." I said, "I've been around for 5 years, what is your reason?" He said, "Article so & so & so." I said, "What's that mean?" He's getting hot now. I then asked, "When did I do this evil deed?" He then specified when. I acted like I was thinking and walked over to the calendar. I said it rained that day and I was eating with three friends at W. J.'s house. He called W.J., J.O. & J.D. in and they all swore I was there. (I was there, but not when the incident occurred). This floored Utley. He then played his last card. He had me stand at attention and called for Bobo. He arrived in 20 minutes. Utley said, "Could you remember the other rider?" Bobo said, "Yes." Utley said, "Is this him?" Bobo looked me up and down and said no, this is not the man." So I beat the CO. He said if I ever appeared before him again, he would take all my stripes.

We built a clubhouse way out in the woods; we cut the trees down ourselves, the old fashioned way with a regular saw and after we built this clubhouse I became a member of the Golden Eagles, which I believe is still functioning to this day. I ended up being secretary for the Golden Eagles. We would go out there on Friday nights and everybody would bring some beer. Let me describe this place to you first. It was about a 20' by 20' log cabin. We poured a concrete floor, materials of which were donated or what we could steal. We built a roof and stole a jukebox out of one place that was closed for the winter. We went to the dump and got a whole bunch of couches to sit around on. We built our own bar. We had it good, we had a place to sit down, we had the bar and then we would bring our own booze out there and we would literally start partying Friday night and we'd party until we passed out. Then they would lay you down and when you woke up you would start partying again and you wouldn't stop until late Sunday night. We had some terrific times. We had a lot of ladies of dubious virtue who would go out to the bushes with us and we would fool around a little bit and indulge, come back in and have a good time dancing and drinking. During this time is when I met my best friend, Jim C…….., who is still my friend after about fifty years. Jim and I became pretty good buddies. One night I was drunk as a skunk, couldn't hit a bull in the ass with a base fiddle. Another club member, Art S…., had brought this girl named Julie out there. Well, Julie got the hots for me because of my magnificent Hercules structure and all 135 pounds of me. We were dancing, and we danced close in those days, so close you would try to get on the other side of the person like you're supposed to be when you dance. Art S…. was pretty drunk and he was sitting over there just watching me. Well, we were drinking and pretty soon I had to go to the men's room. Now we didn't have a men's room like you people would think of, we had a one holer way out there behind the back of the clubhouse. Now in route, as you came around the corner of the clubhouse, there was a tree and there was a branch that was set about 5 feet above the ground, so you had to bend down a little bit to go underneath the branch or you would run into it with your head. So I told Big Jim that I had to go to the latrine and I would be back in a minute and to watch over Julie. I went out and went around the corner, ducked down and walked forward and all of a sudden "Wham," something hit me on the top of the head and I saw stars. I said, "Damn, I must have hit that limb." So I tried it again and ducked a little bit lower and "Wham," I hit it again. I said, "Damn, there's something wrong here." I couldn't go around the other side of the tree because it was too bushy. I went back in there and Jim saw that my forehead was real red and asked what happened. I said, "I walked right into that stupid tree twice and I stooped way over before I went through." He said, "Let's go out there and try it again." So he stayed behind the clubhouse and I went around the corner and, while I was going underneath the tree, Art S…. was standing on the other side of the tree and every time I went under there he would whack me across the head with a young limb and knock me back down. Well, by the time I got hit twice more Jim had figured this out and pulled me aside and went around the corner and beat the hell out of Art S…. and we were friends from then on. We had quite a lot of fun.

I don't want you to think that's all we did was play. We did good work on our aircraft and we were launching more and more of them. We were learning more and more and we were the second bomb wing to get B47's. The sister bomb wing was the 306th, which was on the same base. There was always a competition between the two of us. At times, we would pack up all of our gear and we would fly off to either Limestone, Maine or to

French Morocco to fly one mission. Six airplanes would fly over there, make a simulated bomb run, land and then we'd turn them around and they would fly back to the United States. It was wonderful, the camaraderie was wonderful and these were real guys. This is not to speak down of the guys nowadays because, God Bless them, they're pretty good warriors and they all pull their load. But we were an older breed and a hard drinking and hard fighting group. Nowadays they don't do that; they study their courses, but by God, they are wonderful, wonderful troops.

About this time W.J. Wright worked in JEBU (Jet engine build up) for a Sgt. Railey Myers. There was a chance for me to be introduced to him. Sgt. Myers had been Gen. Curtis Emerson Lemay's (head of SAC) crew chief, flight engineer and top gunner in the 305th BW during WWII. He was like a bear and meaner than any Sgt. I had ever met. I got my favorite saying from him: "If you are looking for sympathy, you will find it in the dictionary between Shit and Syphilis, now get back to work."

Well, it was promotion time and A2C, A1C & SSGT were promoted in the squadron. Col. Utley called all shop chiefs, including Sgt. Myers, together and said, "We will go over the airmen's records and we will vote on who gets promoted. Sgt. Myers said, "Do what you want, but I wan 6 two stripes, 4 Buck Sgts., and 2 Staffs, you all can have the rest." Col. Utley said, "No, I will pass them out and decide who gets what." Sgt. Myers got up, went to the telephone, put in a Priority 4 call to "Lemay" and told him the problem. He then passed the phone to Col. Utley who meekly answered "Yes, Sir" and hung up. Sgt. Myers got his promotions and the squadron got the rest.

That was in the old days.

At the time we were still running around on our motorcycles at night. I ran into a girl named Ginger. Her father owned a bunch of stores in town and a sausage factory. She loved my little motorcycle and she rode a big Harley, so she would always want to ride my little motorcycle and I would ride her big Harley. Well, unbeknownst to me, she would disappear 2 or 3 days a week and nobody would tell me anything. I'd say, "Where's my girl Ginger, where's my true love?" We were together like two peas in a pod and boy, we could dance and whoop it up and have a good time. She took me to all those nice places like Six-mile Creek on the other side of Ybor City, which is the Cuban part of town. She said, "We're going to go out there. They have a good time and they have a lot of fun out there at Henry's Restaurant." We got out there after driving all the way through Ybor city, not looking to the left or to the right because nobody like our looks. We got out there and they were playing cops and robbers in the place using real cops and real robbers. Somebody had tried to hold up the place and guns were going off all over the place. I suggested we leave the area and go back to the Pelican club on Del Mabry, which was much safer. Anyhow, as I was saying, Ginger would disappear for a couple of days at a time and nobody would tell me….and they all loved me because I was the leader of the motorcycle gang and I was easy to get along with and a lot of fun. I got us into a lot of mischief, but no trouble. What they didn't tell me was that she was sleeping with a dude named Israel Johnson, who was a truck driver. This guy was built like an ape; his knuckles damn near drug on the ground and he only had one eyebrow and it started on one side and went clean across to the other side. He carried a big hog leg in his truck and he was just plain mean. So, one night I pulled in there and I looked and she was dancing with this knuckle dragger and I said, with all 135 pounds of me, "I'm gonna go whip that guy's ass and get my true love, Ginger, away from him." So, they pulled me aside and said, "Look, we told you the two toughest guys in town were Tommy Morgan and Israel Johnson, and that's Israel Johnson." Well, about that time somebody had passed a remark to Ira at the bar and he hit him one time. This guy levitated off the ground and went right through the screen and right through the window out into the parking lot. I said, "Goodness, I'm gonna whip his ass? I better leave the area while I can." So, I went out and got on my motorcycle and was getting ready to start it up and I feel this giant paw holding me and he said, "Are you T.K.?" I said, "Yeah, you can see it on my back" because I had a big T. K. painted on the back. He said, "I understand you've been fooling around with my girl. I'm Israel Johnson and Ginger's my woman." I said, "No, no, no, no, no, we've just been riding motorcycles together. There hasn't been any fooling around." So, being not too swift, he believed me and he said, "Come on in, I'll buy you a beer." I really didn't want to go drink a beer with the son-of-a-bitch, but the windows were already out so if he knocked me through the window, it wouldn't hurt too much. We went in there and we later became friends and passed the girls around. We passed another girl named Little Bit around back and forth at the motel some nights when we would go to Sarasota or to the Daytona races. We went to Daytona once a year; this was a big deal. We would all go up in a gang wearing our Golden Eagle uniforms with knee-high boots, black jodhpurs with a yellow stripe up the side, and black shirts that said Tampa's Golden Eagles on the back. We looked sharp and we had the best looking bikes from all around. One day, at a club meeting, I heard about this other guy, Tommy Morgan. He was described as about three ax handles across the shoulders with a very small waist. So, while we were having our Golden Eagles club meeting, the door swung open and this guy stepped into the doorway wearing black motorcycle britches and boots and a t-shirt. He was a giant, a good-looking guy, but he had a little mean look to him. We became quite good friends. He wanted to ride my motorcycle at times and I rode his Harley. He really enjoyed the hell out of that and like I said, we became great friends. He was a good guy to have on your side during a fight.

THE GREAT FIGHT AT "EL MORRO"

One night at the "El Morro Club" we were invaded by a group of car drivers. This was a no-no as the El Morro was for "Marlon Brando" types; (the Wild One's) cycle riders. So, after they drank their beers we invited them to leave; me with my massive 140-pound frame backed up by TJ, Ernie, Leroy and Tommy. A scuffle broke out. As we were fighting, I had picked on a skinny guy but he was stronger than hell. In fact, I was on the losing end. I hollered for Tommy, as he was having great fun throwing guys out the front door. He came over and went back to back to keep extra people off me. I then proceeded to whip "Skinny's" ass and help him out the door. All had a good time but without Tommy it could have been a disaster.

I used to come home to Jacksonville on some weekends. Milton Ricks, who owned the B.S.A. shop, would let me do work for him, such as: pulling an engine and transmission out & dismantling it; grouping parts and keeping all different types of bolts for a different section, i.e. valve covers, valve linkage, head bolts, base bolts, etc. I got so that I could tear down an engine in 45 minutes. One Saturday, while I was at work, a State highway patrolman rode up to the shop. He came in and asked, "Is that Thomas Kaye's BSA out there?" Milton said, "Yes, and it's the fastest in town." The highway patrolman said, "I heard it was fast and I would like to race him." (The shop was located on Beach Blvd. And it was nine miles to the beach with no crossroads). I came around the corner and said, "If I raced you and beat you, you would cheat and call the cops on the other end and they'd put me so deep into jail they would have to pipe sunlight in to me." He said he wouldn't and crossed his heart and swore he wouldn't.

Milton said, "Do it." I told the highway patrolman we would start racing when we get to 95mph. We would be side by side and then turn on. He said okay and away we went. We got to 95mph and he signaled to me to turn it on. Hell, I was still in 3rd gear, so I ran away and got 4th gear and went into my rider's crouch: feet on back pegs, knees tucked in laying on the gas tank, and left hand holding the forks. The only thing sticking out was my throttle hand. I looked back and he was way back. I said I would back off the throttle, sit up and slow down. When I backed off the bike started a high-speed wobble. I poured it on and it stopped. I screwed the steering dampener down, tried again, same thing; pour it on, sit up, same thing. Miles are going by and the beach bridge is in sight. I had better get it slowed down soon. Still running 110 mph I started easing down on the back brakes and slowing down with the throttle still on. Once I got below 90 mph everything was fine. I turned around and went back to the shop. When I pulled in the highway patrolman asked where I'd been. I said I was going so fast I couldn't slow down and told him my story. He said it must have been true because my eyes looked like saucers.

He ended up having Milton build him a Full House Flash and rode with us on weekends. His little son ended up working for me 25 years later.

About this time, I was getting quite proficient on the airplane and they decided to send me to Tucson for three months with a SAC evaluation team. They flew three B47's out there for a week to a strange base. We would have to repair them, fix them and launch them and they would fly a unit-simulated combat mission, come back. We would turn them around and another crew would take them and we continued on like that for three months, just during the week, the weekends were free. So we decided to go to Tucson a couple of nights in a row and I met up with a fellow airman named Tarcen. I had been stationed in the Navy with his brother, so we became fast friends out there, and he, being of Mexican heritage, could speak the language and he would take me into the bars and that way I wouldn't get my head stove in. We met a lot of girls and had a lot of good times. They didn't have any bushes to take them to over there, so we would have to nail them in the car if we had a chance. We spent three months over there. It was a fabulous three months, and besides that, I was getting TDY pay, which was another $30.00 a month on top of my regular pay. This amounted to a total of $90.00 for the three months I was there. Tuscoon was a strange place, weather wise. In the morning we would be freezing and in our big parkas. By 1400 we had shirts off getting a tan. By 1800 we had our parkas on again. I saw it got so hot the tar got soft and the airplanes (a few) sank thru the tar. We had to use lifting bags to pick them up and put steel plates under the wheels and taxi them to concrete pads.

"IN BETWEEN"

One day, after returning to MacDill AFB from Tucson (Davis Monthan AFB), we went on Alert for USCM's. We were all in the shops, so card games and dice games broke out all over the squadrons. I had my $90.00 TDY pay in my pocket. I was to apply it to my cycle payment when I went home after the missions were over.

I was lying on my side on top of the wall lockers watching a game called "In Between." It took no skill, just blind luck. Everybody ante'd up $2.00 apiece in the pot. With seven guys the pot was $14.00. Everybody was dealt two cards. The ideal cards were Ace (low) and King (high). You would then bet a portion or the whole pot that your next card would go in between the Ace, King combination. The only thing is if you got another Ace or King you would lose all your money into the pot. If you had any other card you would win. However, there were a lot of losers and the pot grew by leaps and bounds. Some winners bet a little piece of the pot. I said the hell with it; my TDY pay was extra so I was going to get in the game with the big sergeants. So the lowly Corporal climbs down and within 2 hours had everyone's money; their paychecks, grocery money, booze money, etc. I had between $600 and $700 when the game was over. I had all the money in the game. I lurched off as I probably had $50.00 in coins in my pocket. This, plus my TDY pay, allowed me to pay my motorcycle off a year early. Never again did I see this game played for this amount. I introduced it at other bases while riding in a launch truck. When you had five or ten planes leaving within a few hours, the fastest and the best specialists would be in a bread van type truck. We parked next to the aircraft to be launched. We would play cards to kill time. Seldom was it a money game as my reputation had preceded me.

After paying off my motorcycle I traded my BSA in on a Triumph T-100C. This was a motorcycle that had raced in Daytona. It was running first place for a couple of laps and then my friend Johnny Wilson missed a gear, over revved the engine, and he blew the bottom of the engine out. I had told Jack Kulan, who had built it, that if he would fix it up I would swap my motorcycle in on that Triumph because I wanted to ride it. So, I got the motorcycle rebuilt. It had two carburetors on it, and a remote float bowl. I had brought a tach-drive back from England from a gold star and he cut the cases to make it fit. Now I had a tachometer and knew when to shift properly and I would not over rev the engine. I had upswept megaphones on it, small competition pipes and a small solo seat and piggy pad flanders and risers and it looked just about like my BSA Super Flash. It was even faster, with a smaller engine than my Super Flash had. It was really a good motor scooter and it would fly. About this time, the General's aide met me one day. He was called Barefoot Stew, he was a Captain and he said, "T. K., I've heard about you. You're the secretary of the Golden Eagles club. There's only two or three of you on the base that are in the Golden Eagles club and we would like to set up a motorcycle club on this base. Thereby we would be able to train everybody to ride and give them a course to set and they would have to get a motorcycle license." Now, he was called Barefoot Stew because he hated shoes and he would slip his shoes off every chance he got. He would ride his motorcycle in his bare feet; he would drive a racecar in his bare feet. He was a big, good-looking guy with gray hair. He also, if you're old like me and remember the Vitalis hair commercials, made a Vitalis commercial where he was combing his hair using Vitalis and telling another boy he needed to use Vitalis for his hair. He was introduced as Barefoot Stew and he was the first one that ever skied on his bare feet; that's really where he got the name Barefoot Stew.

Capt. Stuart McDonald was the epitome of a General's aide. With him we started the MacDill Jet riders club. He got us a building on the side of the base close to Dale Mabry Ave. He got us help from AIO Squad (Air installation squadron). We made a fine obstacle course to test people to get a base license. They made ditches, a gravel street (for stopping), a water pit 30' long (for stopping), and everything else we could test them on. After they passed there was no problem. He probably pulled strings so I could make Buck Sgt. Major Utley never forgot me. So it came from above.

In order to cut down drag racing among the men, we set up the first timed ¼ mile in Florida. As a fact, Don Garlets was there when we had our first runs. We ran Timed ¼ mile for several years. As a matter of fact, Jack Kulan, who built my bike for the Daytona race, built up a 40 cubic in. Triumph for Quentin Wall to ride plus he had a Triumph dragster in the open class. People were upset I took the 500cc trophy, Quentin took the 650cc trophy and Jack Kulan took the open trophy.

CHAPTER 4
TDY TO SIDI SLIMANE, NORTH AFRICA

Next, we got ready to take the whole wing TDY. We were going to go to Sidi Slimane, North Africa. Sidi Slimane was located in French Morocco. There being two Morocco's at the time, one was French Morocco and one was Spanish Morocco, they were side-by-side but are now the same country. Now at the time, the French were governing it and Algeria. The FLN, who were the people who wanted to become independent from France and run their own Arab country, turned around and were cutting French men's heads off left and right. So, we were kind of leery about going into town. When we landed we had our motorcycles in there and we immediately started turning our aircraft around, getting ready to launch them and it wasn't but about 24 hours when we had 45 aircraft on the ground ready to fly. Now, I'm going to just cover some things like what we lived in. We lived in what was called a Dallas Hut. It was actually made from 12 pieces of 4' by 8' plywood made into a box and the upper 4' would be nothing but screen and it would have a door that would flip down over the screen so when you had a sand storm you would drop that down. Sand still came in; it didn't help worth a shit. In the middle they had a square built of about 3' by 3' and a bunch of dirt and in there sat an M43 pot bellied heater for the wintertime when it got cold. Of course, we all had parkas and we had just a wooden roof on there and it would rarely rain. We had our footlockers and, of course, no wall lockers and we would have to ride the bus to go to the chow hall. Those of us who didn't bring our motorcycles were the ones who had to ride the bus. Now, let me describe the bus, there was an alcoholic dog on the bus that belonged to a guy from the fighter squadron and this dog would get up in the right front seat of the bus when we were going down to the chow hall, and god help anybody that was sitting in his seat because he would snarl at them. The bus driver would then tell them to get out of that seat, because it was the dog's seat. He would climb up there and look out the windows as we rode around in the bus. When we got to the chow hall he would be the first one off the bus and he would go to the chow hall, meet his master, then his master would go in there to eat and he would bring him something to eat when he came back. Then the dog would get on the bus, go back to the barracks, and sleep until about 5:00 p.m. Then he would ride the bus down and get off at the NCO Club where his master was hanging out and his master would give him a bowl of beer. He would drink the beer and sleep under his master's feet and by the end of the night he had two or three bowls of beer and he would be a little bit tipsy, just like his master and he would ride the bus back to the barracks and go to sleep. Now, needless to say, a dog with a hangover is a pretty irritable son-of-a-bitch at 7:00 in the morning when he got up with his master to go get breakfast. That was very unique.

Now, we were having many missions where we would go TDY. The next mission we had to go on was to another base named Ben Guirrer, which was also in French Morocco. We had to teach the people in transit maintenance how to service a B47 and how to do minor repairs on them just to clear the red crosses in order to get the aircraft in the air and back to the home station. We were over there for about two weeks. There was Jack C....., Robert E. R....... and I as representatives from the hydraulic shop and the pneumatic shop. So, we went to the NCO club one night and C..... said he was feeling lucky, so we hit the craps tables and the slot machines. Jack got up there and started saying, "Shoot $2.00, shoot $2.00" and he would win, so Jack would drag $2.00 winnings, put it in his pocket, and still leave the $2.00 there. Well, this one big son-of-a-bitch turned around after Jack took about $10.00 off of him and he said, "Shoot 10, shoot 10 you son-of-a-bitch, shoot 10." He was getting obnoxious to the three of us. He was a permanent person over there and he wanted us to shoot $10.00 so he could make up his losses quickly. Well, C..... wouldn't do it. He kept saying, "Shoot 2; shoot 2" until this guy got quite overbearing. Robert E. R....... had a snoot full of liquor by this time. Robert E. R....... was one tough cookie; he was half Indian and had a very good build and was very strong. I saw Robert getting mad. The guy was standing there in front of Robert and Robert dropped a dollar bill onto the floor, reached down there to pick up that dollar bill, made a fist around it, then brought his fist up and hit that guy right in the mouth. That guy's teeth were sticking through his lips and I started counting and said if this son-of-a-bitch doesn't fall in about 30 minutes, we're all in deep shit. He didn't fall in 30 seconds; he just shook his head and came after us. Well, needless to say, he whipped all three of us and he threw us out of the NCO club. We didn't lose any teeth and neither did he, but he was leaking blood all over the place. Anyhow, we trained those people on that mission and went back to Sidi Slimane for a day or two and then they said we were going to Wheelus, Tripoli in Libya to train those people over there. By this time we had a pretty good team going so we went over to Libya and set up the same sort of class and school. We went down town a couple of nights and again I found another black cat night club to go into, and we had a good time and we were whooping it up over there. We couldn't find any ladies of dubious virtue because they were Arab women and they told us, don't mess around because you can get hurt over there with the Arabs. Right there in the middle of town there was an old wall that was full of machine gun bullet holes, cannon holes and everything and they said it separated the new city from the old city, and whatever we did we were told not to go into the old city. Well, anytime you tell a GI not to do something, you know exactly what he's gonna do. So, we were at the black cat and we went out and rented a couple of horse and buggies and had a drag race down the main street of Tripoli. Then we had them take us to the entrance through that wall into the old city. Now, in those days we had a curfew. We were supposed to be back at the base by 12:00 a.m. and in bed by 1:00 a.m. We were in the middle of this great big place with girls all around us, drinking champagne and, let me tell you, there were some beautiful women there. They were all beautiful women, because like I explained before, they wee displaced persons and they couldn't get a regular job because there was no work, so they sold their bodies. We were such good GI's and tried to keep their economy going. About this time it got to be around 4:00 a.m. We had our jackets off because all we had to wear was our blue uniforms. We looked up and there were four AP's (air policemen) glaring at us. Robert E. said, "We're in for it now." They said they were going to take us back and throw the NCO in the barracks under lockup and the two corporals were going to go to the jailhouse. I said, "No, you can't do that." He said, "Why can't we?" I said, "Because we have to leave and go to Turkey at 6:00 a.m." So, they stuck us in the back of a weapons carrier, which is an oversized jeep, and it was cold. They drove us out there and took us right to the airplane and just luckily our friends had packed our bags. They threw us out of the weapons carrier right in front of the airplane. We got in with our heads still smoked, went inside the airplane and went to sleep. We took off and flew up to Adana, Turkey; it's called Incirlik now. While flying to Adana from Wheelos, we had a young navigator who must have been about 22. He wasn't doing very well. I was listening on the spare interphone from the Port scanner's position. I always volunteered to be scanner so I could hear everything. They, the aircraft commander and copilot, kept asking where they were and what heading to take (we were over the Mediterranean Sea.) He would get up on stand and use sextant for 3 shots, come down and try to figure out where he was. Finally, the A. C. told the boom operator to come forward and take the sextant shots and help the navigator. This he did and squared the kid away. I was very happy now.

That's when I learned boom operators were trained to navigate in a pinch. We landed there and we were checking into the place and found there were only two buildings on the base. One of them was the chow hall and the other one was the medical place. It wasn't a hospital, it was just a bunch of medics in a big Quonset hut and the chow hall was just a giant Quonset hut. At 6:00 p.m. they would just pull a big curtain across the middle of it and one-half became the NCO club and the other half became the Officer's club. It was a very high-class place; this was when it was tough over there. This was when they used to gig you for buffalo shit on your bow and arrow. As we were checking in the First Sergeant told us to go by the chow hall and get four coffee cans for each of us. So, we each went and got our four coffee cans and didn't ask any questions. We were sleeping in tents, so we went back and found us a tent to go to sleep in, and as we pulled in there we saw what the coffee cans were for. You would put a coffee can under each leg of the bunk because, when it rained, it got very muddy. It got so soaked that if you were lying on the bunk and didn't have the coffee cans to distribute your weight, you would sink down into the mud and be laying and sleeping in the mud. We were learning fast. We also went out and started teaching the people about the airplane and we saw the Oscars, which were the enlisted men in the Turkish army and the Turkish air force. God Bless them, they were treated like dogs. If they made the NCO angry, all the NCOs would get in a circle and literally beat the offender into the ground, then the other airmen would pick him up and take him back to the barracks and nurse him back to health. That's they way they maintained their discipline. Now, the Crew Chief on the F86's that they had, slept on the airplane. The only thing he had was a big piece of canvas and four big rocks and they were very precious to him because he would make a tent out of the wing of the aircraft and the four rocks would hold the canvas down and that's where he slept and ate. They would bring him a little food. They were a tough group of people, the Turkish pilots were utterly fantastic, and their courage was unbelievable in what they would do with their airplanes. They could fly like the Blue Angels; they were wonderful. Now, these poor Oscars would be given a ticket once a month and they were put on a bus and sent to Mersin. In Mersin there was a big compound, which is a giant place about a block square with big high walls. It had broken glass on top of the walls inside the concrete so nobody would try to get in and nobody would try to get out. Inside here were apartments full of some beautiful looking women, but they had crossed paths somewhere with the government and were sent to prison. This was their prison and the only way they could get out was to fornicate their way out. They got so many tickets for the guys (the Oscars) that they serviced. Well, we were working there and we decided, after about a week, that it was time for us to go and check out Mersin and go to the compound. Well, we hired us a cab, I think it cost us about $20.00 for the whole day, and we drove into Mersin. At the time it was 8 Turkish liras to the dollar and you could go into the compound and get yourself a girl and do the beast with two backs and it would cost you all of a dollar. You couldn't drink whiskey because there wasn't any whiskey; all you could drink was wine and champagne. I would go in there and spend a dollar, come out and go get a souvenir for somebody and then go back in and spend another dollar. I spent $5.00 on that stuff the big boys were getting. I had a very enjoyable time. Then we would eat and we were warned not to eat anything but eggs and French fries and then we would go watch a couple of floor shows, which were pretty good, then we would go back to the base. We did this about three times during the two weeks we were there. After we were there for the two weeks we got on a KC97 and we flew back to Sidi Slimane. We would volunteer for all these TDY's just so we could go to another foreign place and see another foreign place. Because of all of these TDY's they told us we were going to go on an R and R to England for five days. R and R meant rest and recuperation, but it was in actuality I and I, for intercourse and intoxication. So, about 55 of us got on a KC97 and packed our little AWOL bags full of stuff. We took some nylons with us that we had bought in the PX because you could always swap them for something. We then got on the airplane and took off. We landed in the upper Hayford in the middle of the night. Now, out of this KC97 came 55 horny GI's. They were already aware that we were coming so they had about 15 taxi's waiting for us. We all piled into the taxis and we were passing the bottle around and were racing to London. The cab driver was going to take us to Piccadilly Circus. We were racing to London, passing the bottle back and forth and I was sitting facing aft. It's quite unnerving when you look forward and see that you're running on the wrong side of the street and you're half hit in the ass. So after about an hour and a half we got to London and we got us up to Piccadilly Circus and all the cars pulled up and disgorged us 55 horny GI's, who pole-vaulted out of the cars. I started looking around because the next day was my birthday, I would be 23 years old. As I was walking around I came up behind a beautiful girl. She was a little blond with a pageboy wearing a blue suit with nice high heels. He name was Kay Lisa Martin and I remember her until this very day. I said, "Hi there" and I started blah blah blah, as I always had the gift of gab. The next thing I did was ask her if she wanted to go have a bite to eat. We went to the Wimpy's, which was the McDonalds in those days, and we had a couple of hamburgers. All I had had to eat previously was covered in sand, because we had been eating down in the desert while on TDY. Then I said I wanted to go dancing some place so she took me to the Lycium, which was a proper dance hall. It had a dance band on a big giant stand and they would play for an hour, and then there was another band playing the same song as it swiveled around. There were four bars, one in each corner downstairs and then there was a balcony with four more bars upstairs. We danced the night away until about 12:00 a.m. and I said, "I don't have any place to stay, do you know any place where we could go and stay?" We went to the Southway Hotel on Gillingham Street, 1014 Gillingham Street in Victoria. I still have the receipts for the hotel. It was a pound ten, which was $4.00 for a double at night. I went back there and visited the place again this year. Of course, the rooms now are $60 to $70 a night. So we went up there and they had a radio built into the bed and we made the beast with two backs many times because I was a horny little devil from being out there two or three weeks without being with a woman. I woke up the next morning and I had this beautiful little blond girl on my arms and I said this is the best birthday I've ever had in my life. I will remember this forever and ever and ever. We stayed together for three days, and then I caught the train and went back to upper Hayford. We got on back to Sidi Slimane and we checked back into the squadron and went to bed that night. I got up the next morning and I noticed that my crotch and skivvies were hard, as if they had puss on them. I threw back the covers and I looked and the skivvies were green. I said, "Uh oh." I ran to the latrine and looked and I went to urinate and, oh my God, it felt like a hot logging chain coming out. I said, "Uh oh, I've got the clap." I knew I would really remember my 23rd birthday because I got the clap off of that beautiful little blonde girl. I put my clothes on and wrapped my schlong up in a red rag and they went up and checked in with the medics. While I was at the medics, I was looking and there were about 50 of the 55 guys. They were all sitting up there coughing. They said, "Well, we must have gotten a high altitude cold coming back." I said, "High altitude cold shit, you've got the same thing I've got. You've got a dose of the clap." I went into the back and they had a Mexican medic and he said, "What's the matter, gringo?" I said, "I think I've got a dose." He said, "Well, let me take a look. Yeah, you've got it." I said, "Well, what are you gonna do?" He said, "I'm gonna give you a million units of penicillin." I said, "Wait a minute, I've had the clap before and they used to put me in the back of the hospital and I would have to take my meals back there. They would give me a shot every day of about 100,000 units." He said, "Well, we've got this new deal. What we're gonna do is give you one million units and it will knock it out." He whipped out this hypodermic needle. It was the size of a small fire extinguisher with a knitting needle on the end of it. I said, "Good Lord man, you can't put that thing in me. That needle will come out the other side." He said, "Shut up gringo, I show you how we do this. Drop your drawers." He put it in at an angle in my thigh. I wrapped my schlong back up again in my red rag and I went on back to work. They told me I was on the launch team again that day, and to go launch that KC97 which was taking another crew up to upper Hayford. So I was out there getting ready to launch the aircraft and the guys were standing around and asked me, "What did you think of London?" I said, "It was utterly fantastic, with beautiful, gorgeous women." They said, "Well, where did you pick them up?" I told them where we picked them up and he said, "Did you have a good time?" I said, "Sure did" and I opened up my one-piece fatigues and said, "This red rag wrapped around my schlong really proves it. I've got the biggest dose you've ever seen in your life." Everybody laughed and got on the airplane and figured they were going to use condoms. I said, "One day, someday, I will get back to England and meet that little girl again.

TIME IN NORTH AFRICA, SIDI SLIMANE AIR BASE

As I told you before, the Arabs were killing all the Frenchmen and we were kind of afraid to go to town. They told us not to go to town unless we had about twenty GI's together and not to break away from the group because we were liable to get our heads cut off. Several times in the three months we were there, actually four months, they had heads roll up to the front gates because they would cut off a Frenchman's head and roll it in there to scare us. They did a pretty damn good job of it. Anyhow, I had one friend in the shop named William Robins. He was from New Iberia, Louisiana and he spoke Cajun, which was French and he said, "T.K., T.K., I've got us a deal." I said, "What kind of deal is this?" He said, "I've got this one civilian and he said that he will take us to the little city of Petijone about 30 miles away and they have a big cathouse there. It's built like a fort and they have about 12 or 15 girls in there and a bar. When we get ready to come back they can get us a cab and bring us back in the cab." He said, "I'll be able to talk the price down, so we can spend quite a lot of time there and get laid a whole bunch of times." So I said, "That sounds very good to me. What time are we going to go?" He said, "We'll sneak out about 9:00 p.m." The days were long and we didn't want to be seen going out. He came back, we gave him a couple of mille (thousand francs) for gas and he took us to Petijone. Sure enough, this place was like an old fortress. It was like the ones the French Foreign Legion used to build out of the big stone they got from the quarries and it had a big door in the front. Like the old Robin Hood days, once you got inside of one door, they had a big beam that could be dropped down. It was held in place by some angle irons and in each window there were shutters that could be closed off and you could drop a bar down on them. We didn't think too much of it at the time, but it saved our lives. Anyhow, we were sitting at the bar, drinking and talking. The girls in there were left over after the war. They were French girls, very few Arab girls, and there were Italian girls and German girls because they were DP's left over from World War II. DP stands for Displaced Persons. This was how they made their living. So, I'd get one and I'd go upstairs and do the dirty deed then come back down. Then we'd drink some more and dance and William would go back up and he was getting it for very cheap prices. We were laughing but I don't think we were rowdy or anything. After about three or four hours there we heard someone beating on the front door and we heard a lot of people hollering. They went and looked in the peephole and said, "Uh oh, the Arab's are here. They think you are French men and they're going to kill you." Immediately William and I ran and we dropped a big beam so they couldn't push that front door open and we closed all the shutters on the first floor and said, "What the hell are we going to do now?" We took the girls and went up to the second floor where they had their rooms and we broke beer bottles and wine bottles on the steps. We figured the Arab's had bare feet and they would cut their feet when they were coming up there. Again, I was really worried about what was going to happen to my motorcycle back in the states. We were very, very, very frightened. We barricaded ourselves into one room onto the street in the front and all of a sudden we heard a BLAM, BLAM, BLAM, and we opened the window and looked out and right below the window where we looked was a half track (that's a vehicle where the front wheels turn and drive and it had a track like on a tank on the back). It was the Foreign Legion and they had a 50-caliber machine gun up on the front of the truck bed and they were shooting up in the air down the street and all the Arab's were backing off. They were telling us to jump, jump, jump. I was saying, "Jump shit, it's 20 feet down there." They said, "Jump or you're a dead man." I didn't have to do too much thinking so I jumped first and hit the deck and collapsed and Willie did the same thing. They threw the truck in gear and took off. They asked where we were from and we told them City Slimane Air Base. They took us to the air base and didn't even slow the vehicle down; they just opened the back gate. When we got near our gate they just threw us out into the sand. Needless to say, we didn't go back to Petijone anymore. But I would like to make a dedication in my book to the French Foreign Legion because this little boy wouldn't be here if it weren't for the legion.

Well, about this time the TDY was over. The three months had gone by and I had visited every place I could – England, French Morocco, and one weekend we had gone to Spanish Morocco. There I bought a little black Pekingese in Laratchie, Spanish Morocco and I snuck that back in from my NCO. I kept the little puppy inside my pocket and I just kept my hand in there and he remained quiet while I went through customs when I came back. We had also gone to Adana, Turkey, we had gone to Ben Guirrer, and we had gone to Libya. Hell, we couldn't have had a better time. So, we got on the airplane and we were coming back home on a C124, which is call Old Shaky or 30,000 Rivets Flying in Loose Formation. It was a big four-engine reciprocating with four 4360's. It took off at 174 and flew at 174 and landed at 174 miles an hour. It was quite a gigantic airplane. So, the airplane was bringing back Toulene thinner and aircraft paint. There were only 24 of us on the airplane; that was all we could crowd on. The thinner and paint were sitting right in the middle of the airplane and we were sitting long ways on both sides of them. It didn't matter because we were going back to the ZI and I was going back to get my motorcycle again. So we flew and we landed at the Azores and helped launch a few more airplanes through there that had gotten sick and came on down. We flew from there to Bermuda and we landed and refueled and took off again and ran into a big storm. It was really throwing that airplane around and we were struck by lightning and it melted the two antennae on top, which went to the horizontal stabilizers. It was beating on the side of the aircraft and sounded like something trying to come through and then when the lightning struck it also put a ball of what's called St. Elmo's Fire, which is a blue sphere of energy about a foot in diameter, into the airplane and it just bounced around the inside. Now, the airplane was full of thinner. It wouldn't have taken too much for it to blow up. Well, all I could think of was who's gonna get my motorcycle if I blow up. That's all I was worried about. Eventually it bounced around three or four times through the airplane and it went out through a sidewall of the aircraft and it just burned a little pinhole. We turned around and went back and landed and I still had little Liratchi in my pocket and I got on through customs. Sergeant Shaw took the little dog off my hands and gave it to his wife. Everybody was happy and I was ready to go home and get my motorcycle. I so enjoyed England and I was going to figure some way I could scheme to get back to England. By this time I had made Buck Sergeant and another guy in the shop was a Staff Sergeant and he was a journeyman level also and he said, "T.K., do you want to go to England?" I said, "I sure would love to." He said, "Well, why don't you take my shipment." I said, "Can it be done?" He said, "Well, we are both five-level, we'll just go see the First Sergeant and we will just swap and you can take my shipment to Brize Norton, England." I said, "Sure enough, old friend." So we went to see the First Sergeant and he swapped us around so I got a set of orders to Brize Norton, England. I went on home and put my motorcycle in the bedroom up on a concrete block and that's where it stayed for the four years I was gone.

CHAPTER 5
BNAFB, ENGLAND

I got on a train in Jacksonville, at the big beautiful train station and rode that train up to Philadelphia and then I took a bus from there to Maguire Air Force Base and got on an airplane, a C54, and fourteen hours later landed in Prestwick, Scotland. We had to wait for a day or two until they got enough people together and then we would ride the train back to London and then back to our base. Well, we were living in the train station; it was called the station hotel. We were living in the hotel rooms above the train station and all the trains came in down underneath there. We were again whooping it up and we could go dancing at Bobby Jones dance hall every night; there were the most beautiful Scotch lassies you've ever seen in your life and they could all dance. It was a big, beautiful dance hall and you would start heading for one beautiful girl and when you were half way there you'd see another one and you would change angles and head for her, then you'd see another one and then by the time you finally got to one, the prettiest one there, the song was over so you would have to start all over again. We danced there three or four nights and I met a beautiful girl named Jacqueline Ford. She was a model for some kind of perfume. I told her I would come back and we would stay in contact and we would write and we did write. Eventually, we turned around and got on the train and took the train all the way to London, and from London we took the train back to Oxford and then they had buses waiting for us that took us to the base. Now, I was in a strange outfit. The normal outfit there was called the 3920th consolidated aircraft maintenance squadron, but I was assigned to the 3915th.

Nobody knew what the 3915th was. So, all the guys from the 3920th went and checked into the squadron, which was just forming and was brand new. So, the rest of us just hid out in the barracks; nobody came and got us so we went to the airmen's club and to the chow hall. It was a beautiful, gorgeous base and finally, after about three weeks of laying around, we were getting tired so finally one guy went to see Sergeant Miller, who was the First Sergeant of the 3920th. He asked, "Where are we supposed to go, we're the 3915th?" Lord have mercy, he came up from those barracks like a dose of salt and said, "So, this is my lost squadron? You guys are all on my shit list now. You've been hiding out." I said, "Look here, nobody ever met us and we're 3915th and you're 3920th." He said, "Well, you're gonna be attached to the 3920th. If an emergency war plan is enacted, you will go to Bodo', Norway and recover aircraft and steal fuel wherever you can; any kind of fuel (gas, kerosene, diesel, perfume), anything you can put in the tanks to get the airplanes back." Then some other guys of the 3915th would go to London airport and to other airports surrounding and do the same sort of thing. This is part of the emergency war plan and that's why we were called the ghost squadron.

Explaining tactics of EWO (Emergency War Operations)

Fighter-bombers would blast their way in with small nukes taking out Radar & Russian aircraft bases for their fighters. Then, Blue cradle EB47E would lead the way in for B47E's to finish the job.

The purpose of Brize, Greenham, Fairford, Upper Heyford, Lakenheath, Mildenhall, Bruning-Thorpe and Chevelston was to launch bombers in case of war.

Wings go TDY to those bases to keep personnel and supply proficient.

Brize had 68th wing for 3 months; 384th for 3 months, and the rest for 3 months. We would go TDY to Lakenheath & Mildenhall to support wings that were TDY there, then back to BNAFB to receive 100th BW for 3 months then 380th for 3 months. Then we started permanent reflex. Wings did not come over any more. We maintained 15 aircraft on full time alert strip loaded and ready. Each week 3 planes would fly in from 2nd on 308th Bomb wing in Savannah. They would then send 3 planes back. We rotated planes like this to keep aircraft flying time the same, as an aircraft just sitting and not flying will start leaking.

We also maintained 15 Blue cradle A/C, from 301st & 376th BW. These planes had a special pod inserted in the bomb bay with two Ravens-crows ECM (Electronic Countermeasures Operators) to jam soviet radar as they led bombers in.

During one break (90 days) I went TDY to support Bomb Wing at Lakenheath. They were from Lincoln, Nebraska. I was riding the launch truck, launching the days training missions. Planes were also landing at the time. A B47 came in and instead of landing with fore and aft gear touching at the same time he hit nose gear first. The aircraft started porpoising (bouncing) as he tried to get it under control. He popped the drag chute, which didn't help and he crashed into the munitions dump. This was where all nuclear weapons were stored. He burst into flames and we all cleared the base. The nukes were stored underground in large revetments, covered with 20' of dirt. However, nothing happened except the flight crew was killed and we were a little scared.

While I was stationed at Lakenheath, the main highway bisected the base. On that road was located "Mickey's Tea Bar." They sold tea and sandwiches. It was also a hangout for some local girls of the evening (who also worked daylight hours). They would service young lads TDY from the states. We would not pay for it. There was too much free stuff about. There was one beautiful redhead, called Lakenheath Annie, who operated out of there. One time, she went into the barracks for the night, selling it for 3 pound 10 shillings (10 dollars). Sunday night when she left the barracks she was selling it for 10 shillings ($1.40). When she left she had every bit of money in the barracks. She came to the Tea bar, laughing, talking to us permanent people, saying she had made over $700.00. I think she rested for a week, went to London, bought a bunch of clothes and was back to work the following week. About a year later, I was walking down the main street of Brize and spotted a good-looking redhead pushing a baby carriage with a little A2C with her. She had gotten married and had a kid with him and was going back to the states. Yep, it was "Lakenheath Annie" and she probably made a good wife.

We went back to BNAFB as we were getting another wing.

Well, about this time we finally drew a payday and I said I was going down to London. In the meantime I had gone to the PX and for $40.00 I ordered a handmade suit. I picked the material and told them exactly how I wanted it made. I had a beautiful blue suit made with a one-button roll, cloth covered buttons, patch pockets, drop loops for the belt loops, pegged about sixteen inches, and I had bought a beautiful pair of suede shoes and got a couple of shirts and ties out of the PX. I was ready to go to town; I was looking good. In those days when you went to town, you went in a suit, shirt and a tie. You didn't go in Levi's or fatigues or anything. You did not leave the base unless you were in blues or you were dressed in a suit because we had to worry about Anglo-American relationships. We had to maintain a good rapport with the people of England. So, anyhow, we went and caught the bus and went down to Oxford and then we showed our ID cards and got a roundtrip ticket to London for a pound, which was $2.85 at the time. We hit London and I had already been taught by Kay Lisa Martin how to use the tubes, so I jumped on the tubes at Paddington station and rode the Paddington Line, which is the Baker Lou Line, to Oxford Circus, changed to the Central Line, then went to Bond Street and then changed to the Piccadilly Line and I came out underneath the Piccadilly and came up and did a Piccadilly Circus and there I was. I started looking around and I found a place that would hand make shirts for me up on Shasbury Avenue, so I ordered a couple of shirts. As I was walking around I went to Wimpy's and who did I bump into but Kay Lisa Martin again. So I grabbed a hold of her and I said, "Look here, little girl, do you remember me?" She said, "Yeah, I remember you. We spent your birthday together." I said, "Yeah, and you gave me the biggest dose of the clap that I have ever had in my life. Did you get it fixed?" She said, "I never had it Thomas." Yeah, like she was a virgin; she was using her cherry for a taillight. So, anyhow, I had some 32-ply rubbers that were like Michelin tires so I said, "Let's go back to that same hotel again and we'll spend the weekend together." So we spent the weekend together, except I used rubbers this time like the people always told us. I met her the next three or four weeks in a row, having a large quantity of condoms with me.

Not having a car yet for transportation, we rode the trains. English trains were two types; one had a hallway down one side like you see in the old movies, with a series of compartments where six or eight people could sit in each compartment. The older trains had no hallways and the compartment went all the way across the train. If you had to go to the bathroom, you were doomed. You would have to wait until the next train station in order to get off, then run int6o the train station and take care of business, and then come back out and get into the train again. So, Googee K_____ and I were riding into London and there was one Englishman in the compartment with us and we were just passing the bottle, a 40-ounce jug of whiskey, and we were chasing it with orange juice. We were smoking and carrying on having a damn good time not bothering anybody. The Englishman was just watching these two crazy yanks. We'd light up a Pall Mall and he'd light up a Player's cigarette. Their Player's cigarettes were about the size of a pencil in thickness. They were packed very hard and they were half the size of a Pall Mall. We would smoke our Pall Malls down and throw them out the open window. We looked at him and he was still smoking that Player's cigarette. We started getting nervous and had another drink or two and we looked and he had smoked that cigarette so short I don't know how it didn't burn his lips. The ashes were falling behind his teeth, that's how small the butt of the cigarette was. When he finally finished it and dropped it onto the floor, nothing hit the floor but ashes because the little bit that was left passed through the air, rapidly burned it to a cinder, and there were just ashes floating down. Well, anyhow, we hadn't stopped and we weren't going to stop because we were on the express train and the first stop was Paddington from Oxford. I said, "My God, Googee, we have drunk all this booze and I've got to pee and we don't have a stop. We still have another 25 or 30 minutes for the ride." He said, "Why don't you just pee out the window, T.K.?" The window was open; it was a window in a door. So I stood up with one foot on each seat, hung my schlong out the window, and urinated out the window. As it happened we started going through West Broadway at about 50 miles an hour. Everyone was standing on the platform and here goes a rotten G.I. with his schlong hanging out. I urinated on half the people on West Broadway. But that was good clean times. Needless to say, we had another wild weekend. Well, about this time I found and located a good place to go and it was called the Grand Chester. It was in Lancaster Gate between the Paddington tube station and Lancaster Gate tube station. This guy named Mr. Peters had bought this big giant hotel and inside this hotel he had five clubs. Now, we're not talking about nightclubs with dining and dancing and everything. But you could go in there and dance; there was a jukebox and a bar. On the second floor there was a beautiful Polish girl named Sedonia and she had the bar on the upper floor. Down in the cellar there was a tiny bar. In the back of the bar was a closet, and in that closet, behind a screen, was a snake. It was a giant boa constrictor and consequently, the name of the bar next to it was called the Snake Pit. In that bar they had a jukebox and a piano. Someone would be playing the piano and there would be a big sing along and you could whoop it up. Then you would go back up the stairs and go over to Muriel's bar. She was a pretty little girl. She had a real nice bar with a pretty big dance floor in it and a jukebox, of course. Underneath that was another club called the Sea Farers and it had a beautiful dance floor and a real nice bar. Coming back out of that place, and going next door down into the cellar was a number two club, which had a lovely dance floor and everything. I'll get into that because that is where we had a big battle one New Year's Eve in which I partook and got my ass beat and cut up and everything else. Anyhow, K_____ and I were going to these places and we would always pick up a girl. We were staying at this one hotel called Elizabeth's Hotel. It was three blocks away and it was on Linester Terrace. It's now called the Craven Gardens Hotel. The lady who was the manageress (that's proper English) just loved me because I was such a sweet young lad. She would give me the key so we could open the front door and sneak the girls in the middle of the night. Anybody else would have to ring the bell and she would have to open the door so they couldn't get any girls in. We had it made in the shade; at least we thought so for a while. Then we started going to another nightclub over on Harrell Road; it was called the 2-4-2 Club and I met a lovely Spanish girl over there and I had good times with her. We were out one night at the 2-4-2 Club, Robbie, Googee and I, and we picked up three girls. My girl's name was Joan Cherry. Of course, I would get one named like that. The other one's name was Doris and I forgot what the third one's name was. They were pretty good looking hammers. We got in the cab and we went on back to the Elizabeth Hotel and we snuck into the front. I had the key and we went into the three rooms and we all shacked up for the night. The girl looked because I had a little paper bag full of condoms and she said, "What are you gonna do with these?" I said, "We're gonna us them all, baby, we're gonna us them all." Her eyes rolled up and she damn near passed out. But I didn't use them all. By that time I was 24 and I was starting to slow down already. So when we got up the next morning we went out and took them to breakfast and the girls were saying, "Why don't you guys get a flat in town?" I said, "We would but we don't have time to go looking for one." She said, "Well, give us your addresses and we will find a flat for you up there by where we live. We live in Cricklewood, which is up on top of the Kilburn High Road." When we left them at the train station that night, we kissed them good night and locked tongues and swabbed tonsils with them for a while and pinched them on the hiney. We got on the train, hung out the window, and waved bye to them. We figured that was the last time we would see or hear from them. About Wednesday we all got letters in the mail saying, "Look here, we found you a lovely flat for 7 pounds a week (that's $20.00 a week); it's up on 118 Fordwitch Road right off the Kilburn High Road." So Robbie had a little bitty tiny English car and we loaded our clothes in there and drove on in. We looked at the flat and said we would take it. We were in the process of meeting the landlady. Now, as God is my Judge, this is the truth. Her name was Mrs. Szylidio. She lived at 66 Biddulph Mansions, Maida Vale, in London. If you remember the wicked witch from "Somewhere over the Rainbow", she looked identical to her, complete with the big wart on her nose, except she was big and fat. She was Polish and she found out that I was of the Polish heritage. She would grab me and hug me and squeeze me to her bosom until she would about break every bone in my young body. I was elected to have to carry the rent to her every month. Anyhow, the rent was $20.00 a week and the flat had three bedrooms, a giant kitchen, small refrigerator, gas stove and a big couch in it. Now, for the gas in any one of the rooms, you had to put sixpence in the little gas meter so the gas would come on for a while. Now, the bathroom had a bathtub that was about the size of an Olympic size swimming pool. To heat the water, they had what was called a geyser. This was a very unique device; you put four pence in the gas register deal and that would allow a pilot light to come on. Then you would light the pilot light. When you turned on the water, due to falling water pressure over a diaphragm that would open the water, it would allow water to come in through these heating tubes and allow a big flame to go up between the heating tubes, instantly giving you hot water. It was a magnificent device. It damn near killed me one time, but it was a magnificent device. So, I was quite enthralled and we decided who was going to get which room and then we started bringing in records and record players and our clothes. We started having wonderful times every weekend. We kept it a secret because we didn't want to have anyone else coming up and breaking up our parties. The flat opened up on the top floor and I said, "Well damn, we'll get some more GI's in here and we'll start taking over this house." So I got my buddy Phil and Al and another guy named Joe. They rented the flat on the top floor. The flat below us came open and I got Tommy Dunn, Milt Boldeck and Paul (I don't remember his last name).

Once we had GI's on 2nd, 3rd, and 4th floors we really started living good. Our flat had a Giant kitchen and refrigerator. Of course, I was the only one who could cook so I would hit everyone up for a Pound on Friday night and I* would go to grocery shop around the corner and get lard, bread, eggs, sausage (walls), Canadian bacon, tomatoes, etc. I would start breakfast at 8 or 9 o'clock and feed everybody. The ladies thought it was fabulous, as they never were fed like this before. We were the talk of Lancaster Gate area. At about 1200 I would hit everybody up for $2.00 and we would drive to Grosvenor Square to the Navy PX and buy beer at $2.00 a case and more food for Sunday brunch and Spaghetti for evening meal. We would eat late and clean up our apartments and the house would be quiet during the week. Occasionally we would invite a neighbor over to cement Anglo-American relationships. In fact, Eddie Mangone from a fighter base at Weathersfield, who lived on the 2nd floor with T. Dunn, and M. Bolduck, invited the family from two doors up. He ended up marrying their daughter, after they saw what fine fellows we were.

A Chinese family, on the ground floor, occupied the only flat we didn't have at the time. We had a circular staircase going up to the fourth floor and the fourth floor became the party room. The living room on the fourth floor was just devoted to nothing but partying. We built us a bar up there and had it stocked with all kinds of booze. We probably had over 150 45-rpm records, and I mean that place jumped from Friday night until Monday morning about 4:00 a.m. About this time I decided it was about time for me to get a car. Doc P (Chubby) or Phil was selling his '52 Ford. So I bought his '52 Ford while he got a new MGA. We were really shitting in tall cotton (that's where the cotton wipes your ass as you straddle the road while you're picking up the cotton). We had this big Ford and the English girls just loved that big car. We were staying with these same three girls for about two or three months. It was getting about the time to venture forth and get some strange stuff because this girl was just getting old. I told the guys, I said, "Look here, I'm going to break up with Joan. You guys keep on with whom you want." They said, "You can't do that, Thomas." I said, "Why can't I?" They said, "Because she cleans the house for us during the week so we can pass the Captain's inspection with Mrs. Szylidio on Friday." I said, "Well, look here, if you want to keep that going you're going to have to turn around and you're gonna have to police up on her. I'm going to go get me a little Spanish girl at the 2-4-2 club." So they got quite angry and hostile with me, but anyhow, I broke up with Joan. She was a wonderful girl. She liked good music and we used to spend our Saturday afternoons out at the park lying on a blanket smogging (that's kissing). If it were winter we would light the fire and play my 33-RPM records of good music. I broke up with her and started going with this Spanish girl named Lolita. I went with her for about two or three weeks. I would bring her nylons and she would just get all twitterpated because even in those days you couldn't get nylons. Everything was still tough over there. In England in 1955, 56 and 57 they still had rationing going on. The country still hadn't recovered and in London, probably ¼ of the city was still bombed out, with bombed out buildings everywhere you went. But they were wonderful, happy people, always smiling and they didn't have shit. They were always smiling and the girls were wonderful; tall, elegant looking, didn't have a lot of money but they dressed well and they had the most beautiful legs of anyplace in the world because they walked everywhere. They had gorgeous calves. All the time that we had the flat we were going down on Lancaster Gate and we were going to the clubs down there on Grand Chester. We had a regular courting of girls that when they saw us coming they knew the party boys were coming. I ended up having one girl named Cecile that I was indulging in sex with. Then her sister wanted me so she sent her sister over to meet with me and then we both played the game one weekend where I had both of them at the same time. It was just a fantastic time, everything you could ever dream of we did over there. The other boys had policed up on a couple more ladies and they were having good times too. Now, at the same time that this was going on, on Wednesday nights at the base we had what was called pig night. They would bring a busload of girls from Oxford and a busload of girls from Cheltenham to the NCO club and they would have dances. We would go up there and police up on these girls, buy them a meal and some drinks and then dance with them. At the end of the dance we would try to get them to go out to the bomb shelter because there were still bomb shelters left there from World War II and we would try to get a wall job standing up on the wall. Some of the girls would be the nice little girls that they were and gave the young guys a wall job and others wouldn't. Well, I met this one lovely girl named Mavis. She was probably 5'9" or 5'10" tall, built like a brick outhouse with the most gorgeous legs and calves that I've ever seen on a woman and she was a good dancer. I said, "Oh, oh, oh, I want that." So I tried to get her to come into London and she said, "No, if you want me, you have to spend the weekend in Oxford." I said, "No, no, no, no, I am in London. Now here's my telephone number in Gladstone 2462 and I'm at 118 Fordwitch Road and if you ever come in, just give me a call. Otherwise, we'll just keep dancing and this is all the further it will go." So after about four or five months…now, I'm going with other girls at the time…but one Saturday afternoon my telephone rings and I answer it and say, "Gladstone 2462." She said, "Yes, is this Thomas?" I said, "Yes, this is Thomas K., Sergeant K." She said, "Well, this is Mavis." I said, "My God, hi there girl, where are you calling me from, Oxford?" She said, "No, I'm down at the Paddington Station." I said, "Well, you just wait for me there. I'll be down in the V-8 Ford." So I leaped down into the car, spun wheels and I drove on down to Paddington, which is about four or five miles away and she was waiting for me by the cabstand. I came sliding up and screeching to a halt, put the parking brake on and opened the door. She looked absolutely elegant; I can see her blonde hair to this day. She was pretty well endowed and she filled that blouse magnificently. She had a black suit on, I'll never forget that, and black high heels. I thought, I'm gonna get some of that, gonna get some of that tonight. So anyhow, we got in the car and we went back to the pad (to the apartment). I said, "Well, I've got to take a shower. Here are some records. Play these records while I go get cleaned up and we'll go out this evening. We'll go dining and dancing and have a good time. Then we'll come back." She said, "Yeah, we have to go by and pick up my bags at the railroad station." At the railroad station they had a place where you could leave your bags and they would be under lock and key. So I got all dressed with my shirt and tie. I looked good because, boy, I was a dresser. By that time I had acquired about six suits and all my shirts were handmade by Cecil G's on Shaftsbury Avenue in London. I had handmade Italian shoes from Oxford Circus. We looked quite elegant. We got in the car and went down to Paddington. She dashed in there and got her overnight bag and came back out. We went to the Bayswater area, parked the car and sauntered up to Queens Way and found a very nice restaurant, had a nice meal and then we got in the car and drove back up to Lancaster Gate, parked the car, and started hitting all the five or six clubs in the area. By 11:00 p.m. we had had a good time and she was a dancer par excellence (fantastic). The whole time while I was dancing with her and holding her and dipping her I'm thinking, I'm gonna get some of that, gonna get some of that, gonna get some of that. We went back to the apartment, I lit the fire and threw the quilt on the floor and had a bottle of Chianti and had a couple of glasses there. I was stripped down and ready for action with a sheet covering me and an erection that was so great I couldn't close my eyelids because they were skinned back so far. If it had gotten any harder I would have passed out because all the blood from my body was engorged in my dorcus americanas. She walked in and she still had her high heels on and her garter belt, no panties, just a bra and her breasts were just lying in the bra. There was no top half on the bra and the nipples were like two little cherries in a martini glass. Oh my God, I thought this was gonna be the greatest thing in my life. She lay on the floor and we were locking tongues and swabbing tonsils, enjoying the hell out of each other. Finally, it was time for me to thrust home, like they say in a sword fight. Well, I thrust home and she said, "Oh, oh, it hurts." I said, "It hurts?" I'm thinking I'm hung like a stud field mouse and she's saying it hurts? I don't feel anything because this lady had a problem in as much as she was very, very loose. There's an operation to repair it now. I looked behind me and I thought maybe there's somebody big behind me doing something that's helping me because I'm not doing this lady any good and she kept saying it hurt. Well, anyhow, we indulged in other ways that night, which sufficiently took care of things.

VIGNETTES

This story takes place in Oxford, England. My friend Joe and I were at Whites Bar, carousing one evening. We picked up two ladies of dubious virtue and headed out to the back woods. We were in my '52 Ford. When we got out on this back road, it was an all gravel, single lane road seldom used so we had it made. We flipped a coin to see who would get laid in the car; the other got the outside. I lost so I was the outside man. We locked tongues and swabbed each other's tonsils for a while and I got her knickers (panties) off and sat her on the trunk deck lid with her high heels hung in the bumpers. I eased on in and set my feet and started laying pipe. Damn. I was losing traction in the gravel, and had to reset my feet. This went on and on. I felt the car shaking. I thought Joe was really getting it so I looked in the back window and saw the two of them laughing at me. What Joe had done was slip the gears into neutral and I was pushing the car down the road for a hundred feet or so.

I had a good friend named Ralph S. who was an instrument tech by trade, and a horny GI by night. He never would go to London or Oxford. He always went to Chelteman, 20 some miles away, to the Horse and Groom Pub. He always dressed quite well and had a cab waiting at closing time for him. He would pick up a girl, go to the cab and he would drive to the outskirts of town and deposit them at this special haystack. Yes, I said haystack! He had a tunnel and a cave in the haystack complete with battery operated lantern (large 6 volt lantern with red cover) and blankets and Scrumpy's Cider and VP wine. The cabbie would pick them up and drop off the girl and bring Ralph to the base. He did this for three (3) years, never shacking up in a bed.

I also had a friend named Blue. He was a typical GI. He had very little topside when women were involved. He was at the Horse and Groom and policed up on a real dog. She said, "Let's go to the graveyard and get some." Blue being drunk, sat her on a headstone and started laying pipe. It was getting good and something tapped him on the shoulder quite hard. He looked and it was a "Bobbie." He said, "Here, here, what are you doing?" Being drunk, Blue got argumentative and the "Bobbie" locked him up for desecrating a graveyard. The Commander and First Sergeant went crazy when they got him out of jail.

About this time we were into reflex, instead of bringing complete wings of 45 aircraft and maintaining 15 of those on alert, we changed posture by just maintaining an alert strip. These planes were cycled in every week, (3) three at a time. This saved a lot of money. Instead of moving 3,000 people, permanent people maintained the aircraft on alert. We started with Bombers from 2nd & 308th BW at Savannah, GA. As we came up to speed we needed someone to lead the way in by jamming the radar, SAMS, etc. A special wing was set up in Columbus, Ohio; actually two wings, the 301st and the 376th. They would feed aircraft for Reflex at Brize Norton and Greenham Common, in Oxfordshire, England. As we went into operation and since I was already checked out on the two air conditioning systems, one in Aircraft Pressure vessel (AC, Copilot, Bomb Nav), these aircraft had a special pod that was hung in the Bomb Bay with two electronic warfare operators (jammers of Radan, etc.), one was an officer and one was enlisted. I never could figure that out, nor could I ever find out. These people talked to no one.

I volunteered to go to Greenham to check an airman out on Air Conditioning and Pressurization in the pod. At this time is when I met my lifelong friend Bill Bocz. He was from Pennsylvania. We got along real well. We trained and partied for my 90 day TDY, plus I got an extra 30 dollars a month. These were great times. This was when Bill received his nickname "Big Bad Billy Bocz" and he sure earned it.

EXCERPS FROM THE MEMOIRS OF BILLY BOCZ

IV
1959/1962 RAF Greenham Common, England

Other than RAF Woodbridge, RAF Greenham Common was the only base That I was stationed where the morale of the base flowed from the enlisted ranks to that of the officers, not vice versa.

Greenham Common was unique in that it had so many gamblers. At any given time you could get up a bet on just about anything, even the weather. The story you are about to read happened, the names have been changed to protect the innocent.

It all started a couple days before Guy Falks Day, an English holiday celebrated to mark the attempt to blow up the Parliament building. A group of fellows decided to see if it was possible to live off the English economy over the holiday without spending any money. At a hundred dollars a head we paired off. The ground rules were, we would shoot darts at a map and whichever town/city it landed nearest was where you had to go. The only financial aid was a train ticket there and back. Being trustworthy gamblers that we were, a certain amount of proof would be required upon return. My partner was nicknamed Doughnuts and we drew Liverpool. Although the stipulation was "no money", nothing was said about cigarettes. At this period of time American cigarettes were at a premium. Armed with clothes and an AWOL bag full of cigarettes we took off. It wasn't until we were on the train that we came up with a game plan. It was decided that we would write a book on better Anglo-American relationships.

Arriving at our destination, we headed for the first pub that we could find. On the way to the pub, we managed to pick up a couple note pads and pens. Upon entering the pub, we pulled out our butts and lighting up, we let everyone get a look at the packs. Offering the nearest lads one and lighting them up, we engaged in small chitchat talk, eventually getting around to the book theme. This immediately got everyone's interest. We spent two days and a night and had a great time. Armed with names, addresses and phone numbers we headed home. That was it, or so we thought; little did we know.

We presented different items and addresses to verify our claim and easily won. It started three days later. The mailroom called us to come pick up our mail. Both bags were stuffed and there were two bags full on the floor. We carried it all back to the shop. We poured all the mail out onto a workbench and started sorting through it. After a while I looked at Doughnuts and said, "Oh, Oh, I think we're in big trouble." Everything was quiet for a couple of days with that feeling of impending doom. It arrived on a nice sunny day. The first shit called down to the shop for us. We were told to report to the base commander's office (PDQ) as in Pretty Damn Quick.

On the way to his office I said to Doughnuts, "I think we are in deep dog shit." Entering his office the secretary ushered us straight in. Reporting in as ordered, he says to us, "Troops, tell me about your book." We kinda looked at one another and said, "Book, what book?" About right then I truly believe he got the idea of what was going on. He kinda got that funny look on his face. His next statement was, "What you're saying is that there is no book. Do you both know what you have done?" Breaking out in laughter he says, "There's a T.V. station that wants to interview both of you. Also, a book publishing company wants to print the book." At this point we went from scared to super scared. We just knew our shit was weak. When he got done laughing, he called in his secretary. He dictated a letter, which he had us sign. One was to the newspaper in Liverpool. The others were to the T.V. station and the book publishing company. To show that God really does protect drunks and fools, nothing more was said about it. I consider us very lucky to this day that we didn't end up in jail.

V
THE GHOST OF WOODBRIDGE

For many of you non-believers (I was once one myself), you are about to read about a situation I was personally involved in. I still don't want to believe in them, but then I'm no longer a disbeliever either.

Within the first week of arriving at RAF Woodbridge, an incident occurred that would have everyone talking. We had a building used by the orderly room, commander's office, flight crew's lounge, and job control. CQ (Charge of Quarters) was pulled in this building rather than the barracks. The reason for this was we were used not only for CQ, but also to guard the safe. This kept the AP's from posting a man there.

My first introduction to the ghost was on hearing that one of the squadron's troops got hauled away in a wrap-around jacket to RAF Lakenheath. The base contained the nut ward or funny farm, whichever sounds better. He was pulling C.Q. the night before. He was a young trooper with dark black hair. When the orderly room opened in the morning, they found him badly shaken with solid white hair. It seems that he had a run in with the ghost. This instant was duly recorded by orderly room personnel. Needless to say, the squadron personnel were not too happy about pulling C.Q. in it. It was not until my third year there that they stopped it.

My first experience with it was also my first time pulling it. C.Q. started at 1700 pm by relieving the orderly room and ended at 0800 am the next morning. After receiving my briefing and everyone cleared the building, the first duty was to insure all doors and windows were locked. The evening started off quiet enough, then around 2300 as I sat there reading a paperback book, I started hearing windows and doors banging. I got up and made the rounds. All the windows and doors were still secure. This really rattled my cage. I never really saw anyone, but it left a lasting impression.

My first sighting, if that's the proper word, was while working on an aircraft. I was the only one in the revetment. The opening was an open archway without any doors. Having problems trying to hold my flashlight in my teeth, I happened to look up and see this officer in the open archway. Distracted for just a couple of seconds to remove the flashlight from my mouth, he was gone. He didn't have enough time to cover the distance to the gate. So much for help. I managed to finish the job, and upon leaving I asked the guard where the officer went. His answer was, "Sarge, you were the only one in there.

Two other incidents come to mind where the ghost was identified. The first involved the AP's. They chased him running down the runway at 35 mph, firing live rounds at him. The second involved another of our squadron personnel. Upon starting C.Q. they issue you a .38 revolver (unloaded) with six rounds. Unable to stay awake, he soon fell asleep. The smell of cigarette smoke woke him up. A non-smoker, the odor woke him up and he saw a smoking cigarette in the ashtray, but what scared him the most was the loaded .38 laying on the counter pointed at him. What he saw was a Major in a WWII flight suit walking through the double doors leading outside. What makes this action so unique is the fact that the doors had a logging chain through the handles with a padlock. These situations and many more were logged in the C.Q. log.

One other event strikes me as funny, especially at the time it happened. A friend of mine drew C.Q. this particular night and for once I was not out late. At 2300 I was woke up by Snyder calling asking me to bring him out a pack of cigarettes. I said I would, but knew he wanted me to stay out there with him. Knowing this I loaded up the wife and two kids. When I got there, there was Ralph. He had a case of beer on the floor and his full-grown Labrador dog with him. As I suspected, he tried to talk me into staying.

Shortly after this we stopped pulling C.Q. in that particular building. The AP's were now stuck with their ghost. Fact or fiction? Did we really see the (Major) ghost? I feel like I did. What's your guess?

VI
1959/1962 RAF GREENHAM COMMON, ENGLAND

Of the many occurrences at Greenham Common, these two meshed together.

It started out with a visit from the commander of (SAC) Strategic Air Command, General Curtis Lemay. It occurred just a couple weeks before Christmas. He used our base to park his aircraft while he went up to South Ryslip for a conference.

Now the first sequence of events took place. The air police assigned a young troop to stand guard over the KC-135 the General used for traveling around. His instructions were that no one but the General was to approach the aircraft. So, later in the afternoon when a Captain approached the aircraft, he was refused entry. He insisted on being permitted aboard, that he was part of the General's staff. Not having the proper security pass, the airman 2nd class calmly drew his .45 automatic and had the Captain spread eagle on the ground. The situation was soon defused.

Afterward this airman was reassigned to guard the back gate. This gate was utilized by many of the officers to get to the "O" Club, which was located off base. The problem with this was that you still had to cross through a high security area. A security pass was still required to pass through this gate. The next evening a staff car returning from the Officer's Club decided to use the back gate. The staff car was being driven by none other that our Captain. In the car with him were the General and a couple of ranking officers. After acknowledging the car in the proper military manner, he informed the Captain that they could not pass through the gate without a security badge. The Captain proceeded to inform the Airman that he had the General on board and did not need any badges and that he was going through. Now the man coolly drew his .45 and ordered the Captain out of the car and on the ground. Again his supervisor was called out to defuse the situation. Now higher-higher decided that it might be prudent to let this young airman off, at least until the General left the area.

Now, the second part takes place. It's time for the General to leave. Take-off time was at 1100 hours and about a dozen of us were standing outside the Instrument shop to watch the takeoff. We had a long paved runway with a thousand foot of gravel and a thousand foot dirt extension at the end of the pavement. We watched as the plane lined up and poured the coal to the engines, and released the brakes. When it passed the point of no return, everyone was saying, "pull that sucker up, pull that sucker up." It started kicking up gravel and the gears finally started to retract when they got to the dirt. Now at the end of the dirt was a tree line. We watched as the aircraft flew through the tops of the trees.

On a return trip a couple months later, some of the troops got to talk to the crew chief. Apparently when they got back to their base, they had to clean the tree limbs from the landing gear. It had amounted to a Christmas shopping trip, as the plane was badly overloaded.

A footnote to all this: The young Air police airman received an automatic promotion for his standing fast to his determination to properly perform his job.

BACK TO T. KAYE'S MEMOIRS

About this time we had our beloved B-47's at the base and things were getting kind of critical in the World with the Russians. We had 15 aircraft on the base parked on the alert strip, loaded with four 25-megaton bombs, and the crews were on alert in little houses right behind them. They could be off the ground in 10 or 15 minutes. At the same time this happened there was a problem that arose in the Suez Canal, where the Egyptians were closing off the canal so it could not be used and the British and the French got together with the Israelis and they were going to kick the shit out of the Egyptians. The Israelis were going to do all the work and at the last minute the English bombers would come in and bomb the hell out of the Egyptians and we would get the Suez Canal open. They were fighting Abdul Nassar. He was a very radical leader of Egypt at the time. In fact, he caused them to have about three or four wars where they got the shit kicked out of them four times over there (in 1948, 1956, 1965 and 1973). Anyhow, it really got uptight because the Russians were making threats and we had all the aircraft locked down on the base, on alert, and they told us we couldn't go to town anymore. Now, we don't mind fighting the war, but don't ask us to give up our cooter and booze. So, we were going to go to town and a couple of the boys stuck their clothes in my car. They were allowed to go down to the Beehive Bar, which was right outside the gates. They weren't allowed to go any further than that. I had the car and I could get on and off the base so they threw their clothes in the back of the car and I went down to the Beehive and picked them up and we started heading for London. Now, God help us if the war would have started and we weren't there. Of course, the airplanes were in perfect condition and they would have gone on their mission and it would have been doubtful that there would be anything left to come back to. So we said the hell with it and we were going to keep up Anglo American relationships and we were going to town. So we went to the town of London and went to Sibones at Lancaster Gate and had dinner. There was a beautiful French girl with black hair. I was bs'ing with her because I was the guy with the biggest line of bullshit. The boys were sitting over there watching the ole' master at work. So we parked the car and went to the Grand Chester club and later started to walk down to the 55 Club. All the stewardesses hung up there because that's where the officer's territory was, and they would always try to police up on an officer first. As we were sauntering down laughing, joking and carrying on, I looked on the other side of the street and spotted that beautiful girl who had been working at Sibones. She had a couple of letters that she was going to mail. I dashed across the street with great vigor, come up behind her and said, "Hi there, my name if Tommy Kaye and I'm a Sergeant out at the base. Are you going up to the post box?" She said, "Oh yes" with that lovely French accent. I said, "May I walk with you and talk with you for a while?" I waved to the boys to go on up to the 55 Club. We walked up to the post box and I started turning on the charm and started talking and talking and talking. I found out that she was from Paris and she had come over here to go to school. She had come from Paris to go to a cooking school in London. She was a delight. I can remember to this day, she was wearing a light powder blue suit, nice high heels, and she had long black hair and was well endowed. We talked and talked and talked and I looked and saw that the boys were coming back down the street so we walked across the street and saw that things were closing down. The boys jumped in the back of the car and I said to her, "I'd like to sleep with you tonight." She said, "I'd like that, Thomas, I'd like that very much." So, being a gentleman, I opened the door and helped her get into the car and then drove on up to 118 Fordwitch Road, where the boys went on into their bedrooms. I went down and made us some coffee and we had a bit of coffee and talked a little while. Then I put the records on the record player and we started stripping down for some action. She had the most gorgeous body. She made Marilyn Monroe look like a piker. She had the most gorgeous breasts; they were like ice cream cones. I swear you could have put coat hangers on the end and hung up a suit and they would have held it. So we got in the bed and we played all sorts of games, such as 34 ½ and ride the pony. It was a wonderful night. Unbeknownst to us those two rotters in the back bedroom had got glasses and put them against the wall and were listening to the two of us carrying on, sighing like wounded Billy goats or a wounded steam engine. Anyhow, we indulged until the wee hours of the morning and then caught a little bit of sleep. Then she woke me up and said, "I've got to get to school." I woke up the boys and told them to get ready because we had to take her to school and we would go into town and get a bit to eat. So, as we're driving back down Edgeware Road, and this is the God's truth, I looked over and I held her hand for a minute and then I said, "By the way, what is your name?" That's when she told me that her name was Sonya. That was the fastest con job I had ever done on a girl, because I got her to spend the night with me and I never even knew her name. Anyhow, I dated her quite a lot of times after that, and took her to a lot of parties. She eventually married a guy from New Zealand and she immigrated to New Zealand. I like to keep up with all of my old girlfriends.

After this episode we went and snuck back onto the base. The next weekend we were due to go to Upper Heyford to go to B-47 school. Finally, after all these years in the Air Force, they were going to send me to school on the B-47, which I already knew like the back of my hand. Googee K_____ went up three or four days ahead of me, and Zipjack came up and John Henry Thomas III and a couple of other guys rode up with me. We brought K_____ clothes up with us because he went up there on a bus and he left his clothes in my car. When we got there it was at the beginning of the school day and we noticed K_____ sitting in the far corner of the room. We said, "Googee, what are you doing over there in the far corner of the room?" We walked over to him and he smelled kind of bad. We looked at his knees and his elbows and you could see there was a little bit of cow shit left on them. He had gone into town and picked up a WRAF (that is a Woman's Royal Air Force girl) and they went out into the fields to get a little and he got his knees and elbows in cow shit. When he came back he cleaned it up the best he could, but he was still kind of rank and they wouldn't let him sit in the regular part of the classroom; he had to sit in the back. Needless to say, K_____ caught up with me about two years ago and he's now a deacon in the church and he sings in the choir. He doesn't smoke or drink or anything anymore. He's got religion and a mighty big strong life. Anyhow, we went through school during the week and, being that we were in school, we could go to London on the weekend. Well, Zipjack didn't have any money so he didn't want to go. John Henry Thomas III and I went to the Grand Chester and, while we were in there, John Henry Thomas III picked up on a girl named Rose. She was Zipjack's girlfriend and he had been trying to get in her drawers for a couple of weekends and he had never succeeded. So, John Henry Thomas III from Pittsburgh, Pennsylvania policed up on her. I brought Kathy, Cecilia's sister, since I couldn't hit up on anything that quick anyhow, and I wasn't going with anyone else. We got in the bent-eight roadster (that means it is a V-8, hence the "v"), we swooped on up to the apartment and we got in our respected rooms and turned on the jukebox. We had the sounds and we were indulging and having a good time. We spent the weekend there and had the normal, wonderful, wonderful weekend and then we came on back. About Tuesday, John Henry pulled me aside and he said, "T.K., I think I've got the clap. I'm going to the medics tomorrow morning." So he went to the medics and, sure enough, he had the clap. Of course, they had the new one million units and they were going to cure him. I said, "Are you going to tell Zipjack, because it's his girlfriend?" He said, "Hell, no. If I got the clap I'm gonna let him get the clap too." I said, "John, that's rotten." He said, "Well, we're G.I.'s." So anyhow, we loaded Zipjack up this weekend because it was after payday, and he went in and got his true love Rose, and we picked up a bunch of girls and went back to the pad and partied. We had a couple of cases of beer and we were dancing and everything. Zipjack went and he finally got some cooter off his girlfriend. After all, she had given it to his friend. Again, we had a good time. We left about two or three o'clock in the morning to get back to the base to go to school. Now, I have to describe Zipjack to you. He's a little short fellow about 5'4", looked like a cherub, a little angel with the blonde curly hair and a round little face. He was a Polock from Chicago. On about Tuesday, he said, "I've got to go to the medics this morning, I think I've got a haircut on my dork." I said, "Why, what's the matter, Zipjack?" He said, "Well, it must be a haircut." I just looked at Thomas III and shook my head and said that son of a bitch has got it too. So, we dropped him off at the medics on the way to school. He came into school and I said, "What you got?" He said, "I've got a haircut on my dork. They're going to give me a shot for it tomorrow, they want to make some checks on it." I just looked at John Thomas III and we both shook our heads because we both knew he had the clap. So, about Friday he said, "I'm ready to go to town." I said, "Zipjack, have the medics turned you loose? Because you had the clap." He said, "What do you mean I had the clap? I had a haircut." I said, "You had a haircut, shit. You had the clap because John Henry Thomas took Rose home last weekend and got the clap off of her." He said, "You dirty bastards, you didn't tell me that I could get the clap from her." I said, "No, what's good for one friend is good for all the rest of the friends." We went back to the big city and needless to say, Little Zipjack didn't go to Rose anymore. He pulled her aside and told her what he had caught off of her. We picked up about three or four more girls and we partied again. It was just like that every weekend. Outside of the rent, which was $20.00 for the flat, we might spend $20.00 each for partying each weekend. It was the loveliest city and you could do anything you wanted in the world there, cheaply. Now, it's a different story, it's one of the most expensive towns in the World. In fact, every time I go back to the big city I visit 118 Fordwitch Road. You'll see the pictures of it in the book. Between my flat, the flat above it and the flat below it, we had three rooms. They have now taken each room and turned it into a flat and added a little bathroom and a tiny shower. Now they have twelve flats where they used to be just four, and they charge $800.00 a month for each of those little tiny flats. It's amazing the costs of venturing out nowadays compared to how it was in the days gone by.

Another thing that happened prior to us getting our flat happened about New Year's Eve of 1957. You will see a picture in the back attributed to this wild ass New Year's Eve. Now, needless to say, we GI's were kind of dumb and we didn't know that New Year's Eve was open season on GI's. Everywhere in London there were Englishmen who were called the teddy boys because they were gangs that dressed in Edwardian style suits. It was open season on GI's because we had the money and we had all the girls. So, at midnight, they would beat the hell out of all the GI's. Well, needless to say, Vetter, who was in my barracks, and Sam Giovino, who was in my barracks, and I all decided to go to the Big L. This was right before we got the pad. We were staying at the Elizabeth Hotel. Anyhow, we were down in the Number 2 Club. Now, Vetter looked like an Englishman, he was very pale, he did not have a tan; he looked like a bloke. He was standing with his back against the wall next to the jukebox. Sam Giovino looked like a typical Italian with the dark hair and dark skin. And then there was good ole' skinny T.K., who by this time had grown from 135 pounds to about 175 pounds. Again, we were all dressed very well because it was required that we dress before we left the base. I don't think there was a pair of Levi's on the whole continent of England. I was just not done; everybody got dressed and wore white shirts and ties. So, we were in there in this little bar. Now I have to describe the bar. It was down in the cellar; there was one way in and that was coming down the stairs from the upstairs hallway. So, there was one way in and one way out. This bar was probably 16' wide by 32' long; the bar went all the way across one end. There were little small coffee tables, couches and chairs all the way around the outside and then there was the dance floor in the middle. By this time, we were pretty damn drunk, but we were having a good time. I was dancing, and God knows who I was dancing with; I was policing up on any lady who was there. Again, we did not know tonight was open season on GI's. Vetter put his bottle on top of the jukebox, which had an angle going down of about 15 degrees. Since the bottle was wet on the bottom, it slid back to the backside and then fell to the ground and broke. It just happened to be almost empty. I went up to the jukebox and put a sixpence in there and was playing Elvis Presley's new song "Love Me Tender." I was leaning over to get a couple of more to play and this bloke walked up there and put his bottle up and said to Vetter, "Go ahead, break my bottle, Yank." Vetter said, "No, this is New Year's Eve, we're just having a good time." So, the bloke took his bottle and turned around and smacked Sam across the top of his head and later it took eighteen stitches to close up the wound in the top of his head. Another one spun me around and hit me right on the nose and broke my nose. I guess he didn't like "Love Me Tender." He then hit me again and I fell to the ground in the middle of the dance floor. I managed to get turned over because I knew what they would do next because they would link arms and kick the hell out of you and stomp you while you were down. So, I pulled a couple down on top of me. Now, Vetter hadn't done anything. Sam was fighting for his life with blood leaking all over him. They also kicked me in the knee, kicking my kneecap around to the side. Vetter said, "I'm gonna go help somebody in this fight." He looked and here was a pile of people on the floor and he sees this hand coming out trying to pull himself out. Vetter thought, well, I'll strike a blow for the Americans and he leaped into the air and came back down and stomped on that poor bastard's hand. There was a big scream and about that time I pushed up and erupted out of the blokes because they were of smaller stature than me. I got up and started throwing them off. I was really getting angry, my adrenaline was pumping and I said, "Let's get the F-- out of here." We were fighting our way back to that little doorway. We got in the doorway and fought our way across the hall and went up the stairs. It was a piece of cake once we got on the stairs because we were kicking them back down the stairs and as one would fall, he would knock down three or four more. So, we came out the hallway and were running across the street and they came out carrying cases of empty beer bottles and started throwing them at us. They sounded like mortars coming in crashing. I got in the middle of the street and, since my kneecap was around the side, my leg locked up and I fell in the street. Sam was holding a rag over his head and Vetter didn't pass a lick; he didn't do a damn bit of good. I said, "Sam, Sam, partner, come and help me." He said, "Hell no T.K., if I come back to get you we'll all get killed," and he took off running along with Vetter, who didn't have a scratch on his body. Well, about that time, I got up and, with my stiff leg, I passed the other two bastards up. We got back to the hotel and, God Bless Rose, there was a doctor living in the hotel and she brought him down. He brought his kit and had to shave part of Sam's head to put eighteen stitches in it. He didn't have to do anything to Vetter because he didn't strike a blow for the Americans. Then he came to me and, by this time, my nose was swollen and my eyes were black and he just fiddled it around and put some tape across it. He took my kneecap and pushed it back where it was supposed to be. He said, "That's going to give you a lot of trouble later on in life." Then he put an ace bandage around it and started checking my ribs. I had three broken ribs so he taped me up. We were really a good-looking crew so we went up to our respective rooms and went to sleep. About 10:00 a.m., Sam and Vetter came to my room and we were talking about the battle that we were in and I said, "Boy, we sure got the hell kicked out of us." Vetter said, "Well, I fixed one guy. I stomped his hand. He'll be hurting today." About that time I took my hand out from underneath the blanket and my fingers looked like old bananas; they were yellow, brown, blue, green and purple. I said, "Yeah, you son of a bitch, you stomped my hand. You didn't strike a blow for anybody." So anyhow, that was New Year's Eve of 1956-1957.

A couple of weeks later Sam was getting ready to go back to the states so we had a bottle of whiskey in the barracks and we were sitting on a footlocker. Sam brought out this bloody handkerchief and we took a knife and cut it in half and on my half he wrote, "To my buddy T.K., a wonderful night in the Big L, New Year's Eve '56 – '57, from your buddy Sam Giovino." I did the same thing on my half that I gave to him. I still have my half; there will be a picture of it in the back of the book. It was all good memories.

Now I'm going to tell you about one of the big parties that we had. It was in the winter because there was snow on the ground. Two of our friends were going back to the states, Joe G_____ from New York who ended up being a bible salesman in Miami and Hero, who was what we called a jockstrap soldier because he worked in the gym and he was going back to Washington State. We were going to throw a going away party for them that was going to be unbelievable. We bought all the booze at the Class Six store, which means that we paid anywhere from $.80 for a 40 ounce jug of vodka and gin or $1.60 for a bottle of V.O.; a bottle of champagne was $.88. In my car we had three cases of champagne and twenty 40-ounce jugs of whiskey in the back on the floor. We had swiped out of the chow hall a gross of hardboiled eggs, twelve loaves of bread, four gallons of mustard, four gallons of mayonnaise, four cases of tomato juice, a great big cheese about ½ the size of a small wheel and we had one full length of bologna, salami and liverwurst. There was a case of Spam in big square cans about 12" long, 4" by 4" square. Damn, we would never starve, we ended up eating fried Spam & eggs for breakfast, Spam sandwiches during parties, Fried Spam and spaghetti, Spam and veggies; there was no end to the use of it. I still love it to this very day. Anyhow, there was so much shit in that car of mine that only two of us could fit in there. My good buddy Albert Emil Schultz from Chicago (may he rest in peace), and I were the only ones who could fit in there. The rest of the car was full to the brim and the trunk was full to the brim with all this stuff that we had purloined and bought. So we were going to London and here were all our friends who were coming to the party and they were hitchhiking on the side of the road in the snow and all we could do was wave to them. Doc Pringle had taken two guys in his little two-seater so the three of them wee in London waiting for us when we arrived. By that time they had 100 pounds of ice and they had broken it up in this giant bathtub, which was the duty bathtub for the whole house. We put the three cases of champagne in there and took all the booze upstairs. We had everything laid out on a big table that we had rented for the food. It was unbelievable; we had four cases of tomato juice for the hangover on Monday morning. We went downtown to the PX and bought a couple cases of beer. When we had everything laid out and right, we had a big cake that said, "Bon Voyage, Joe and Bon Voyage, Bob Hero." About twelve of us went to the 55 Club that night to pick up some good-looking girls for this big party – Joe G's and Bob Hero's going away party. Well, Bob had a very good voice and he used to sing with a little four-piece band. He would sing some Frank Sinatra songs and he was very, very good. Joe G_____ was like me; we were the dancers of the outfit. So, we partied and were working on some girls. I picked up this little itty-bitty girl in a white dress with funny sewing all over it. Her name was Ruth, a pretty little thing about 5'2" tall, weighed about 95 pounds. Everybody else had the girls and we piled in the car and in the cab and we took the van with us. One English guy snuck in there; his name was Collin. I later became great friends with him, but he wasn't invited because we didn't want any blokes, it was only for GI's. So we went up and started partying. The wine and whiskey were flowing. The sounds were going on. There was a light snow falling outside. Everyone was taking pictures through the night and around five or six o'clock in the morning Doc looked over at the mantel piece and said, "Where's my Leica camera?" Leica was a German camera, very good at the time. Another guy said, "Where's my Argis?" Argis was an American made camera. I looked around and said, "Where's the bloke?" Well, two other blokes had snuck into the party. We went rampaging down the stairs, got out front and one of them was running away with the cameras. Doc Pringle ran, leaped in the air and body tackled him and got the cameras back and beat the hell out of the guy. After that happened a little bloke came down and he was trying to go out the front door and Joe G_____ got him in the corner. Joe G_____ would pound him until he got tired and then he'd look back because the circular stairway was filled with girls and observers. This was the first time, I guess, that Joe G_____ had ever won a fight in his life. He'd punch him for a while, then look back and smile at the ladies, then pull him back up and punch him some more. Finally, when Doc Pringle got back he opened the door and threw him out on the front steps. About that time, another bloke who had been hiding in the kitchen (the aforementioned Collin) came out with a big knife, menacing everybody and everyone backed up the stairs. I had one boy that was going with me to Psychology classes at the University of Oxford three nights a week, who's name was Joel P. Murray. He was from Salt Lake City, Utah. He was normally a very quiet individual. So I was down by the door blocking the way along with Joe G. so the bloke couldn't get out there. He came down the stairs and was standing right beside the banister. He couldn't go through the two of us and thank God he didn't try by cutting us. Joel P. Murray eased down and made like Douglas Fairbanks, Jr., putting one hand on the banister and vaulting over the banister and kicking that bloke in the head with one foot and he kicked the knife out of the hand with the other foot. Then he stood him up and beat the hell out of the bloke and threw him out of the front door. Anyhow, we got our cameras back and went back up and started partying again. Well, about 5:00 a.m. I deemed it was time to go to bed and get some of the good stuff before all the beds got taken. So little Ruth and I went down into my bedroom and got into my big bed. This little girl, I swear I don't know what she had, but I've never gone as many times as that time. She just reeked sex and we would indulge and climax and in then minutes I'd be ready to go again. After I went about three or four times, Doc Pringle came down because he wanted a bed for this girl that he later married. She was a beautiful black haired girl named Jackie. So they ran me out of my big bed and we went into the back bedroom and got into a smaller bed and went a couple more times. All in total, in a period of 30 or 34 hours between little bits of sleeping, I think I climaxed about nine times. That was my world record never to be surpassed. I don't know what she had but whatever it was, I never experienced it again. We just made it back to the base. It was a wonderful going away party.

Right around now is when I fell in love with three girls at the same time. That's something a male should never do, especially one who drinks. I was dating a beautiful blonde with elegant breasts named Joan. I was also dating a young little redheaded girl named Jean and then another girl name June. I was working them pretty good. I would work one on Friday, one on Saturday and one on Sunday. I went on pretty good for about a month; I was just enjoying the hell out of myself. This one weekend I got drunk and I called Joan by June's name, and Jean by Joan's name, etc. etc. I blew three romances in the ass at the same time.

I also have to regress back to that little girl, Ruth, who just radiated the sex. One weekend I was coming into town by myself for some reason. We had ham that afternoon in the Chow Hall so by the time I got to town, and we met at my flat, I was starting to get very sick. She said, "Let's go over to my flat and I'll take care of you there." This was Friday night. So, we drove over to her little flat and I went inside and starting barfing and then the diarrhea started. I was going from both ends; I could have literally filled a 55-gallon drum. I had a terrible fever and she nursed me through all of this. It was just endless; I was dehydrating and she would force me to drink water and took care of me all through the weekend. All that time, while I was so sick, I still managed to diddle that little girl three or four times. I'll never forget that as long as I live. So about Sunday afternoon, I was coming out of it and we went to town and I had some poached eggs on toast. That little girl actually saved my life. When I got back to the base, I found out that we had some bad meat and there was about 60 or 70 guys what went to the hospital for stomach poisoning. That was quite a deal. I went with Ruth for maybe another month or so and then we just drifted apart. She was one sexy little girl.

About this time we got involved in a little bit of black marketing. We almost put the hiatus on my career in the military. Since I had the car with the big trunk and everything, the guys would get whiskey and put it in the trunk of my Ford. Now, let us talk a matter of economics. You didn't black market cigarettes because there wasn't enough profit in there. You'd pay around $4.00 for a carton and you could sell it for $8.00; that was only 100% profit. But you could get a bottle of Philadelphia whiskey, which is rotgut at the best, and you'd pay $1.40 for that bottle of whiskey and you could sell it for $10.00 downtown. A bottle of vodka and Gibley's gin, which we paid $.80 for, we could sell for $7.00 downtown. Now I don't really understand why anybody got upset about all this shit because we weren't sending the money home, we were spending the money on the economy. We were lubricating the economy with our excess pounds that we made. Also, we were keeping a lot of small bars stocked. When you went in there and asked for V.O. or Seagram 7 or some other drink, what you were getting was Philadelphia poured out of our bottles down in the cellar. So, a lot of guys were airmen and they couldn't buy whiskey so they would get an NCO to buy it for them or they would get an officer to buy it for them. We had dentists buying it for them, and doctors buying it for them. We had the base security officer, Toby (I forget his last name), who bought it for a couple of his AP's. So every time I taxied out the gate on Friday night I would have a load of booze in there and, being the good little Sergeant I was, I never would participate. And to this day, luckily for me, I still have my ration card (you'll see a picture of it in the back) because we could purchase four bottle of whiskey and four cartons of cigarettes a month, but you had to have a stamp plugged out on the ration card and that's what really saved my butt. This one day I said, "Damn, I need some extra money. I think I'll go by the Class Six and pick up a couple bottles for the black market." So, luckily for me, I spent the whole day on alert strip working on an airplane. I couldn't get any booze. Being on the flight line all day, we were a little bit late going out. I had a low right rear tire that was low on air. A kid named Tyce was going with me out the gate and a Sergeant named Brewer says, "What you got in the trunk?" I said, "I ain't got nothing in the trunk. My right rear tire is low, that's all." He said, "Turn that car around, I want to look in the trunk." Tyce looked at me and I looked at him and thought, I'm in the shit now. We pulled over and he said, "Open the trunk." I took that little brass Ford key and I tried to break that mother off and there must be stainless steel on the inside of the brass. So, he opened the trunk and he says, "Sergeant Kaye, you have a problem. You're only authorized to take one bottle of whiskey off per NCO in this car and as I count it, you're 41 NCOs short." In other words, I had forty-two 40-ounce jugs of whiskey. So, I was heading for Fort Leavenworth, the military jail. He said, "Follow me." They took all my whiskey and as we were passing it out we were putting it on tables and I was trying to mix it up and they saw that it was all Philadelphia and just eight bottles of vodka and gin. I didn't say anything and they said, "You're free to go because you're a non-commissioned officer and we can't throw you in jail." So I got in the car and I went to the Big L and I said, "Oh, woe is me, I'm going to the cross bar hotel for damn sure." All my friends who were in the house, whose liquor it was, said, "Don't worry T.K., we'll claim a couple of bottles here and a couple of bottles there and everything will be all right." Yeah, in a pig's ass everything will be all right. So, Monday comes and the Colonel comes down and calls me and he says, "You're in a lot of trouble. But, you've done good work for me and I'll stick by you. Anytime they stay on you too long, just call me. Here's my phone numbers."

So they started questioning me and I explained that this belongs to this guy, this belongs to that guy, and the rest belongs to all these other guys. They said, "Well, we've called all these other guys and they said they don't know nothing about nothing. They don't even know who T.K. is." I said, "Well, they're lying. They're living in the apartments with me." They all ratted on me and ratted me out. So here I'm stuck having to account for all of these bottles of whiskey and I can't account for one of them. Now, they know they've got the biggest black marketer in 20 years, but they can't prove anything because they never caught me selling it to anybody. In fact, it never left the base, so technically I never broke the base regulation. But this went on and on and they questioned me on and on and on and finally I told them, "Damn right we were going to go black market and I'll tell you where I was going to go black market but you can't do a damn thing to me." By this time, the guys were starting to drift away and were being sent back from overseas and Doc P went back and so did Toby, the base Provost Marshall, who bought some of it. They traced every bottle of liquor back to who bought it. Again, it proved that it wasn't me because they had numbers stamped on the top of every one. So they knew who purchased every bottle of liquor and they knew that none of it was mine. I was just the stupid idiot with the car that was carrying it. So, anyhow, that drifted down and things quieted down a little bit.

Now, of course, I had vacancies in the apartment so I moved Matheny and a couple of other boys in. They were sharing the flats with me along with Albert Emil Schultz, my buddy from Chicago. He stayed with me right until the end. I quit hanging at the 55 Club because I wasn't gratis there anymore. Because some of the officers had gotten in trouble for purchasing this liquor for the lower grade enlisted men. So I went back and was hanging out at the Seafarers Club down on Lancaster Gate. Matheny and I were sitting in there one day at the bar talking and these two beautiful, elegant ladies walked in the door. I shall never forget them; it was Elizabeth and her girlfriend. Now, Elizabeth was the daughter of a missionary from China. She had been raised in China. They were both wearing Cheongsam velvet dresses with the high Chinese collar with the little, they call them frogs, where they button it, with a slit down the one side, then there was a slit by the leg. They both were absolutely gorgeous. I looked at Matheny then I looked at that blonde, and both of their hair was in a Swiss roll where it was up, pulled back and rolled in very nicely. They were very, very elegant. I looked at Matheny and I said, "You see that blonde there? She could sit on my chest and eat saltine crackers and drop the crumbs in my eyes until all I could do was holler help, help, help." So anyhow, those girls walked in and they went up to the bar. I had to go to the bathroom and when I came back the girls were down at the bar with Matheny. So Matheny said, "Let me introduce you." I didn't even think about the one wearing the gray Cheongsam, I was just thinking about Liz because she was just like an actress. She was so beautiful. He said, "Liz, this is T.K." We started talking and I started dancing with her and as I was dipping her she looked right up in my eyes and said, "T.K., I've got a box of saltine crackers at my house." And there I was, shocked, she just totally blew my mind. I took her out of the dip and I picked her up and said, "You really amazed me. You shook me up there." So we danced the evening away and then decided to go to a friend of mine, Reggie's pad, and we partied until the wee hours of the morning. I took her home about 7:00 a.m., we never did diddle. A couple of months later I took her to another party at Reggie's and I was dancing with her. I said, "You know, I always wanted to sleep with you to see what you looked like first thing in the morning." She said, "Well, there's no better night than tonight." So, we indulged and when we woke up in the morning there was not one hair out of place on her head. I don't know how she did it, but I mean she was something, absolutely gorgeous. She later married a technical rep from North American and moved back to the states.

About this time is when I met my first wife. I was still under a lot of pressure, still worried about the whiskey deal. C.I.D. was following me to see if I was going to do anything dastardly. I was just coming to London and it ended up that Al and I were the only ones who had an apartment. We stayed in the apartment together as all the other apartments had gone back to the English people because the GI's were all gone. We had pretty much settled down and he started going with one girl who he married later on and had two children with. She named them Rory Albert Emil Schultz and Cheyenne Bodie Emil Schultz; I'll never forget that. Then she left him and went back to England. He drank himself to death. He died very young, about the age of 36. He loved her dearly.

About this time, Matheny and I were sitting down in the Seafarers one night. Now, John Wayne was my hero and he always married girls from the orient and I always had a liking for women from Burma or India or some place like that. It was very exotic and I was raised on Kipling and Gungaden and all the pictures from over there; the purple plane with Barbara Luna and Gregory Peck. I just had a thing for those girls. One night I was sitting at the bar and I looked and this beautiful woman walked in. She had long black shiny hair done in a pageboy. She was Anglo Indian. Her father was a Scotsman and her mother was an Indian. She was wearing a lavender light coat with a white dress with lavender flowers and lavender high heels. What a set of legs she had. She was really a looker. Anyhow, I diddly bopped up to her, bought her a drink and asked her if she would like to dance. So we started dancing and talking. She danced like a dream. At closing time I took her in her car and we went to the Golden Star downtown and had breakfast. Then I took her home and said, "Well, I'll see you the following night." She stood me up the following night and about a week or two later she met me again. So we had another date and then I stood her up. We played that game for about two or three months and then we started going together seriously. In fact, we got going together so steady that you know, you sort of drift where the only thing holding you together is the sex. But anyhow, she was staying in 41 Palace Court and I was staying at my apartment. Another guy had moved in. His name was Wes Shales and he moved in with Al in the back bedrooms. So, Lorna and I went out one Saturday night to Reggie's to a party. Reggie had the ideal party room. It was down the cellar, with red lights and everything was just right. So, while we were there I felt like dancing and she had met another old girlfriend of hers. So, they were sitting there bullshitting. I don't know what they were bullshitting about, but anyhow, I met another girl named Terri. Terri was a good dancer so we were dancing. About 2:00 a.m. or 3:00 a.m. it was time for me to go home and go to bed. Terri said, "Why don't we slip off and go to my place or your place and get a little bit?" I said, "But I'm with her." She said,

"Well, go ask her if she's ready to go home." So I went over to Lorna and I said, "Look, let's go on home." She said, "No, I'm talking to my girlfriend. You sit and wait." I said, "Well, kiss my ass" and I went back and told Terri, "You ease out the back door and I'll ease out the front door." We met outside there and jumped into the bent eight roadster and we drove quite swiftly back to the flat. We got up to the flat and Wesley was in the back room with his girlfriend. Terri and I got into the front room. I put the jukebox on, had the lights down low, and we got stripped down to action and were just getting ready to get a little bit and I heard this taxi come to a stop. You could differentiate the engine of a taxi from anything else in England. I heard Lorna talking and then the door slammed and I could hear these high heels coming across the front and start coming up the steps. I said, "She's here." She grabbed her clothes and I was still in my shorts and T-shirt and I grabbed her clothes and her and put her into the back room with Wesley and his girlfriend, hoping that I would get by with it. I jumped in the bed and was lying in there listening to music. Lorna went by the kitchen and picked up a big bread knife (rusty, of course), which would have given me lockjaw. She came charging into the room saying, "You no good G.I., you ran off with that Irish witch. Where's she at? I'll kill her I'll kill her. I'll cut you up, you no good G.I." I was playing the innocent roll and said, "No, I've just been home here." So, in the meantime, she was checking the bathroom and the kitchen and here's Terri in the back bedroom with Wesley and she's in her panties and bra, holding her shoes. They knew Lorna was coming in there and would look underneath the bed, so what they did was put her out the window. Right down about four feet below the window was the roof for the kitchen of the apartment underneath, so that's where they put her. The picture also evidences this; you'll see an arrow drawn showing exactly where she was on that roof. This poor girl, in the wee hours of the morning, was out there in her skivvies holding on by her fingernails. Lorna came blazing into the room and looked around, looked underneath the bed and said, "Well, she's not here. I don't know where she's gone but I'll get that Irish bitch one day." Then she slammed the door. Of course, they brought Terri back inside, got her clothes, then they eased out of the blat on the back and took her home in Wesley's car. Lorna was quite upset emotionally. I was also quite upset. By that time I pretended I was asleep and she leaped into the bed. I did end up, eventually, after a few more adventures, marrying her and had two children with her.

WHO DAT?

There were two places over which we flew the RB-47 regularly, that required we pass very close to Soviet airfields on entry and exit. One of those was the narrow strait between Sweden and East Germany as we exited West Germany and went into the Baltic Sea. At both locations, we were always intercepted by Soviet fighters and watched very closely. It created a problem for the Soviets because fighters out of the bases involved had enough fuel to permit flying into a NATO country and defecting.

We learned that there were only two or three pilots at each location that could be trusted to make the intercept and return, because the fighters had enough fuel to make it into Sweden or Germany. Each time they came up, they used different names, call signs and such in an attempt to fool us. But analysis of the voice recordings revealed that the same guys were being used all the time. Sometimes they would come up in a four-ship cell with two of the regulars and two new guys. We guessed the regulars were ordered to shoot down the other two if they tried to defect.

Our pilots usually greeted the Soviet pilots with the middle finger gesture. Soon it became routine to look off your wing and see a grinning Russian giving you the finger. That started a game between us. First, just as the MiGs were about to close on us, the two pilots would duck down so they couldn't be seen and the navigator would fly the airplane with second station. That shocked the fighter pilots, especially when the RB-47 made a turn, and they reported us as a 'Ghost Airplane'.

Then we got full gorilla masks, that slipped over the head, and the pilots acted like apes were flying the airplane (that wasn't too far from the truth). One of the wives found slipover Khrushchev masks and sent them to us. The Soviet pilots laughed their heads off and saluted when looking over and seeing two Nikitas flying the RB-47. We also put blow-up plastic women in place of the pilots.

That game continued for quite a while and we became more and more creative. But we got the greatest shock of all when a MIG-17 pulled up less than three feet off our wing and was being flown by-Lyndon B. Johnson. We have no idea where a fighter pilot in the Soviet Union was able to get a slipover Johnson mask. Both pilots saluted the Russian and from that point on it was quite common for us to be intercepted by Lyndon Johnson.

The gorilla suits and masks also caused quite a stir when we landed at other bases (where they had never seen an RB-47H) and taxied in with the pilots wearing them.

Quite often, getting back to our base was more of a challenge than the enemy defenses. We filed no flight plans and because we kept the airplane completely blacked out and often had no markings, visual identification was almost impossible. That got real sticky, especially in Turkey, England and a few other places. The Turkish pilots were crazy and unpredictable as they answered to no one else. The British were trigger happy and rude. Once we were intercepted by an RAF pilot and he got quite nasty. He made a few attempts at establishing radio contact, but we couldn't answer. We had no markings but were obviously a B-47 type airplane. Finally he said, "Unidentified aeroplane, if you do not establish your identity immediately I am going to open fire." Our copilot pointed the 20MM cannons at the bloke and let the radar go into lock-on. He immediately replied, "Tally ho, identification received and understood. Have a jolly day chaps."

I'm including an excerpt here of a book by Colonel Bruce Bailey, with his permission. He was the best Crow that they had in the United States Air Force in the 55th. He did more for improvements and making the mission go easier and better. Of course, if you read his book, which is called *Flying The RB47*, by Bruce Bailey you will be able to truly understand a large part of the Cold War; the things that they did, and their comrades who were shot down and were killed. The people in the United States never knew this was going on. They were brave, brave men and I take my hat off to them always.

The time is still 1957 and this is a little quick vignette of me on a B66. The B66's were just coming out and were twin engine, fast attack bombers that had two J71 engines, had a three-man crew and I'd never seen one before. We got a work order for a hydraulic leak on a hydraulic pump on the number one engine. I grabbed Tice and said, "Let's go out there and fix that leak and we're going to find out how fast that Mother goes." So we went out there and we took one fitting off, put a new Teflon backup and a new 6290 seal, screwed it down in there, tightened the fitting back up and we decided to get it pressure checked later when the crew came out. Now, the bomb bay doors were open so I walked into the bomb bay and I looked and there was a crawl away that goes right from the bomb bay all the way up to the pilot's seats. There's no co-pilot on this aircraft, there's just a pilot and a navigator/bombardier and a tail gunner. At the end of this was the instrument panel and I could see the Mach meter and the air speed indicator. I told Tice I was going to crawl up there and to keep a lookout. He said, "You'd better not go in there, Sgt. Kaye." So I said, "Okay, I'm going to be careful." So I got up on that little crawl away and as I crawled forward there was a ladder, a stairs, built into the fold down fuselage, a part of the fuselage where the flight crew normally entered. I shook that three or four times and it seemed like it was latched to me. As I was crawling across it, it opened up and it fell straight down and I fell straight down and landed right on my nose, which I broke. I also blacked both eyes and blood was leaking with enormous quantities all over the place. I said, "Well the hell with it. I didn't want to know how fast it went anyhow. Let's go back to the shop." So we went back to my hydraulic shop and I got some rags and I'm holding my nose and laying down and trying to get the blood to stop. Well, the blood wouldn't stop by about 5 o'clock so I went up to the medics and the doctor looked at me and he said, "You broke your nose." Well, it's been broken before so he just pushed it back to where it was supposed to be and put a little bit of tape across there. He said, "You're really leaking enormous quantities of blood so I'm going to stuff wicks up there." I said, "Stuff wicks?" He said, "Well, they're like a woman's Tampax. You put them up in there and as they absorb the blood they kind of seal everything off." So I said, "Okay." So he put the two wicks up in my nose and I went on home. Of course, when I got home I was accused of everything by my lady friend who I was spending time with at the time. She accused me of being at the NCO Club and being in a fight. She just simply would not believe that I had fallen and broken my nose. So I got up the next morning and went to the base and we stood roll call, we checked out all the aircraft, went to the alert strip and checked them and I turned around and went back up to the medics. The medic pulled the wicks out and by now they are dry and everything so I thought, "Well, they'll come out and it will be all right." As they came out the one on the right was sealed up but the one on the left was still gushing. He said, "Well, you know what we're going to have to do Sgt. Kaye? We'll fix this." So he went in there and he whipped out what looked like a handy dandy, 88-cent Japanese soldering iron. I said, "What are you going to do with that?" He said, "We're going to cauterize the inside of your nose to stop it from bleeding." I said, "No, no, no, no, no, we're going to NOT do that." I guess I got so frightened that it closed off the blood vessels and I haven't had a bloody nose since then. That's the end of that vignette.

Now, we had some new aircraft on the alert strip that were from the 301st Bomb Wing. They were called Blue Cradle aircraft. These were special, they would lead the bombers in and they had a special capsule in them two ECM operators, one officer and one enlisted man, two Crows. Basically, this aircraft was a one-way ticket. It was to lead the bombers in and jam everything and open the way for the bomber electronically. They jammed the radar, jammed the guns, and jammed everything else. Now, this was coming from the 301st Bomb Wing in Lockbourne, Ohio and they sent an individual over named Morton Cherim, who was a young Buck Sergeant and an ex Navy man so we got along well. Morton and I are still friends after 50 years and he was the one who started teaching me about air conditioning and pressurization, because we had a guy assigned to my shop who was kind of squirrelly and he just didn't look right. You couldn't say what was right or what was wrong with him; he just didn't have a full deck. Anyhow, Mort started schooling me every day and we'd go out on the jobs together when the aircraft reflects in and we'd go over them and check everything until I got a good understanding of how the air conditioning and pressurization went and then we started working on liquid oxygen and water alcohol injection. So I learned everything from him. About that time, one morning we had roll call and I asked if everybody was there. They said, "No, the pneumatic man isn't here, the pressurization man isn't here." He's the one who was assigned to my shop who wasn't all there. I said, "Well, go to the barracks and see if you can find him. I'm not turning in a false report." So, C.W. Palmer went up to the barracks and came back and said, "He's not in his bed, Sgt. Kaye. His bed's not made, you've got to see this." We jumped in my Bent 8 roadster and went back to the barracks and found that his sheets, pillowcases, and everything else was gone, and the bed mattress was rolled up and his wall locker was empty and open. I thought that was very strange. I went to the 1st Sergeant and turned in my roll call and said, "my pneumatic man isn't here and I'm not going to say he's here because I don't know where he's at." So, he told C.W. to leave the room and when C.W. left the room he said, "Sgt. Kaye, that guy that you had wasn't right. He exposed himself to some little girls coming out of the movie last night and he exposed himself to the base commander's daughter. I got a call about him and I called the OSI and we took all his clothes and everything and put him on an airplane and he's on his way back to the States now, but not a word of this is to get out." So, nobody ever knew what happened there.

About this time, we had a new squadron move in with us, they were TAD also and were the 4080th Strat Recon People, who came from Del Rio, Texas with the U2s and the RB57Ds. These RB57Ds were a very unique aircraft in as much as the wings were stretched to about 100 feet and the J65 engines were removed and J57s were put on there. This gave them an altitude of over 100,000 feet, about 103,000 feet, towards the end of the mission when they were light in weight. They were strictly an electronic and photo- reconnaissance aircraft and they had a two-man crew. They were painted black on the bottom and white on the top, which I never could figure out. The U2s were all black. These aircraft were never talked about; we were able to find out very little about them. They were very unique as they kept power on the aircraft at all times. They had three of them over there and they took over the one hangar and the hangar doors would open and they'd drag one out with the power unit attached and running. They would start up the engines, pull the power unit, and he would taxi out and, without sitting at the end of the runway or anything, he would turn around and get on the end of the runway, go about 800 feet and then go straight up and out of sight. When he would come back he would taxi in and they would hook a power unit onto him, then they would open the opposite hangar doors and let him in the back side. In the meantime they had taken the one in the middle and moved it up to the ready line. It wasn't till many years later that I found out what was actually going on and the reconnaissance they were doing. They only made 21 of these aircraft and the aircraft didn't last very long because there was a great amount of stress on the wings when they landed and the wings were cracking and they just got rid of them about four or five years later. About this time we were still working our blue cradle aircraft and our regular 15 alert strip aircraft and the 55th Strategic Reconnaissance Wing was coming in there with their RB47H's. These were very, very nice people. I remember this one Sergeant who was in charge, his name was Flowers, and we worked quite well with him. I would help his little pressurization man, all he had was an Airman 3rd for a pressurization man and I got in pretty tight with the people. I noticed that when they were changing the tires these big alligator jacks that we had, which had two pumps on them, would take about 20 minutes to jack up the aircraft in order to change a tire. So I went to see Sgt. Flowers and I said, "Sgt. Flowers, if you can acquire a B47 hydraulic pump for me and a relief valve and a relay, I will build you a pump that you can plug the MD3 into and jack your airplane up in about 30 seconds. So he said, "Great, T. Kaye. Let me get to work." He got all the parts that I needed and we took it into the shop, put a couple of T fittings in there and used the same reservoir and mounted the hydraulic pump on one side and the relay and the relief valve on the other side with a control switch, and they could just take it out to the airplanes, stuffed it underneath the strut, plugged the MD3 into it and hit the switch and swoosh, it went up. He was quite enthused with that and he gave me a letter of recognition for it, to be put in my files. I did this again later at Westover, and I did it up in Portsmouth, New Hampshire and I received awards for each one that I did. This time here, after working, we went to town and Googie and I (Sgt. K_____ and I) went down to the Grandchester and we policed up on a couple of ladies named Trina and Charmaine, never forget them. We had gotten a room; this was before I had gotten the apartment up in Cricklewood. We couldn't get into the Elizabeth Hotel so we grabbed a room on Queen's Way with some old guy as a night clerk. We came back with Trina and Charmaine and we were going to get them upstairs. This place was very unique in as much as there were balconies outside of each room and the balconies are interconnected to the ones next door. There is a picture in the book as you can see. I kept the guy busy, slipped Googie the key, and he snuck the two girls in and we got up into the room. About that time the guy must have gotten an idea of what we were up to so he came up and started beating on the doors. We turned around and put the two girls out on the veranda on the porch. Unbeknownst to us, there was a sleazy bunch of soldiers over there from Germany living in the next room and they had a big party going with the booze and the girls. While we were in there arguing with the manager and he was looking underneath the beds and in the closets and looking all over, they policed up on our girls. When that guy finally left we crossed over to the party and tried to get our girls back and the soldiers wouldn't let us have our girls back. They said they were going to throw us over the balcony. Discretion being the better part of valor we said well the hell with it, another day. The next day, I'll never forget, Googie and I went down town and we saw Viva Zapata with Marlon Brando. It was quite a wonderful movie. That evening we went out and we went to Jo Jo's bar up on Queen's Way and we met this RAF type who had a car and he was going with Jo Jo's sister. At quitting time I told him I always wanted to swim in the Thames River. Now, the Thames River is now clean, but at that time it was a dirty, filthy river. So he said, "Surely Yank, we'll go down there." So we went down there and were right by the river and we took all our clothes off and handed them to the ladies, who put them in the back of the car. We were down to our skivvies and gave the girls our T-shirts. We went down the stairs and we leaped into the Thames River. Well, might I tell you, that was one FILTHY river, but we had to be showing off that we were the GI's. We swam around in it for a while and then came back up and used our T-shirts as towels and dried off, then threw our skivvies away, put our clothes back on and went on down the road. That was another little adventure.

We had an instrument man named Ralph Sanders who like to go to Cheltenham, which was about 20 miles the other way from Oxford. He would go into the Horse and Groom and police up on some young lady and he had this set up with one particular taxi driver. At closing time, which was 11:00 o'clock, the taxicab would pull up and Ralph would escort his lady out to the car, and they would drive out to the edge of town where the haystacks were. Ralph had burrowed a hole in the haystack, and inside that haystack he had a big 6 volt battle lantern with a red cover over it, and he had about 4 or 5 blankets in there, and a couple of bottles of VP wine, and he would go in there and shack up with that girl all night in that haystack. At about 6:00 o'clock the taxi driver would come by, honk the horn, and they would come out picking the straw out of their hair and everything, then they would drop the girl off in town and he would bring Sanders back to the base. Ralph never shacked up anywhere except in that haystack.

We were now living in the apartment in Cricklewood and Googie had a wild idea and said, "T. Kaye, why don't we suds up Trafalgar Square?" I said, "What are you talking about?" He said, "Well, I bought half a box of Duz and we'll go down there in the middle of the night and we'll pour it in there and let the pumps circulate it and it will suds it up." Well, we went down there and we drove around and made sure there was nobody around, and we put the Duz into Trafalgar Square. The next morning we went back to see what happened all three of the fountains were full of suds, and it made the Overseas Weekly and it made the Mirror and all the other ones. They had chemists trying to find out what caused the water to suds up and I said, "Well, my God, if we ever get caught we'll go to a dungeon somewhere and we'll never see the light of day again." One Wednesday we decided to go to town, Joe G_____ and I, so we got in the car and went down to Oxford to White's. About that time we policed up on two young ladies of dubious virtue and we asked them if they'd like to go out on the back roads and get a little bit. Girls were very easy in those days and they didn't play any games. Now, I mean to tell you, these girls were beautiful girls and quite well dressed and they all worked and had jobs, but they would lie down with you if they liked your looks. As we got out, I went down this one back road with gravel on it, and we stopped and parked and I told Joe G. "Let's flip a coin. The guy who loses is going to go out in the back and get his and the guy who wins is going to get his inside the car." Joe G. won and they got into the front seat. I go around to the back of the car, take her knickers off, hooked her high heels into the bumper of the car, put her buns right up there on the trunk deck lid, and just walked right in there with my enormous schlong. I would pump three or four times and then I would have to move forward, I would pump three or four more times and I would have to move forward again; I couldn't understand why I was losing so much traction. I knew there were rocks down there. After about ten minutes I looked up and I saw these two clowns leaning over the front seat looking at us out of the back window, and what Joe G. had done was slip the car into neutral and as I was humping it I was pushing the car forward and so after every three or four strokes I would have to move on up. When I looked behind me you could see where I had come down and pushed my way about 150 feet down the road.

By this time I was living with Lorna at the flat, and I decided well, everybody was gone now but me and Al, and Al was getting married, so I decided I might as well go ahead and marry this girl too. She was quite a beautiful woman. So, I went and requested permission to marry and they wanted to see her passport. Now, remember, she was from India and she was raised in Communist held territory. She had lost her passport so that meant we would have to apply to the Indians to get a new passport for her, and that's just about a lost cause. That went on for about six months, and then when I finally got the passport I got permission to get married. We had lost her visa so that once we got married we could get back to the states. This was going on and on and on and on so I'm getting ready to marry her and I find out I'm going to get a dowry when I marry her of 1,000 pounds, which was $2,700 at the time, plus a big giant leopard skin that I wanted that the father had shot and had hanging on the wall. We were going to have the reception at the Douglas House near Grosvenor Square. I didn't have to pay for anything, we went right by the book, I paid for the boutonnieres and I paid the preacher. Everything else was done right by the book and the night before, of course, I was going to have a bachelor's party at my buddy Skee's pad. We had it set up from two or three weeks before and I brought a Jeroboam of Champagne, which is like three or four bottles of regular champagne. I left about 7 o'clock. We were staying at her Aunt and Uncle's house, who were footing the bill for this wedding. I went to Skee's house and the minute I hit the house my clothes were laid out, and I changed all my clothes because I knew that I would be getting checked out when I came in. We went out to the 55 Club and to the Oak Room and to the Grandchester and a few other places and we partied. We picked up a bunch of young ladies of dubious virtue and brought them back to the pad and partied and fooled around until about 5:00 o'clock in the morning. At 5:00 o'clock in the morning I jumped in there and took a bath with the lady I was with and I put on my own clothes, got in the car and drove on back, went in at daylight into the aunt's house and both of them immediately checked me for lipstick and all that other stuff. I changed into my blue suit with my vest and everything and I was ready to get married at 9:00 o'clock. We got married at 9:00 o'clock and we went down town to the Douglas House and had a lovely, lovely dinner and then we went to the bar. Now, the father, who had lost all his money and lost his tea plantations in 1949 and 1950 in India, couldn't afford all this so the Uncle, who was a broker for Jute, he controlled all the Jute that came out of India and Pakistan, footed the bill. Well, they were drinking doubles and triples and they were about twice as strong as English liquor. The father-in-law was getting upset emotionally so as Lorna and I were getting ready to leave outside, the father-in-law and the uncle got into a fight. I jumped in between the two of them and ended up getting smacked in the eye and got a black eye. We got into the car and slowly rode on down the rode into married life not so happily.

In the following weeks I received a package from Father-in-Law. It was a leopard skin for wall mounting and a check for 1,000 pounds @ $2.85 to the pound. It was Lorna's dowry so now you know someone who received a dowry like the olden days. The skin was what I had always dreamed of having on a wall.

During this time, Mort Cherim was with me for about six months, and he made a good air conditioning and pressurization man out of me. I repaid him by letting him go to Europe without taking a leave and spend ten days in Europe. He went to Spain, France, and Germany and he went over there with the swim club and he swam in like the junior Olympics, in which he did quite well.

During my time while stationed in England, I lived in a place called The "Studio" in Enysham Oxfordshire. Many tales were told of lovers and death. The house was two stories, shotgun-style, with the front and back door open you could see straight through the house. After moving in I checked security, all windows had double locks and the door had the same old key lock and a new Yale and a chain. The house was secure. We just drank tea, no coffee. The first night we heard dishes rattling downstairs. I went down – nothing – went back to bed. Lorna was reading. She woke me up – dishes rattling & smelled coffee. I told her I'm not going down again, let Charlie have the first floor after dark. This carried on till 6 month lease was up and we vacated quickly to another house.

The next vignette is from Billy Bocz's story of actual, documented ghosts left from WWII.

ANOTHER EXCERP FROM THE MEMOIRS OF BILLY BOCZ
RAF WOODBRIDGE, ENGLAND

While stationed at Woodbridge, England 1965-68 with the 79th TFS, a part of the 20th TFW, stationed at Weatherfield, England, we shared the base with the 78TFS from a sister wing stationed at Bentwaters, 2 miles as the crow flies away.

The many things that happened to the personnel are almost beyond imagination, one of which I was asked to write about was the week that the wing lost seven aircraft. At least, to those of us involved, they were lost.

One of the commitments of the wing was to supply close air ground support for the army in Germany with our F-100's.

Our orders were cut for the TDY to Ramstein AFB and on a Sunday morning the support personnel and equipment were loaded up on a C-130 and we took off for Germany. Our arrival at Ramstein should have been a warning that things were not going to go well. There were no aircraft on the ground and the ramp was diner eating clean. The C-130 pulled onto the ramp and, without cutting its engines, lowered the back ramp and dumped us and our gear in the middle of the parking ramp. No one met us to let us know what to do or where to store our equipment. Having been in similar situations, we hauled out our big long logging chain and tied everything together. Except for two senior NCOs, we all packed up and went into Lanstrul partying. It must have finally dawned on the local yokels that they had a big pile of junk in the middle of their now clean ramp. I can imagine the panic this must have caused. The only personnel that they could track down were our two senior NCOs. While we were drunkenly unaware of these happenings, the two of them had to move all our gear to an empty building a short distance away.

Monday morning, waking up in various stages of hangovers, we were amazed at the number of generals going by in staff cars followed by many more staff cars with full colonels. It was very apparent that something big was going on. After a few questions asked of some of the local troops, we found out that General Box, commander of 3rd Air Force Europe, was retiring and having a parade. This explained the lack of aircraft and the clean ramp. We were unaware the F100s we were expecting actually flew to Ramstein, but was refused permission to land. They were sent on to Hahn AFB a short distance away. It was decided that due to the ceremony, the above-mentioned aircraft were delayed a day. We all considered this our good fortune and took off to party some more.

We thought since we probably wore out our welcome in town our next target would be the NCO Club. About 14 of us took off for the club. Monday was an off night for the club so about the only ones there were the band and us up on the stage practicing their routines. While listening to their music and reestablishing various stages of intoxication again, we started getting the band into the mood of things. It got to where they were playing for us. Not meaning to speak evil about a person but God must have put all the leftover shit together when he made her. She was so ugly that at one point in her routine, she put a mop head over her head and blackjack gum on some of her teeth and it actually made her look better. You had to give her credit though, she could really sing.

Tuesday – We woke up in pretty much the same shape as Monday. We had decided to meet at the base OPS building until the aircraft arrived. The day was spent between pitching horseshoes and playing cards. After a very boring day we still hadn't gotten any aircraft so it was "party time." This time we hit the German club on base. We spent the evening drinking German beer.

Wednesday – With hangovers present we managed to make roll call (at the OPS building) and another day without aircraft playing cards and pitching horseshoes. The partying continued again that evening.

Thursday started off like the other three days. After roll call the day went pretty much like the rest. Just after lunch, not having received the aircraft, it was decided that maybe we should call back to Weathersfield and find out what the problem was. Our senior NCO, a MSGT, was chosen for this task.

Now the next player enters the picture. The conversation after making contact with higher – higher back at the base went something like this. After identifying himself, our leader asked, "when were we going to get the aircraft?" Answer – "You don't have the aircraft?" Answer – "No, we don't have them. Don't you?" This wasn't going well as the base was going through an ORI (Operation Readiness Inspection), the other player in this cluster fuck. We were told to hang loose, that they would get back with us. Later in the day they did call back. It would be Sunday before they could get us a plane. I will always be curious as to what was said to our leaders over our situation.

Friday and Saturday were spent pretty much as anyone can guess; conserving what little money we had left. A lot of the guys ended up tapping our leader's checkbook for eating money. Some just went on a forced diet.

Sunday at noon, we left our good times at Ramstein behind. After getting back to Woodbridge, all this nonsense came together. We understood what happened to the planes and crew, and were highly amused that the inspectors were on base at the time. Life was great even if for a short time only.

CHAPTER 6
WESTOVER AFB

Now, my tour of duty was up and I was going back to the ZI, the Zone of the Interior, and I got my orders and I was going to Westover AFB in Massachusetts. I wasn't too happy about going to Yankee territory where it was cold. I had put in for two bases in Florida. We had a little dog, a Chinese Toy Pug, that I had given to some Army people who were going home about two months before us. The little dog was taken and was in Washington, D.C. waiting for us, along with my two friends who were in the Army. We got there and got the dog and I went shopping for a car. With the amount of money I had I could only afford this big 1951 Packard Patrician. God, what a boat it was. It had a big old Straight 8 engine in it. I took it and had it put on the rack. They changed the oil, they checked everything and everything looked good, so I picked up Lorna and the dog and we took off for Florida. We drove on down to Florida and we spent 30 days down there with my mother, who was living in my house at the time, then we turned around and drove back up to Massachusetts. I arrived at Westover and got into the hydraulic shop. We had 48 B52 C's and D's. We had a gigantic shop. We had 146 men in the shop and were working three shifts a day, seven days a week. They found out that I knew Pneumatics and water injection, so I was assigned to the Pneudraulics shop, which took care of air conditioning, pressurization, liquid oxygen and water injection. While I was there, guess who I ran into; my friend Morton Cherim who had been with me over in England TDY from Lockbourne, he was there. I also met a young man named Edouard DeSelles, who was a real go-getter and he really wanted to learn the airplanes and was a lot of fun to be with. He liked hotrod cars. He had a dechromed and primered 1951 Chevy and I had a dechromed and primered 1952 Ford so we got along real good. We worked together and we learned the Turbo Alternator Drives. We learned them so good nobody else could handle them like we could. Any problem that was there, that came up, we got them. These turbo alternator drives were four axial flow, which means that the bleed air from the engine was run through an axial turbine, like the back end of a jet engine, that turned the gear box, that turned the alternator, that generated the air conditioning for the aircraft, the 200 volts ac/400 cycles. Now, there were four of them on the aircraft, and the unique thing about these was that they had to be paralleled; they didn't run just a portion of the airplane. There was a certain way you would start them up in sequence, you would get the phases just right, and then you would parallel them until all four were feeding into the bus at the same time. There was a very quick reaction, very unique units built by General Electric. I really loved them and, boy; there wasn't anything we couldn't do to fix them. That's what I liked, because everything was located externally and you could change your start pump, your main pump, you could change your over-speed valve, you could change your electronic control box, the controller, the servo valve; everything could be changed. We very seldom had to change the drives, except every thousand hours they were changed, whether they needed it or not, for a time change. DeSelles and I had very many adventures working on them at the end of the runway and fixing them and getting them going good.

Another individual, his name was Maxi Kessler, was a crew chief on B52D #6-666. One memorable night at the chow hall everybody was in line. Now, Maxi had three other men on his crew, a Japanese guy and two black guys. He walked into the chow hall and saw that big line and he just hollered out at the top of his voice, "Gang way for the United Nations crew, a Jap and a Jew, Cassabubu and Namumba." They went right up to the head of the line and nobody said a word. That night we were working on a B52 where we had to swing all the landing gear, so we had to jack it up. This takes a total of six body jacks, a tail jack, and four jacks on the wings. Normally it's a twenty-one-man crew, but there were only two of us. One guy was working the manifold to run the jacks up, I was running around monitoring the pressure on all the jacks and then trying to pump the tail jack up at the same time to keep 20,000 pounds on it. Well, we had a Major for a maintenance chief. He was a magnificent looking individual and he was what you'd call a wing-knocker; he was a West Point man and you could damn sure tell it about him. As he was walking through about one o'clock in the morning he said, "What's going on, Sgt. Kaye?" I said, "Lookee here, Sir, we need somebody on the tail jack. Can you jack that while we are jacking the aircraft?" He said, "Well, aren't you supposed to have a 21-man crew here?" I said, "Yes sir, but we don't want to call the guys out of the barracks, we can handle it." He said, "Well sure, I'll jack it up." So, I put him on the tail jack and explained how he had to keep the pressure at 20,000 and then run the lock ring down constantly as we were going up. So we jacked the aircraft up and we got the plumb bob where it was perfectly level, everything was correct, and we thanked him and he went on to his office. I don't know what he was doing but he was probably writing some reports or something in the middle of the night. Now remember, the Cold War was getting very hot at this time. About three hours later we were done swinging the gear and doing everything we had to, and he came walking back so we asked him if he could please do it again. This time he would be lowering the jack being very careful to keep the ring about two inches ahead of the piston and keeping the pressure at 20,000. He worked out pretty good as a tail jack man. One night we were working at midnight and it was cold and rainy and damp and he always told us, "If you ever need me you just call me. It doesn't matter what hour of the day it is." So I took my night crew and we went up to the chow hall at about midnight, and we got into the chow line and we got through the line and the guy gave me two eggs and two pieces of toast and a little dab of grits and two little pieces of bacon. I said, "Lookee here, we're out here in the cold and wet and we need some chow." He said, "Well, all you're going to get is one ration, Sarge." So I said, "I want to see your boss" and the boss turned around and backed his man up and said, "Just one ration, that's it Sarge." So all my men went through and I went and got on the telephone and called the Major up. About ten minutes later here he comes in with his hat on with all the lightning bolts on there and his beautiful tailored overcoat, a pair of boots, and his pajamas underneath there and he went in there and kicked ass, he started off with the top guy and went on down there and he said, "You guys get all the chow you want. You're out there working in the snow and rain and everything and these guys are sitting up her fat catting. Now go back up there and get all you want." Well Lord have mercy, after that we were top dog.

We had an airplane go down up at Griffiths because he had lost two alternator drives and of course, we jumped into a station wagon and took spare alternators with us and a spare drive and proceeded to drive up to Rome, NY. We got up there and I tried to start the drives. I had the engines running and tried to start the drives and it was a very simple problem. I had to remove some shims on the over-speed switch and that took about five minutes and I had that one fixed and going. There was a loose wire to the exciter fields on the other one. In about ten minutes we had it fixed and we were on our way back. They could not get over how fast we fixed these. But see, they had G models and they didn't have treble (?) alternator drives; their alternator drives were built right into the engine, which made it very simple.

About this time we got a call and I was with my friend Motley, he was an old-time like me but he stuttered and we are still friends to this day. He lives out in Enterprise, Alabama. We had a B52 on Chrome Dome that lost his air conditioning and pressurization, so it had landed in Sidi Slimane so they stuck us on a KC135, the two of us and all the gaskets we could take and everything, and we flew onto Sidi Slimane. When we got there the flight crew was waiting for us; they were getting tired of just sitting around there. We got them to fire up the four and five engines and Motley was up on the stop-deck working the air conditioner and as he went from hot to cold he found a blown aluminum duct so we shut the engines down, pulled the duct out, and took it to the welding shop. They guy who could weld aluminum bubble gum welded it back together again and we put a bunch of epoxy over the top of that and put it back in with the new gaskets that we had brought. They fired it up, pressurized the aircraft on the ground, and everything checked out fine. I asked if I could fly back with them and they got permission to let me fly back. That was my first ride on a B52 outside of the Chrome Dome mission. I sat up between the pilot and the copilot in the IP seat, who was the inspection pilot, and let him sleep. I was up there like a big dog, watching everything and checking everything out. It was a wonderful flight; it was just very exciting.

I flew two Chrome Dome missions, now that's a 25-hour mission, in order to get my flight skins. It's not very nice, when you take off you're strapped on top of the toilet. This is where the eighth man seat is. All you can think of is when you're landing is man, if we crash I'm going to die in a bucket full of shit, and that's no lie.

This aircraft was very unique in a couple of aspects; the engine drove nothing. Everything was operated off of engine bleed air. What they did was take air from the compressor section of the engine, the twelve stage, and ran it into manifolds up and down the wings and up and down the fuselage, and into the fuselage it went to the four alternator drives, it went to the two air conditioning packs, one big one up forward and one all the way in the back for the tail gunner, and then we had ten hydraulic packs and systems. Four of the hydraulic packs worked everything on the wings, the tip protection gear, the inboard spoilers and the outboard spoilers. Fuselage one, two, three and four packs worked the four main gears and crossed over, nine and ten work the pitch trim in the back by the tail gunner. We also had to take care of the water injection pumps. These were again very unique devices, driven by engine bleed air and built by Thompson. They spun 100,000 RPMs. What you did was fill the leading edge of the wing full of water with fish oil in it. The fish oil is what lubricated the two water pumps on each wing. One water pump fed two engines and the other one fed the other two engines. The one was in front of the other and wouldn't you know it, the one that burned was always the one in the back, so you had to pull the front one out also. What we would do if I had to go in and pull the back one out, I'd pull the front one out and I'd get two pumps and I'd put two brand new pumps in there and try to preclude going back in there later and doing it again.

As I said before, the Cold War started getting hot and General Lemay didn't like the idea of us having 48 B52's at one base so what they were going to do is take 18 of them and take them to McCoy, Florida in Orlando. Well, I thought wow, that would be a nice shipment but I'll never get on it so I won't even put in for it because all the brown nosers will get it. So, all the brown noses got on the list to go and they went up to this Major Schoolcraft, as I remember his name was Schoolcraft, and he looked at that list and he knew that all of these were no-load people, they were non-producers; they were the guys who worked the paperwork. So, he sent the list back down and said this is no good. He said that from every shop he wanted some other men, good men. So they turned around and put all the dumb ones on the list, and all the trash, just to get rid of them. These were all the guys who were always in trouble. Well, the Major looked at the list again and he turned around and sent the list back again, and said, "I'm coming down and I'll pick my people who are going with me." So he came on down and, very luckily, he picked me and he picked Motley, and Selan Massey from downstairs, who was an air conditioning and pressurization man, and a couple of the other guys who were the real workers and the real producers. So we got to go to McCoy AFB on a transfer. Well, about this time DeSelles' wife came up pregnant and of course, my wife wanted to be pregnant because Eddie's wife was going to have a kid. She couldn't get pregnant for some reason so Eddie's wife took her to see the obstetrician and he said her womb was turned, so he reached up and he turned her womb back. Boy, that was a horny time. I'd come home from work and I'd be attacked. I'd be attacked two or three times every night until she got pregnant. Well, about the time she came up pregnant was about the time that we were going down to Orlando to McCoy AFB. At the same time I also had my Chinese Toy Pug that I had bought in England, and it's mate and she had turned up pregnant as well.

RECON AIRCRAFT

U2B	alt. 90,000ft
RB570	alt. 100,000ft
RB47-H	alt. 44,000ft
RB45-C	alt. 51,000ft

Martin RB-57 (Don Rawlings) "D" Model

Boeing RB-47 "Stratojet" "H" Model

RB45C

USS Franklin D. Roosevelt (CV 42) underway, October 1973.

P4M MERCATOR by Martin

NTRA. SRA. DE MONTSERRAT

MONTSERRAT - 22/25 El Santuario desde San Juan

CW - TK - Tico - Thompson

U.S. AIR FOR

Thompson in front of shop

BNAFB

3920 HYD SHOP

WELCOME HYD SHOP

My crew on bomb trailer

Mort on Alligator BNAFB Airlines

U.S. AIR FOR

Always dragging ass Sgt. Cherim

(24)

To My Buddy T.K.
A Faboulous Memory New Year's
Eve 1 Jan 1957

No#2 Club

Lancanster Gate
In "The Big L"

Sam Giovino

P.S. Your Half of The Battle

65 club

To French
Marocco

BOEING RB-47H "STRATOJET"

CW-TK-Tico-Thompson

BNAFB

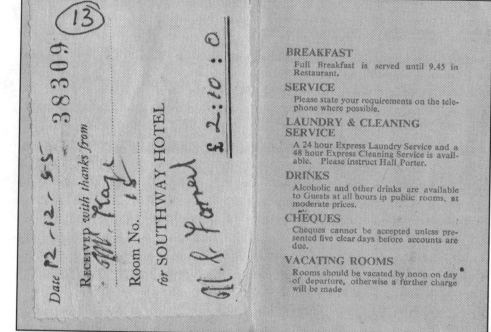

Date P2 -12- 55   38309.

RECEIVED with thanks from

M. Roy.

Room No. 15

for SOUTHWAY HOTEL

M. S. Farrel   £ 2:10 : 0

SGT. T. Kaye leaving for England 1956

SGT. J.J. Motley & AIC D. Sprague on Mactan Island, Phillipines 1966

SGT. T. Kaye leaving for England 1956

The Gang 1954

C133 B

The shop

B36 Builton, Midway Isle.
-Handcarved props
-Seven fuel tanks
-Actually the first in the world
to fly with pusher engines

SGT. Bocz & AIC Hellinger at
McCoy AFB, 1964

Midway Isle.
Shop- Hyd, Aircond-Press.
Liquid Oxygen & Water Alcohol

Water Alcohol Div.
78% Water 22%
Methanol 6 quarts
Fish oil ±1%

Shop tool boxes

'Respect Is Earned, Not Demanded'

JACKSONVILLE, Fla. — In answer to letters to the editor entitled, "Above It All?" (April 20 issue) and "NCOs and Labor," (May 18 issue):

The question that the airman raised in the first letter is the lack of leadership abilities of his supervisor (since this is probably the first one). Observe his mistakes, and in the future, when you become an NCO, do not make the same mistakes he made. Strive to be the best NCO in the Air Force. Study, observe others. Remember, "Respect is earned, not demanded." It doesn't go with the rank automatically.

Leadership is the ability to create an emotional bond between you and your men. There are no set patterns for this, as everyone is different; hence, everyone supervises differently, not from a book. The two supervisors I remember most were the ones who knew absolutely nothing about the aircraft we were working on, but used their ability to (make) their NCOs get the job done. That was their way of doing the job. Everyone respected them and enjoyed working for them. They never went on the flight line as long as I knew them.

READER OPINION

My method was the opposite. First, as a shift leader (I was an hydraulic tech in large shops at Westover, Pease and McGuire) I would go out on a work order myself. At once, I established that I could do the work, I knew what I was talking about, I knew how long a job took and how I wanted the job done.

I gave the individual someone to emulate. The doubt was erased from his mind once and for all. He knew who to call when he had a problem. After doing this with each individual, I would apprise them of my standards of work and their appearance and professional bearing.

As a flight line supervisor, I checked constantly on my people, and made them feel that I care about them. Later, when I became shop chief, I made sure my shift leaders operated the same way. My shop always had the highest reenlistment-rate and my airmen are now masters. Even though I am long retired, I still call them and check on them. I learned as much about leadership from airmen second class as I did from masters books and the NCO academy.

Today, a young airman wants to be led. He joins our ranks because he wanted to do so. He was not forced, so it is the NCO's job to motivate him by setting an example. Remember he comes from a society in which authority is not respected, so he must be led by example; I still maintain, a leader cannot lead from behind a desk. He, the airman, needs the benefits of our skills, job knowledge and technical ability. He expects this and it is up to us to deliver.

The last thing I want to cover, as it is never taught, is *moral courage.* It is defined as "knowing and standing up for what is right in the face of popular disfavor." Nowadays it seems to be difficult to get anyone to take a stand in mild dissent. Along with this is *moral integrity.* That is, the ability to make a decision without anything such as personal feelings, friendship, or sickness sway your decision-making abilities.

In closing, I never drank with my men, went out with my men or became friendly with my men. I didn't try to be popular. They knew if I made a decision, it was a just decision. That is the way I patterned my career.

MSGT. THOMAS KAYE
USAF Ret.

RB47 E

AIC Dan Fergeson
-became Comm Pilot

MIDWAY

1st Wife T.K.

SMS Bruce Reichenbach

Its not the critic
who counts, nor the man
who points out how the
strong man stumbled, or
where the doer of deeds
could have done them
better. The credit belongs
to the man who is actually
in the arena; whose vision
is marred by dust and sweat
and blood; who strives
valiently, who errs and comes
up again and again; who
knows the great enthusiasms,
the great devotions and spends
himself in a worthy cause; who,
at best knows in the end the
triumph of high achievement;
and who at the worst, if he fails
at least fails while daring
greatly so that his place shall
never be with those cold and timid
souls who know neither victory or
defeat.

Mar 1952

SR71-Same as A12 only 2 seats

Barracks in the good
old days

SGT J. Charlton
basic 1948

SGT. Bruce Reichenbach
in Saudi Arabia 1968

SGT M. Cherim Receiving Bronze Star

CHAPTER 7
MC COY AFB

So here I was, I had borrowed Motley's trailer, and I had my Triumph motorcycle, which I still had with me, tied in the back of my 1952 Ford chopped, dropped, flopped, whopped and hopped, dechromed, nosed and decked, so it was a good looking little car. I threw my wife and all my clothes and everything in it, and the two dogs in the back, and we proceeded to leave Massachusetts and head on down the road. Well, as we were coming on down the road Lorna came up real sick so she's hanging out the window calling for all her old boyfriends, Huey, Rrroy, and Wyatt Urp and she was sick as a dog because she's pregnant. When we get on the Massachusetts Turnpike the female Pug starts spinning in little circles in the back seat and Lorna asked what was the matter with the dog. I said she was going to have pups and I told her to get the Tech Order; we had a book on Pug's and how you took care of them. I told her to crawl over into the back and take care of her and to take a towel with her. The dog turned around and had one little tiny pup and I told her we'd better go see a Vet close to where we were. Pugs were very expensive at the time; in fact, mine was about the 590th registered in the States at the time. As we were going down the road I saw a big cop car, a Chrysler, and I pulled up next to him and I told him to pull over. Well, he thought someone was crazy; here's come guy telling him to pull over. This guy's in a little Ford dragging a motorcycle and a wife in the back seat, so he pulled over and asked, "What's the problem?" I said, "My dog's just had pups, my old lady's sick as a dog because she's fragrant, can you please direct me to the closest veterinarian?" So he explained how to get to the veterinarian. We drove up to the end of the New Jersey Turnpike, got off, went about two miles and took a right, went on down and went to the Vet's office. We took the dog and the tiny pup, which only weighed about 4 or 5 ounces, in to see the vet. The vet said, "Well, she's only going to have one puppy, so I'll just give her a shot to close her up and everything will be all right and you can just press on down the road." So he gave her the shot, I paid him the money, we got in the car, and we're driving down the road and pretty quickly we got into Virginia. The next thing we knew the dog turned around and gave another squeal and she has another pup. I said, "Oh my God, what's going on now? Well, we've got plenty of time and plenty of money so we'll get a motel and let the dogs rest for about 2 or 3 days and get their strength up." So we stopped at this motel that was owned by an old retired Navy officer so we had plenty to talk about. There was no air conditioning in those days and the dogs were nursing off the female when all of a sudden they started crying all the time. I said, "Well, what's going on? What's going on?" So we had to go find another vet. We drove down the road about 100 miles and finally found a vet and I'm waiting for this vet to come in. I was expecting a guy who looks like a doctor. Well, this vet comes in and he's got hip boots on and cow shit up to his knees and he stunk like a cow. He'd been out there birthing a cow. I'm all excited and Lorna's really cool so I told him what happened. He said, "Well, first of all, here, you take these two pills." I said, "What's them two pills for?" He said, "They are tranquilizers to slow your ass down. You're just too upset emotionally." I took a couple of the tranquilizers he gave me and we went into the room and he was checking the female and he said, "Well, the bitch is dried up due to the heat" because it was July. He said, "I just came back from a big conference and we came back and we brought these little tiny bottles to feed little puppies with. What you're going to have to do is feed the puppies on condensed milk, wine water, and white Karo syrup." So we proceeded to make bottles for them and we bottle fed them all the way down to Orlando and bottle-fed them until we put them on regular food. It was quite a trip and she was still sick. She was still calling her old boyfriends all the way down there, she was sick as a dog.

Well, when I left Motley was driving this big four door Pontiac hard top pillar less coupes they used to call them. It had three two-barrels on it and about a 400 hp engine. It was very, very, very swift. I told him I would meet him as soon as I got down there. Well, we got down there and were riding on the base when somebody in a Rambler pulled up behind me and I said, "Who the hell is that? He's hanging his hand out the window telling me to pull over." So I went on down to find a parking lot and I pulled over and here it was Motley in this Ramble station wagon. I said, "Jack, Jack, what happened to your big Pontiac El Dorado Coupe Deville?" He said, "Ga Ga Ga Ga Ga Ga Ga, that God Damn thing, I I I I I was going through the Baltimore Tu Tu Tu Tu Tunnel and I llllllllost my bbbbbbbbrakes and I didn't make it out of the TTTTTTunnel. I got my bbbbrakes fixed and it cost me tttttttwo hundred dollars. Then I drove on down there and when I got to Augusta, Georgia all of a sudden it just turned right on me and went right through a fence and into a field. Tttttthat's where I lllleft the ggggod damn thing. I went in there and bbbbought me this Rambler." So, my little '52 Ford flat head had made it down there without any problems and his big brand new car had bellied up there. When we got to the hydraulic shop I met my old friend Robert E Reynolds, who was my mentor back in the 305th when I first started off in the B47's. Now I was his mentor, because I was now going to teach him all about the B52's. They still had B47's there, but as our B52's came in, for every one that came in they sent two B47's off to another wing. It was lovely. We had 18 airplanes and it was warm, it wasn't like up there in Yankee territory. Many exciting things happened over there. Again I was working the hydraulic shop, and the air conditioning and pressurization shop, water injection and I was taking care of everything. I really enjoyed it. We were working hard and flying many, many, many hours. One time a super secret aircraft came in, it was called an A12. It was a predecessor of the SR71. This was a single seater operated by the CIA. The pilot was called a "mean little kid" and was only about 5ft. 3in. tall and when he walked around to go to his airplane he was in a total pressurization suit and carrying his own little air conditioners. It was very unique. They took it and stuck it in the fuel cell hangar. Boy, I wanted to see that but I never could. The next night I had a B52 up on jacks and I was swinging the gear by the book as we were doing, cycling on a normal and emergency. I looked and here's that mean little kid. He said, "Hey Sarge, will you take me through your B52?" I said, "Yeah, come on up here." So he climbed up in there and I put him in the copilot's seat and I showed him how everything worked, and I let him swing the gear, turn on the packs, turn off the packs, use the emergency hydraulic pumps, then we crawled through the whole airplane and I showed him the whole airplane and all the drives and air conditioning packs, locks and everything. He said, "I tell you what, I'll show you my airplane." So, he took me over to where the A12 was and he told the civilian guard that I was all right. We couldn't climb and look into the airplane but we could walk around and talk about it, about it's hydraulic systems and it's wheels, and the start cart had two big Buick V8 engines in there coupled together to big superchargers, and that's what turned the air that went into the air starters to turn the J58 engines. When they started up, the engines would be started at an idle and they'd start pumping air in and motorizing engines very slowly, and when he got up to about 30% he would push a button and eject triethylene borane into the engine, and the minute it hit the air it would burst into flame and that's how they let the engines off. I was asking him about this and that and everything and asked how fast it would go. He said, "Well, I can't tell you how fast it will go but I can leave here tomorrow and I can be in California in one hour." I'm thinking to myself, that's 3,000 miles away. This guy is blowing smoke up my butt. So I said, "Yeah, that's pretty nice, it's pretty swift." When he left the next day he set a speed record from McCoy AFB to Merced, California in 58 minutes. That little scoundrel, he was not lying.

TRIP TO OFFUT

I had met a crew chief named John Carson – he rode bikes also. One day he launched his plane and after several hours one drive shut down and on another one the frequency was wavering. So, as per the pilot's handbook, they landed immediately at Offut AFB, which was S.A.C. headquarters. Well, the local electricians and hydraulic technicians couldn't figure out what was wrong. They were not familiar with turbo alternator drives. They (the head shed) called Carson and said, "pack your bag and get ready to leave to fly to Offut. What specialist do you want to take with you?" He asked for me. This was on a Friday afternoon. They said to report to the Trans-Alert and a Gooney Bird (C47) would be waiting for him.

By the time we arrived it was 1800 hours. As we approached the plane, the flight crew asked, "What are you doing? We are waiting for some special technicians." We told them it was us. Boy, were they pissed. We had fucked up their weekend big time. They said to get in back and don't come up front. They wouldn't turn the heat on. We landed at Blytheville, Arkansas and took on fuel and started flying again.

We were met by the flight crew of the B52 when we landed. They carried us straight to the plane. They left the pilot and the copilot of the C47 standing there after Carson told them how they treated us. They were really pissed now. They had to walk in and see to refueling the C47.

Carson and I asked the flight several questions about the problems and they asked how long it would take to fix it. I said, "Hopefully 20 minutes", as the right front drive had a red warning light on, indicating over speed trip. I removed the switch, pulled two shims (making up for wear), put it back together, went to the left forward drive and started checking the exciter leads; one was loose in eye lug. I replaced it and we had the flight crew run engines and check the drives out. Everything was fine. The flight crew was happy; they could leave in about 4 hours. The flight crew of the C47 drove up as we were clearing the 781 forms. They asked if we were complete and we answered yes. They said to get in the truck; they were going back right now. The AC of the B52, who outranked the Captain of the C47, told them we were staying as they were buying us a steak. God, were they pissed. This meant we would have to stay overnight.

We ate and checked when our C47 was leaving and figured we'd better be two hours early, as that flight crew would leave us in a minute. Needless to say, we arrived early and flew back – we had heat (thanks to the B52 Major). We didn't even stop to refuel.

As I was saying, the Cuban crisis was heating up. It was starting where the U2's came into our hangar and they were taking pictures of Cuba and we started getting ready to go to war. Until about 5 years ago I really didn't realize how close we were to doing the deed and snuffing everybody out. It was close. They wanted to bring more fighter-bombers in so they told us that they were going to take our 18 airplanes and we're going to fly up to Albany, Georgia. We'd operate out of Albany, Georgia and fly two Chrome Dome missions a day. Of course they said, "You can't take everybody so the only people that are going to go are Sgt. Kaye, Sgt. Motley, a Buck Sergeant Skinner and Buck Sergeant named Big Bad Billy Boats. He's still my friend some 50 years later and lives down with me in Palatka. So we got all our tools and all our spares and everything and went out to the airplane and climbed on a KC135. We were sitting around and nobody was telling us anything. So the aircraft commander came aboard and he looked about 19 years old and had glasses like Coke bottle lenses. He said, "This is going to be my first flight as an aircraft commander." I said, "Oh, God." He said, "Ya'll ain't got any parachutes and we ain't got no facilities, no seatbelts and seats for you, so you just bundle up amidships and hang on." So I said, "Oh, Good God. We're going to plow a big hole in the dirt and have a big fire and go down in a blaze of glory." He started up and taxied out and he turned around and took the airplane off fine and in 45 minutes we were in Albany, Georgia, but it took him four passes to get the aircraft on the ground. We were pretty happy when he finally landed it. Well, the minute we landed we got all our gear into the hangar and into the shop. As our airplanes were coming in we started turning them around. They were already loaded with the H-bombs so they went directly out to the alert strip. We went out and cleared all their write-ups and got them ready to go and the minute we got all of them ready to go we got the call and we started launching the Chrome Dome missions. We started off by launching the two airplanes and we knew that in 25 hours they would come back and we would have to turn them around. We figured it out that Jack and I would take one shift and Big Bad Billy Boats and Skinner would take the other shift. So we were sleeping in the barracks and things were tight and everybody was scared. We were watching TV all the time just to find out what was going on and seeing Kennedy on there and the paratroops had moved in to McCoy AFB, the F105's had moved in, and we were really close to going to war. The next day the aircraft came in and landed and it landed right when our shifts would turn over so we had four people there to turn the aircraft around and to launch the other two. Big Bad Billy Boats and Skinner would stay there in the shop through the second shift. This went on for a long time, probably 30 days.

One of the funny things that happened with Skinner and Big Bad Billy Boats, on the way from the barracks down to the flight line, were hundreds of pecan trees and the pecan trees had just gotten ripe and we could stand in the barracks when they were going down to the flight line after lunch, and we could watch their progress. We had the old Korean parkas which came down to your knees and they had the sheepskin lining and they had big pockets and you could watch them; Skinner would go up one tree and shake the tree and Boats would pick up the pecans, then Skinner would come down and Boats would climb the next tree and he'd shake it and Skinner would pick up the pecans. You could watch their progress as they went the half a mile down there. I think they must have shit bricks because they sure ate a lot of pecans up there.

EXCERPT FROM THE MEMOIRS OF BILLY BOCZ
TURNER AFB, GEORGIA
DURING THE CUBAN CRISIS

On a deployment by the 4047 Stat Bomb Wing to Turner AFB in Albany, Georgia: This took place during the Cuban crisis, the space at our home base at McCoy needed for the many fighter aircraft being sent there.

Having arrived at Turner Field in late October, there was little chance to terrorize the local population. We were kept pretty busy, as there was only a small detachment of maintenance personnel to maintain them. I got into the town of Albany, into the area that was called Five Points. I'd been in the NCO club drinking a few with a tail gunner from one of the birds, and a couple of crew chiefs. We caught a cab and headed for town. While going out the main gate we all got a laugh. Some of our troops came up big. They repainted the front gate sign, from that of the wing at Turner to ours, the 4047th. I later learned that the base commander took our Colonel out and showed him the sign. He was greatly irritated. I understand he told the base commander that it had to be the local residents, as his troops would have painted both sides. In town, we continued our partying and hooked up with four marines and things got progressively drunker.

The fateful night came around Thanksgiving. Our fearless leader, Jack Motley, gave me and Sinner the day off and, with a couple others, we talked our branch chief into giving us a ride into town. What we didn't know until it was too late was that all the bars frequented by Air Force troops were closed. The only bars open were those that catered to the Marines. Oh well, being off limits to Air Force personnel was not a deterrent to us; in we went. The first thing I spotted was a girl in the middle of the dance floor surrounded by at least eight or nine marines. They seemed to be arguing over buying her a drink. I simply walked in the middle of them and told her I'd buy her a drink. I got her hand and led her to the bar and got us a drink. I decided to use the restroom to relieve some of my previous drinks. That was the best move I ever made. While I was in the rest room, the marines were in the bar trying to decide who was going to use me as a punching bag. My savior was in the form of a SSGT whose shop we worked from. Having recognized me, he came back and dragged me out the back door. Had I gone back in the bar things would have really gotten dicey. The next day at work all these guys were telling me about everything that had happened in town the night before. Apparently we must have raised some hell. All I can say was that I was in town that night and didn't see any of it happen. It took me a while but then I realized it was the four of us they were talking about.

BACK TO THE ADVENTURES OF THOMAS KAYE

At that present time, Lorna had already had the one child and we had purchased a house in Sky Lake in Orlando, a beautiful house. It was a model home and it came with wall-to-wall carpeting, silk drapes and it was only two bedrooms, but it was absolutely gorgeous. I had filled it with beautiful furniture and everything was going good. Now she was foreign wife and everything was really nice because I would come home every night and the food would be on the table and she would be just like in the movie picture shows, dressed up real nice, her hair would be done, the child would be clean, the four dogs would be clean, the house would be immaculate, everything was going beautiful. When we went shopping she still didn't know how to spend American money, I never had taught her, because whenever we went shopping she just said what she wanted and I just turned around, picked it up, and I would pay for it. I ran the money. She also didn't have any credit cards and she didn't know how to drive. Well, all the other guys in the neighborhood would say, "Boy, that Sgt. Kaye, he runs a tight ship in his house and it's always clean, it's not messy, she always looks good and he always has food when he's supposed to and his uniforms are done nice, we're doing something wrong." Well, the wives got together and this didn't go over too well with the wives. They said, "We're going to have to do something about this." Well, about the time when I turned around and had to go to Albany, Georgia for the Cuban crisis, she was going to have to be taken care of, so two of the neighborhood wives said they'd take care of her. They said, "You go get a Power of Attorney so she can cash your allotment check." So when the allotment check came in she had the money. They taught her how to go to the bank, how to cash the allotment check, how to go downtown and go grocery shopping, and how American money was used and everything else. They turned around and taught her what a credit card was and how to use a credit card. They got her a credit card and then they turned around and started teaching her how to drive one of my two cars. So when the Cuban crisis was over and I came home, I had an emancipated foreign wife and everything started going down hill after that.

As I spoke previously, I spoke of the ducts that go through the aircraft and carry the engine bleed air to run the ten hydraulic packs, the four alternator drives, the air conditioning, and they also ran the engine starters and everything. Now, these ducts were running from a standard temperature of ambient, which would be about 90 or 100 degrees, to about 700 degrees which gave them a big coefficient of expansion. They were made of stainless steel. So about every ten feet in the wings you had what looked like a corrugated tube which allowed for the expansion and contraction plus the flexibility of the wing, because a B52 wing would flex up 17 feet and down 11 feet; 28 feet it would be able to go up and down while it was up in the air. So these units started cracking and they came out with what was called Emergency Action TCTO and normally it was taken care of in the factory, but here we had one aircraft that was still on the flight line and it had the four ducts, and they had to be changed. I told Martin, "We'll do it at night. I'll pick my boys so I picked Big Bad Billy Boats, Jesus, Puentes, my little Mexican trainee who was an outstanding worker, and I had Tommy Kovacs who had come to me from the 55th Strat Recon Wing. Now let me explain to you what we had to do. We had to put the jacks underneath the wing and jack the wing to the jig position till it was perfectly straight, just like when it was built. Then we would have to go up there and pull two stress panels off the leading edge of the wing; that would be one on each side of the duct. Then we would have to crawl up inside there and the only thing that would be hanging out would be our legs, from the hips on down. Now, it was hot in there, and what we would do is, I would work the nuts on one side, and big bad Billy Boats would hold the bolts on the other side and we could whip on thru there and we were doing pretty good and we would spell each other off. It was hot and about 8 or 9 at night so we had stripped down to nothing but our skivvies and our brogans, or combat boots. So we were up inside the wing and laying in there working. Well, they were fixing on taking off an airplane right next to us and they had a problem and we were also the launch team, so I came flying out of that wing as fast as I could, which wasn't very fast, grabbed my toolbox, and big bad Billy Boats grabbed his toolbox, and there we are in combat boots and GI skivvies, and we ran over to the aircraft, and the aircraft commander is looking out the window wondering what the hell was going on and who are these two guys in combat boots and their skivvies? He was looking at us and we were over there trying to climb up on the wing and get number five pack started for him, so we had to whip out about 96 screws, which we did very speedily with our apexes and speed handles that we had built, and we turned around and changed the stop/start motor. Now he's still looking out there wondering what the hell's going on, these guys have no shirts on, no uniforms, all they've got on is a pair of skivvies and combat boots. So we turned around, got his airplane started, put the panel back on, and waved him off and went back to our aircraft. I could see him shaking his head as he left. He didn't care because he had all his systems, but he'd never seen anything like that before. So, we went back up on the stands and we were back changing the expansion joints and Boats was on one side and Jesus Puentes was on the other side, and as he was working Tom Kovacs looked up there and Jesus' cods were laying right on that stress panel. So he reached over in his toolbox and grabbed his hammer and he smacked the wing right underneath his cods and he said, "Remember the Alamo, you bean bandit son of a bitch." And he hit that about 3 or 4 times, and Jesus said, "If I could get out of here fast enough I'd cut you up, you gringo." But that was the kind of friendships that we had, they went on and on forever. And again, like I said, Big Bad Billy Boats is still my friend and he lives about 20 miles from me now.

Around this time, after the Cuban crisis, we still had the aircraft on Chrome Dome of course, and we had a B52 with the aircraft Commander a Major Hayes and the copilot was a Captain Veech. It went down and had to land because he had two alternator drives tripped off the line and he had to land in Marone, Spain, which is in the south of Spain, which is known for their big black bulls. They gave us a notice that I was going to have to go over there and take an electrician with me and we got together and, just for drill, we put a whole new alternator drive in the KC135 and a new alternator, because he could always come home on three if we couldn't get anything fixed, plus a bushel basket full of spare parts, because we could work on the drives and get them right. So we went down and loaded everything on the KC135. Now, it's in the middle of the summer and it is hot. The KC135 is a ground-loving airplane, it would be going down the runway using water injection and you would not rotate to take off till you passed the 10,000-foot marker. Now, we had a 12,000-foot runway down there. So, we loaded all of our gear on the airplane and we were standing around talking to the launch crew, and a friend of mine named Moundsy was the jet engine launch man. He said, "Shit, I really wouldn't want to fly on that airplane, T. Kaye." I said, "Why, what's the problem?" He said, "Well, we've had three repeat write-ups on her where we've lost water injection on number two engine on takeoff." Well, if you lose water injection on an outboard engine you're dead, because the aircraft loses control and goes into a yaw and you don't have enough rudder control, this is before we had rudder boost, and things just avalanche and the aircraft usually just makes a big hole in the ground. An inboard engine is not quite as bad but we had maximum fuel load because we were going to fly straight across to Spain. So I said, "Well, Moundsy, what did you do?" He said, "Well, we just retrimmed it and it worked fine, and we ran it for about 2 or 3 minutes at 100 percent and it worked fine." So now, I'm getting my rosary out and start counting my Hail Mary's and Our Father's, so we go up into the aircraft and there's just the two of us enlisted swine and we've got this whole million dollar aircraft as our private aircraft to haul us to Spain. So, we sat down in the back and I grabbed a set of headsets because I want to monitor the inter-phone. So we taxi on out and we're going down the runway and the navigator is calling off the markers 1,000 foot, 2,000 foot, 3,000 foot, V-1 speed, and then you get ready to get up to V-2 speed, then he calls "rotate" and you feel the nose come up and you've got air speed and we'd just got off the ground and the copilots calling and he's saying, "I'm losing water on number 2 engine, I'm losing engine pressure ratio, which means that the engine is not producing as much thrust, and I'm losing fuel flow." Well, all of this is automatic, if you lose water, you lose fuel flow. So, the pilot says, "Okay, I've got it, no problem." We were already off the ground and we were flying so we just flattened out and got up more air speed and took off, so we climbed up to altitude and we're flying merrily along, and I went back with the boom operator and talked a little bit and by this time it had gotten dark. So, I walked on up forward and I looked and the crew chief is sitting in his seat and he's asleep and I looked at the navigator and he's at the table and laying on his arm and he's asleep, and I looked at the pilot and he's got his feet up on the stirrups and he's leaning back and he's asleep. Now, in SAC they had a policy that either the pilot or the copilot would be on 100 percent oxygen, with his headset and his brain bucket on at all times while the aircraft was flying. The KC135 was on autopilot and I look over there and the copilot has his brain bucket on and his wind screen down and I could hear him, since the aircraft is relatively quiet, and he's going UMMMMMMMMMM. This is about the time that TV movie Twelve O'clock High was on, and he thought he was (now remember, the aircraft is on autopilot and he's not doing anything) pretending he was flying a bomb run. I eased on back and got the boom operator cause I wanted him to see this and he came up and he reached across and tapped the navigator and woke him up and told him to shush and listen, and he reached across and got the pilot and woke him up and the crew chief, and then all of us were standing there watching the kid. You know how you can feel when someone is watching you, and he looked around and put his hands in his lap and put his windscreen up and was very embarrassed, of course. It was very embarrassing. We laughed our asses off and, of course, he ended up having a good time with that as well. So we went over there and we landed, and Major Hayes was waiting for us when we got there. I said, "What's the problem?" We were talking to Capt. Veech who had control of the alternators and he said, "Well, T. Kaye, everything was going good for about 18 or 19 hours, and all of a sudden the overload lights came on and I was checking my KWATTS and KVARS and they were virtually uncontrollable and they had max'ed out on the voltage and the voltage regulator couldn't handle it anymore so they tripped off and they shut themselves down. Now, when you get down to two alternators on a B52 the book is outlined in red and says LAND RIGHT AWAY." So, I said, "Well, let's take a look at it." We went and climbed up and it was the right aft and left aft alternator so the electrician got up there and checked all his wiring going to there, and I checked everything to the drives, everything was tight, nothing was loose, all the cannon plugs were on tight, so I said, "Fire up the engines." So he fired up the engines, you have to fire up two engines, then take them up to about 90 percent, that gives you enough bleed air, then we started up all four drives and all four drives worked perfectly. So we sat there and ran them on the ground for about an hour and we could not duplicate the malfunction. So I said, "Well, damn, what we'll have to do is turn around and change the PMG, the controller and the servo valve on both of the drives and then run them again and then we'll go like that, and go back to the states." I said, "Can I fly back with you, Capt. Veech?" He said, "No, we've got four nukes aboard and we've got to go back to SAC" and all that other bullshit. He said, "We've got a bunch of other write-ups too, T. Kaye." I said, "What's that?" He said, "Well, we've got a split in the honeycomb on the back of the left-hand wing, number six hydraulic pack shut down after about 20 hours of flight, and I've got a bunch of flat accumulators and I've got numerous leaks on the brakes and everything, and we've got to clear all these write-ups." Now mind you that we had just flown over and we're tired and we'd been working over there on the drives so I said, "Well, I'll get a sheet metal man to come out there and we'll put some fiberglass up there and scab patch that crack in the wing, I'll flush the gold dust filter on that pack and I'll fix the rest of the problems." So, I got the sheet metal man out there, we whipped up some fiberglass and we made a tin panel and we glued it on over where the honeycomb was broken on the trailing edge of the wing and put four big sheet metal screws through the top of it to hold it in place and we knew it would hold until we got back to the states. I took the gold dust filter out of the hydraulic pack and dipped it in the gas tank of the MD3 to flush it out and clean it out, fired up the pack and it worked fine. I looked and all the accumulators were flat. There were 19 accumulators on that airplane and every one of them bastards was flat. I said, "Well, they've been working all right and they were brake accumulators, they were nothing to do with the flight controls or anything." So I asked Major Hayes again, I said, "We've got everything patched together, can I fly back with you?" He said, "No, no, no, can't do that." So we took all our tools and we were still dead, knocked out, and wandered over to the KC135 and I asked the crew chief what had they done to the number 2 engine? He said, "They just retrimmed it." I said, "Yeah, but they did that three times before." He said, "Well, this will get us back home." So we climbed on the airplane and everybody fired up and we took off and launched the aircraft and launched the B52 and we were flying back to the states. So, we got about 3 hours out and we were laying down and catching a little bit of sleep and the flight crew comes back and kicks the bunk. They said, "I thought you fixed that airplane." I said, "I did. I did. I did." He said, "No, his drives are going out again." So, I got on the radio and was talking to Capt. Veech and I asked him if he could trim them down and he said, "Well, I trimmed them down, trimmed the voltage and the cycles down but they still creep on up and they are getting ready to trip out again, so we are going to go back and land back again." So we had to dump fuel and they had to burn off some fuel, so we landed and went back over there and needless to say, they were kind of hostile and belligerent with us. So, we turned around and talked it over and the electrician and I said, "The hell with it. We'll go ahead and change the alternator out and the drive out on the right aft, which is the easiest one to change." So we turned around and it took us about 4 hours, because we were tired, and we dropped the alternator off and put it in the crawlway, then dropped the drive out, put the new drive in and put the new alternator on, then we turned around and went back to the left aft and we couldn't find anything wrong, no wires loose, no nothing. So, I put a new PMG (Permanent Magnetic Generator) on and a new servo valve on and we ran them up and checked them out and everything seemed to be all right. So, I told Major Hayes, "I'd sure like to fly back with it." So he said, "Well, you know we can't do that, T. Kaye, because we've got four nukes aboard." So I said, "Okay." So we went up and they had a bunch of other airplanes for us to work on. Now we had not been to sleep in about 34 hours. So, we went and we worked and fixed a bunch more airplanes and we finally went back to the barracks and shit, shined, shaved and showered, laid down, and Major Hayes came up and he kicked my bunk and he said, "Sgt. Kaye, you're going to fly back with us on the B52." I said, "Oh, okay." So I laid my head back down and he said, "We're going to be leaving in about four hours." I said, "Okay." So, I'm laying there and I'm starting to think, with a scab patch on the wing, number 6 pack shut down, all those flat accumulators and all them leaks, I grabbed my little tool box and I grabbed that electrician by the butt, and we jumped in a little van that we had and we went on down there and he got a high pack air compressor coming for us and I turned around and had a whole bunch of seals, AN6230B3's if I remember, and I knocked the end out of all the accumulators where the air was and replaced the seals on there, lubed them up real good and put them back in there, and as fast as I was repacking them he had the air compressor going and we were putting the preload back into the accumulators. So, we rebuilt 19 accumulators, went and whipped out a couple of other leaks, and then we found a fuel leak between the engines, we whipped out that line and went to the welding shop but there was no welder there. Now, this is stainless steel. So we went to the hobby shop and we found one guy, he said, "Well, I can't weld stainless steel but what we can do is we can just bubblegum weld it, we'll use some coat hanger and heat it up red hot and melt that and maybe that will hold it." So, we bubblegum welded it with a coat hanger wire, which actually is a very good welding rod for regular welding. We took it back down and put it on the aircraft and it didn't leak, but the moisture would form around where that bubblegum weld was, but with the air passing over it at 600 miles an hour I wasn't worried about it letting loose or anything. About this time Major Hayes showed up at the aircraft and we're leaning against the wheels panting and out of breath and he said, "What are you guys doing down here?" I said, "We pulled our own preflight, Sir. Everything is jam up and jelly tight." So, he looked at the airplane and the people at Marone had a habit that when an aircraft landed when it wasn't supposed to they would paint a red bull on it. Well, so far our airplane had a red bull, then it had a black bull, then it had a green bull (they all said EL TORO DE MARON) and then they had a yellow bull upside down, indicating this was the fourth trip that they had tried to leave. I said, "Oh my God, if we don't make now it now we're going to be SOL." So, I loaded up my toolbox and we were standing around talking and the instructor pilot came over and said, "Sgt. Kaye, I don't envy you going on that airplane with two alternators failing all the time." He said, "Ha, Ha, I'm going back on a KC135." I said, "Yeah, Ha, Ha, you're going back on a KC135 that's lost water on take off for the last four launches in a row," and he kind of blanched and turned a little bit white and went back to check the 781A, and his eyes rolled up and he went and climbed on it. So, we fired up all our engines and took off, it was a real bumpy runway, like a cardboard runway, so we took off and we got about 3 or 4 hours up and I'm sitting in the IT's seat and I'm looking over Veech's shoulder and the alternators are just right where they are supposed to be. He said, "Look at them, Sgt. Kaye, look at them. They're nervous, they're nervous." I said, "There is nothing the matter with them. You have plenty of trim left in there, everything is stabilized, just leave it alone." I took his clipboard and put it over the gauges and said, "Quit looking, you are seeing things. If you have any problems the red light will come on and they will shut down by themselves." We flew on back to the states and we landed and Colonel Hand, who was called the Black Hand (he was a mean motor scooter), he turned around and he met the airplane. As we came out of the airplane he saw those four bulls on there and he went crazy and he said, "I want them off RIGHT NOW!" Then he braced the flight crew and they just pointed at me and he chewed their asses out and he called me over and I told him I couldn't figure out what it was so we put a new one in there and when the other one was all right we changed the PMG and the servo valve. I said, "But we are going to change that alternator just for drill." So we changed that alternator per drill with a spare one the minute that we got back and we sent them to SAMMA, which is an overhaul factory in Oklahoma City, and we told them what had happened and we wanted to know why this was happening, because everything would check out good until it got into the air. Now, the minute the aircraft landed and the ground wire touched the ground they would snap back and be all right. So I explained everything to them and they went and took them apart and they found out that the fields in the alternator, after they are put in position, are supposed to be pegged in with a wedge, and nobody had wedged them. Now, what would happen was, as it was flying, from the vibration it would vibrate a little bit and move, maybe a 32nd of an inch, which was all took to change all the factors on the voltage in the cycles. So, we cured that problem once and forever and when it happened in others we just knew to get a new alternator and put it on.

Vignette to be added in section while stationed at McCoy AFB in Florida

Well, I was the sharpest and most knowledgeable man on B52D's at McCoy AFB (so they told me). I was chosen to go to 8th AF Hqtrs at Westover, Massachusetts to integrate my troubleshooting methods into the Tech Manuals. I had just left Westover six months prior. Well, at least I could see my friend Buck Sergeant Edouard DeCelles and his new baby.

We were to travel commercial airlines and in civilian clothes, but at the meeting with other people from 8th AF bases we would have to wear our uniforms.

I packed my bag, got my ticket and went to Orlando's small airport in the center of town. This was before Disney. They hadn't stolen our base yet.

I arrived at the airport and was on flight 209 National direct to Washington, D.C. I was flying on the new Lockheed Electra, which did not make me too happy. They had recently lost two planes to unexplained disintegration in mid flight. I was to leave at 1300 at gate so and so. I was waiting and saw the Electra taxi up to the gate and the number on the tail was 2209. So I assumed it was my flight and the board said Jacksonville to Washington, D.C. This was strange, as I was told mine was a direct flight. I then went up to check in and as I boarded the airline stewardess looked at me and said to sit over there close to her and she took my ticket and disappeared. The door closed and the four propjets started, then suddenly two on the door side shut down and the door opened and the stewardess said I was on the wrong plane. Flight 209 was behind us. God, was I embarrassed. I had to walk off with everyone looking and go to the plane behind and get on it. I said damn, I foresee a bad flight.

I got on the correct plane #209, which had a few people on it. I found my seat next to a window in the rear. The seats were four wide. Now, who comes and sits in the same row but some gigantic fat lady carrying a crying small child in her arms. I again said "gonna be a bad flight." We took off and in South Carolina we hit some of the worst weather I have ever been in. The baby started barfing all over everything; seats, floor, mother and stewardess. The engines were jumping up and down due to turbulence and the stench was terrible and the brat puked a 55-gallon drum of liquid. I didn't want to try to cross all the barf so I climbed over the seat and moved up three rows. Finally, the weather settled down so I decided to go to the bathroom. Two bathrooms, side by side, said "Vacant." I opened the right door and a little girl was on the pot and she let out a scream and everyone was looking at me like I was a pervert. Damn, this was really a bad flight. Anyhow, we finally got to D.C. I was told to run the length of the airport to Allegany Airlines to catch my Convair 240 to Hartford, Connecticut. After running I made it to the gate as the plane taxied in. The door opened and promptly fell off. Damn!! What else could happen? When we landed I went to the baggage claim section. As they unloaded the plane I didn't see my suitcase (B4 Bag). I waited and waited and the lights went out. No bag. So I went to the airlines. They said the bag was still in D.C. I explained my problem; they said they would deliver it tomorrow. Damn, my notes were in my bag. Well, I had to get to Westover, but the last bus had left. I had to find someone to share a taxi for the 40 miles to the base. I found a salesman so we shared the cab. Upon arrival I called DeCelles who came and picked me up. We called the airline and told them where to deliver my B4 bag. Needless to say it didn't arrive for three days. I borrowed skivvies from Eddie and shirts and had to attend the conference in civvies.

After conference I was selected to represent 8th AF by going to the B52 factory to meet with Tech Reps. I got a lot accomplished and got a few new pages into the Tech Orders; an allowable leakage chart on hydraulic cylinders all on one page (instead of hidden through 12 manuals), and a lot on fast troubleshooting on Turbo-Alternator drives.

I also saw the last B52H made as it taxied out. This was in 1962 and, may I remind you, it is still flying and the backbone of the USAF to this day.

The 4047th Strategic Wing was doing great work, launching many missions with no late take-offs. Morale was good. Bombing scores were good. Everyone was happy.

We had a contest between bases and wings, to see who could launch more "on time" take offs; currently we were leading with about 327 at the time. We had doubled the amount of specialists riding the launch truck to insure quick repair of a faulty item, so we would have an on-time take off. Billy Bocz and I were riding on this fateful day. As I explained before, the B52D had 10 separate hydraulic systems – 5, 6, 7, 8 in the wing & 1, 2, 3, 4, 9 and 10 in the fuselage. 5 & 8 were buried in the wing under panels with 96 cross point screws on the top panel and 60 on the lower panel. Pulling screws was a bitch, but we had made special speed handles with apex drivers on the end to speed up the work. Anyhow, #5 pack on the left wing wouldn't start, so we jumped out and I went and started on top of the wing and Billy on the bottom. The engines were running and #328 launch was waiting and we were flying; our hands were a blur. About this time Sgt. Jack Jay Motley came flying up with a big hammer. He struck the wing a severe blow right below the stop/start motor (a small electric motor that allowed air into the turbine). He must have jarred the contacts, allowing current to operate the electric motor and the pack started up. We had not gotten all the screws out yet. Jack took a look at the amount of screws holding the panels on and said, "Let it go, we'll finish the job tomorrow when it gets back. The aircraft was late so we blew the record. Jack berated me severely and said, "Dddddamn TTTTTTTK, how many times have I told you – hit it with a hammer." I felt like shit; the record was gone; Motley was the here; I was the worm; so I sneaked back into the launch truck with Billy and I swore I would get a big f-----g hammer before riding the truck again.

At this time, Lorna was pregnant with Bianca, my second daughter, and she was about 8 months pregnant. So they called me and said, "T. Kaye, you've got a set of orders." I said, "I've got a set of orders? I just got here about 15 or 16 months ago. Everybody else has been here about 7 or 8 years and I've got orders to go again?" They said, "Well, you've always been the cadre to teach new people the aircraft and you are the most knowledgeable person we have, so we're sending you to Pease AFB in New Hampshire, because they are supposed to get B52's." They had B47s now with the 509th Bomb Wing. He said, "But you are going to have to go up there and teach them what's going on." I said, "But my old lady's fixing to download with this youngun in another month. So they said, "Well, we're try to see if we can get it deferred until after she has the baby." So they tried and here she was 8 months and two weeks and I had to give my new house away. I gave it away to a SMSGT who took over the payments, and later stuck me with the payments, and we loaded up my Studebaker Golden Hawk with my four dogs, Carla, who was 2 years old at the time, and Lorna who was pregnant and normally weighed about 95 pounds and was 5 feet tall but now weighed about 110 pounds, and she was carrying Bianca down between her knees. I figured she was going to download on the trip. We started driving and I would drive like hell through the countryside and then when I went through the cities I would slow on down. I had changed my plugs and points before we left and I had neglected to put the drop of grease on the cam in the distributor so when I got to Maryland the points were chirping with the little fiber block riding against the cam that made the points work. It got to where it was irritating me so much I couldn't stand it anymore so I just pulled the car over on the side of the road on the grass. Lorna said, "What's going on?" I said, "I'm going to take care of that chirping sound, I can't stand it anymore." Now, this had a distributor that was all the way in the back of the engine on the back of the vee. As I pulled the distributor cap off, inside the center of the distributor cap, is a carbon brush and a little spring and that's what transmits the voltage coming into the center to the distributor to where it would feed it back out to the other cylinders. That little spring and that carbon went BING and went off and into the grass. I could not find it anywhere; I was on my knees for 15 minutes. I said, "Lord have mercy, there's no spares, Studebaker was no longer in business, I've got to do something." So, I took the flashlight battery, broke open one of the batteries, took the carbon rod out of that, used some concrete on the side of the road to grind it down, to make the little round brush that would fit in the center, used the wife's nail file to cut it off and cut a groove around the bottom end, and took the spring from a ball point pen and rewound it around the pen to make it bigger, then I attached that to the little carbon brush and slipped it up inside the distributor cap and it fit perfect, then I put a drop of oil on that little fiber glass deal that worked on the cam, put it all back together again, fired it up, and that thing stayed in there for about the next 10 years. That just shows you what you can do if you have to do something.

CHAPTER 8
PEASE AFB

Well, when we finally got up to Pease I had Sgt. Devine, who used to be my sergeant down at McCoy, waiting for me and he said, "I got you base housing." I moved right into base housing and five days later had my furniture in. He said, "T. Kaye, you've got to come to work right away, we are having problems, and I know you know the B47 real good." So I went into the hydraulic shop, met everybody, and checked in with everybody, and they said, "Well, they want you over in the MA shop." Well, while I was checking in at the hydraulic shop I saw Mort Charum again, my old partner from two other bases. So, we got together and we were catching up on how many kids we had and etc. etc. etc. So I told him, "I'm going to go to the MS shop." So he said, "Well, why don't you take me over there too." So I went over to see Sgt. Devine and I said, "What seems to be the problem?" He says, "We've got repeat after repeat after repeat write-ups on air conditioning and pressurization and on the heaters on the KC97." I said, "Well hell, you've got one of the best guys I've ever trained, he actually trained me, over in the shop, Sgt. Charum. Here he is right here. Bring both of us over there and within 30 days we'll have all of your repeat write-ups cleared and you won't have anything coming back." He said, "Great, Great!" So he made the appropriate phone calls and we switched from the hydraulic shop over to the mechanical accessories shop, which is the pneumatic shop, air conditioning, pressurization, locks, and etc. etc. etc. We went in there and the two of us would go out as soon as we had an air conditioning problem, and we would find out what the problem was and fix it, and most of the problems turned out to be a couple of sensing hoses. Now, you have to realize that the air was extremely hot coming to the air conditioner, it's 600 degree air coming from the jet engines and what happened was that it had dried these hoses out to where they were porous and instead of working with full pressure they were working with minimal pressure because they were all leaking air. All we did was go in there and change these two hoses in each airplane and by the time 30 days went by we only had 3 repeat write-ups. Sgt. Devine was just totally enthralled. He couldn't have been happier and he said, "This is great. This is great." While I was working one night they called me to sign off a red cross down on the alert strip. Sgt. Grieves was working down there and he had done the work and he wanted me to sign off the red cross. He came by the house and picked me up and I decided to just slip down there in civilian clothes, slip in there and sign off, so we slipped into the alert strip, checked in and I went up there. He had changed the oxygen converter, so he pulled up the B4 stand, disconnected the bomb door, moved it in, and we checked it all for leaks, we squirted this leak detector all over everything and everything was jam up, so as I was getting down, it was winter time and there was all ruts and ice, and as I jumped down my heel hit on the top of one of the ruts and it slid down in there and you could actually hear, it sounded like a two-by-four cracking, when my ankle broke. So, I hobbled on out and we put the bomb door back together and we went up to the house. I said, "Look Grieves, I've got to go to the medics, I just broke my ankle." He said, "Yeah, I could hear that son of a bitch when it snapped." I said, "Well, I can't go up there and tell them I was on the alert strip in civilian clothes, so take me by the house and I will change clothes and then you can take me up there." Now, this is the God's truth – as I was going in the house he's hobbling and he's on my left hand side cause it was the left ankle, as we hobbled in and I'm going upstairs to change clothes Lorna is sitting there watching television and she says, "What's the matter Thomas?" I said, "I broke my ankle and I've got to go get a cast put on it." So she says, "Does this mean that we can't go shopping tomorrow." Nothing about the ankle being broke, all she's worried about is going shopping. So I went up and changed clothes and went back and got a cast put on there and that took care of that part.

Well, Mort and I went back to the hydraulic shop since we had gotten all the pressurization problems and heating problems all taken care of, so they gave me four young airmen to train. One of their names was Hills; he was a scheming little pilgrim from Boston and he looked like Beaky Buzzard in the old cartoons. Now, remember, that flight line was sometimes 20 degrees above zero, or up around zero, so I would go out with these four airmen and we had what you'd call a BT400 heater and I would hold the heater on their hands so they could work so their hands wouldn't freeze because you couldn't work with any gloves on. Some of them were kind of fumbling and bumbling and everything, so when we came back into the shop one night we had to put our tool boxes in special racks that were isolated from each other and you locked the box in the rack and then locked the rack. You could not see through the rack if you had a metal back on the inside with tool box on both sides and I could hear this Hills talking to Sprague and Jonesy, and he said "Look, if you go out with Sgt. Kaye and it's cold and you don't want to do the work, all you have to do is drop the wrench three or four times and he'll get angry and he'll take the wrench and he'll go ahead and do the work and you can stand by the heater and stay warm." Well, I went over the top of that tool box rack and grabbed him by the throat and he sounded like a squawk and I said, "You little sucker, you're going to be with me for a while and your ass is grass and I'm the lawn mower and you're going to be in deep trouble from now on." And boy, he did stay in trouble. He went into town one weekend and took off on his buddy's motorcycle, got going 80 miles an hour and fell off, and he came back and was covered from one end to the other with road rash and scabs and he couldn't do any work, so we had to make a clerk out of him till all the scabs fell off, for about 3 weeks. He was a real dumb kid.

Now this place up here ended up being Studebaker heaven for me. I found another Studebaker, a Power Hawk and a Flight Hawk and I got them for about $100 apiece. I went through them and redid the interiors, redid the rugs and did the body work on them and I had a regular fleet of Studebakers up there and it was really something. We were out there working on an airplane one day and they had a little Lieutenant who was supposed to keep up with what's going on on the flight line. I was working up on a flap on disconnect unit with another guy, and the aircraft was a flyer but it wasn't going to fly instantly, you know, in the next 20 minutes. The little Lieutenant kept coming back about 3 or 4 times, and I said, "Look, quit bugging us, Sir. Who do you think you are, Jesus H. Christ?" He uncovered his nametag and it read J.H. Christ. I almost fell out. I almost died. We also had one kid in the shop that got into a bunch of trouble. He bought a 61 Ford Fairlane convertible and it was a Yankee car, where they used salt on the roads, and the car was literally rotted off. It was a beautiful car and was only four years old, but the metal was rotted off where you could see all the workings on the inside of the door. They wouldn't give him a sticker to get on the base because it was in such sad shape. The sticker for the base was red, so what he did was he got a red Condemned tag, turned it over, and he very laboriously copied a regular sticker on it with an ink pen and made it look perfect, and then he attached it to the window and drove it around for about three weeks. Then the stupid fool parked in and Air Policeman's parking place and he got caught. Needless to say, he stayed in deep trouble.

Well, it was becoming time for the yearly bombing competition to come up, and it was going to be in Spokane, Washington this time. Sergeant Devine came to me and he said, "T. Kaye, I'm going to send you to bombing competition. If we do well we can use that to get you promoted to Tech Sergeant. I'm sick and tired of seeing these other people get promoted and a good worker like you gets the shaft." So we got one airplane ready, they gave us all new uniforms and nice new yellow hats and all new brogans with the parachute cord. We were sharp. You'll see a picture of me in the book in that uniform. We got in the airplane and flew to Spokane, Washington and landed out there. It was a beautiful base. The minute our airplane landed we went and checked everything out and it was in perfect shape. All we had to do was go party at the NCO Club. This NCO Club was one-half of a gigantic warehouse. It was the biggest NCO Club I'd ever seen in my life. Well, Carlings Black Label salesman was there and so was Hamm's, which was made in Washington State. We didn't have to pay for any beer and we just drank till we could barely make it back to the barracks and go to sleep, get up the next morning and make a preflight and launch the aircraft, go get some breakfast while the aircraft flew its bombing mission. Then we'd go to the club and have a couple of beers, come on back, the airplane would land, and we'd turn it around and get everything ready to go again. After we got done with the third mission we had one more mission to go, but it was going to be 2 or 3 days before that mission went. A friend of mine from the engine shop said, "Let's go downtown, T. Kaye, and see what sort of mischief we can get into." We had civilian clothes with us and we had a little bit of money, so we commandeered the launch truck, put a couple of couches in there and put a bunch of guys with it, and we drove it to town for our own transportation. Evidently, this was done at every bomb comp. When we got down town we found a good place to park it, we parked it and locked it up, then told everybody to meet us back there at 2:00 o'clock in the morning. We went to a couple of bars here and the bars there and they had the most beautiful cars in the world. This was in 1965 and if you remember "American Graffiti" came out, and the cars would just be going up and down the streets, it was a car lovers heaven and they were all done up beautifully. Now, we were sitting down at the bar and looking, and here's all these guys in the corner talking cars, and all these beautiful girls sitting at the tables and not doing anything. We went over and started dancing with them. They were going wild over us because we didn't want to talk cars and cams and everything, and they were complaining, "these guys here all just want to talk cars, and when we go out there to the lake to get a little bit or go skinny dipping and they just want to sit around and talk cars and cams." I ended up with this good-looking blonde in a red dress, and she was fine like Roma wine. She was tall and slender, good looking and a real blonde, too. My buddy ended up with her girlfriend and they had a 55 Ford so we toured several bars, and about 1 o'clock in the morning they said, "Come on back to our house." We figured we'd go back and fool around a little bit. We went back and we were fooling around with the girls in our respective rooms, and the girls said, "Well, we aren't going to let you guys go back to the base. We just love you and we're going to keep you because these other guys don't do anything but talk cars, and you guys you dance and drink and carry on. I said, "Look here, we're lifers, we're 20 year men and we can't give this shit up just like that." Then she let it slip that she was married to some guy in prison. That's all I need was for him to break out of prison and come in the house and catch me with his old lady and blow the top of my head off. I happened to hit the bathroom at the same time my partner hit the bathroom, and I said, "Lookee here, son, these women are crazy." He said, "I know, they don't want to let us go." I said, "We're going to have to scamper on out of here. I'm going to go back and I'm going to get all my clothes on, then we'll talk about maybe we can take them down and get some coffee, then we'll meet in the bathroom. There's a back way out of here through that bathroom window." So he said, "Okay." In about five minutes I went to the bathroom and flushed the toilet about three times, he came in there, we locked that bathroom door, opened that bathroom window, we went out back and went down that alley about 90 miles and hour running, we were laughing of course, but we were running away. We'd cut down one street, over another street, down another street, over another street; we had to find our way back downtown. You could see this car go by, that 55 Ford, with them two women looking for us. They were running up and down the streets. We finally got back to where the launch truck was and got in there and we waited about an hour for the rest of the guys. I said, "Well, at least we won't get caught. Did you do what I told you?" We always went incognito when we were off anyplace, I was Chuck Jones and he was Paul West. We had used those names all over the world. He said, "Yeah, I told them my name was Paul West, because you never know, them bitches might call up at home." We went back and made the last mission and loaded up everything. We came in fourth, which wasn't a winner but it was good enough being 4th out of 48. We went back to Pease and went back to regular work. About a week later this girl had somehow found out Bobby J's real name and turned around and called his house about 3 or 4 o'clock in the morning, and Bobby J's wife answered the phone. Needless to say, Bobby J. slept downstairs for about 2 months before he got back in good with his wife. Luckily, I didn't get captured. Now, it's coming time for promotion again; you had to remember, they would make six Tech Sergeants on a base, with 3,000 people, and about 600 could go for Tech. I said, "Well, I don't have a snowball's chance in hell." Well, Sgt. Devine, who had written my performance reports for years, said, "Don't worry about it." So, we ended up with me making Tech, and Sgt. Cool, who was a Staff Sergeant in the hydraulic shop with me, Bobby J. Goodrich, my friend, made Tech, and our division, Aero Repair, got all six Tech Sergeants on the base. Needless to say, everybody on the base was hostile. Sgt. Devine was drunk as a skunk, because he had written all the performance reports that had gotten all those people promoted. Bobby J. and I went over there and literally, he was small, about 5'2" and an E9, and we just literally picked him up by each arm, took him out and put him in the car, and took him home and put him to bed before somebody whipped up on him. Boy, it was nice after all these years to finally put on these Tech stripes. By now the Vietnam War was cranking up pretty good. Kennedy, and that McNamara, that piece of crap we had for a Secretary of Defense, that bean counter, said "We're going to do away with the B47s because they are no good, they don't have the range" and he didn't know anything about anything. It was still a fine airplane; it flew just as fast as a B52, could do the same mission, but he just wanted to cut corners. They were going to shut down our bomb wing, the 509th, and the other, the 100th bomb wing, on the base. They just turned around and said they were going to send them to the bone yard in November. That's out there at Mazdec in Tucson, Arizona. So we started launching them and sending them to the bone yard and by December they were all gone and I got a set of orders to Midway Island. I found out I could take the family with me after I got housing. We were trying to figure out what to do with my family, so we got in my Studebaker Golden Hawk and started for Jacksonville, Florida. I was on the Massachusetts Turnpike and it died. I checked the points and they were not turning, which indicated a broken shaft somewhere. I called Sprague, who was also going to the Pacific. He lived close to where I was. He came immediately to my rescue. He had wanted to buy my car for a year, so I told him to get me to a rental car place with wife, children and dog and said, "Here's the title, you can have it." He said, "No sweat," and took me to an Avis Rental place, where I rented a Dodge and I signed the title over to him. We drove down in style. I then, while enroute, picked up my Thunderbird in Ludowici, GA. It was a Bob Jones' (who was going to Midway with me) grandfather, who was the crooked judge of Ludowici. If you are old like me you will remember AAA-Post and Collier magazine and everyone said to bypass Ludowici, as it is was a speed trap. When I went to the judge to get my keys he said I couldn't have it until he checked with Bob. I went out and put my extra set of keys in and Lorna drove it to Jacksonville. I sold my T-bird to pay for plane tickets so Lorna and the children could go and stay with her family till I sent for her.

After three days at home I got a call from David Sprague. He said it cost $0.10 (10 cents) to fix the car. I had installed a timing key wrong so he fixed it. He said if I would pay for his way down I could have the car and the title back. Nowhere would you ever find a person like that now; so he came down and we drove around and I showed him Florida – he loved it, especially the Spanish moss. He said that somehow he would come back. We changed liquids in my car, filled the gas tank, and put the car on blocks and pickled the engine (squirt oil in the carburetor of running engine until it dies and remove spark plugs and squirt oil in them; then it would start up when I got back (which it did, with no problem). I bought a Thunderbird for Lorna. My other two Studebakers I had to sell cheap, you had to give the cars away because the whole wing was leaving, so little Jonesy who worked for me, drove the car down to Georgia and left it there, and when we got down to Georgia Lorna drove it the rest of the way home. We were talking with my mother, we were staying at my house there, and she wanted Lorna to stay and wait for me but Lorna said she wanted to go and wait in England. I put Lorna and the two children on an airplane and sent them to England. Little Sprague came down and met me and he and I traveled to California and went to Travis to catch an airplane to Honolulu. When I got to Travis they said, "Let me see your overseas shot record" and I said, "just a minute, just a minute." I was looking and I had lost my shot record. I had to have nine shots. Little Sprague was just looking at me and laughing, you know. I said, "Look here, in my sign off in the medical part, it says that I've had all my shots. Just make me up a new one." He said, "Nope, take your blouse off." So I took my blouse off and he said, "roll up your sleeves" and he hit me with nine shots. Little Sprague had to button my sleeves up, and slip my blouse back on and button me up. Good God, was I sore. We turned around and got on the airplane and flew to Honolulu. When I got to Honolulu I had to catch an airplane to Midway and my little friend, a good trooper, Sprague caught an airplane and he went to Mactan in the Philippines.

CHAPTER 9
MIDWAY ISLAND, U.S.N.S.

Let me explain where Midway Island is. It is on the International Dateline, it's 1,300 miles northwest of Hawaii, it's about 1,200 miles south of Alaska, and it's about 2,400 miles to Japan and probably about 1,500 miles to Okinawa. It's a beautiful island that is about 2 square miles in total. There are two islands, Sand Island and Eastern Island. This is where the biggest naval battle in World War II was fought, right off of this island for this island. Many of the old buildings and the hangers are still there and they are still shot full of holes from when the Japanese attacked. It is a magnificent island; we have Australian Ironwood Pines 150 to 200 feet tall that were planted back in the turn of the century. We have a big giant hanger on that island, which is as big as the Rose Bowl. It's an outside hanger; there are no walls, just a big roof and a center section with all the offices. The island has, of course, all the amenities for personnel and their families. It had 1,200 units for families, including enlisted people and officers. The water around the island was absolutely gorgeous, a powder blue, and that was surrounded by a reef. There was only one problem with that water; in that water were a great amount of denizens of the deep that were going to try to do you in. We had every kind of shark known to man; we had a sea snake, which if he bit you you'd never make it out of the water, his toxin hits the nervous system; we had horseshoe crabs that, if you step on them, the spine goes up into the foot and your foot has to be removed because it's rotted and the poison just runs rampant in you. You can fish all you want inside the reef but you have to throw the fish back because if you try to eat them or boil them or try to do anything with them, you get what's called step and a half, which is like having a stroke where one side of your body goes dead and you do not recover from it. Outside of that the water is absolutely gorgeous and everybody went swimming and fishing and scuba diving, etcetera. I used to go skin diving but when I bumped into a sea snake one day I left the water quite rapidly and never went back in again. We had big, gorgeous picnic areas and we had a school for the children up until the eighth grade, it was a gorgeous school. We had a beautiful brand new church; we had a couple of small hangers and Capt. Sabacour, the navy captain in charge of the island, we all got together and built a nine hole golf course, but you had to play down through the buildings and everything and over the streets. We also started up a model airplane shop there, and a model railroading shop so we had everything to do. Now on the islands were about 160,000 lay a sand Albatross, which are called the goony birds, which you will see pictures of in this book. They are absolutely magnificent looking birds in flight, they have about a seven or eight foot wingspread. They came back every year to nest at the same identical place. I had quarters at Bravo 13, which was the highest point of the island, ten foot above sea level. I had the same thirteen families there for two years, they would come right on back and they would set their egg and etcetera. Now, these goony birds would lay their egg and they would sit that egg and the mate would go to sea to eat, and they ate squid, and then when he got his fill of squid, he would come back and sit the egg and the female would go. They kept alternating until these birds were born. They were the ugliest things you ever saw in your life. The parents would start cycling out to get the squid and they would come back and regurgitate it directly down into the baby's mouth, and that's how they would feed him. In a matter of a very little time this scoundrel grew to be quite large, but he was ugly because he was molting. Finally, when the feathers started coming in, it would be the rainy season and the windy season they would stand on the end of their nest and they would flap their wings to strengthen their wings. After a period the parent goony birds were on the island for about 9 months they would pick up and leave. They would all fly off and clear the island in about three days. The babies that went with them who could fly now would go with them. Some of them, of course, never made it past the reef. They just didn't have the strength and they would land in the water and that's when the sharks would come out and just scoop, it was over, gone. Of course, we didn't go swimming or fishing or anything during that period of time. They would be gone for a period of about 3 or 4 months out to sea, and then they would return back, and after having been landing at sea they didn't have to take off using their feet, so when they came back they would forget how to land so they'd forget about putting their feet down. It was a great delight for us to sit there and watch them come blazing in at about 50 miles an hour and forget to put the landing gear down, and roll into a big old pile with the rest of them. Now, these birds could fly thousands of miles. We had eight doctors on the island studying them. They took one bird and painted his chest with a yellow phosphorescent paint, another one painted with pink phosphorescent paint, and another one with blue. One they put on an airplane to San Francisco in one of our aircraft transitting through, they sent one to Alaska and one to Japan. Within eleven days those birds were back on the nest. They had flown 2,400 miles, 1,000 miles, and 2,000 miles all in eleven days. They were really quite unique.

When we hit the island there was 180 of us from the Strategic Air Command. We were being transferred into MATS, which means May Arrive Tomorrow Sometime, maybe, or as the GI's would say, Many Airmen Tramping in Shit. It later became the Military Airlift Command under General Jack Catten, and he really got it going good because he was an ex SAC man also. We had a Colonel named Johnson who was a very good gentleman, and he explained to us that we had never worked on these aircraft before and we were going to start transitting 400 aircraft a month. I had in my shop Hills, who had come with me, along with Jonesy from Pease AFB in New Hampshire, I had a kid named Foltz, who was nothing but a pack of trouble, and I had a boy named Bruce Reichenbach, who came with me. During that time I found out that I used to ride motorcycles with his father. Bruce Reichenbach to this day is my friend; in fact, I just got off the telephone with him. He went on and I got him into the Flight Engineer program, he became a flight engineer, got a private pilot ticket, a commercial ticket, a multiengine ticket, instrument ticket, and when he retired he was a flight engineer on C141s, C5s, and he was the first flight engineer on the KC10 program. He then went to fly for the Navy in a special DC8 of which he was aircraft commander. After about two or three years he went to Northwest Airlines and now he is flying for American Airlines. He is proficient in the DC8, DC9, 707, 717, 727, 737, 747, 757, and 767. I have great pride in the boy since I had a part in nurturing his military career and his later career. They told us that we were going to be transitting the aircraft at a rate of 400 a month, which works out to about ten or twelve a day. What we did was we were on a 7-day week, 24 hour a day basis, so one of my boys was on each shift and I was on the day shift with them. Most of the aircraft would come in during the day and we had to take care of the hydraulic systems on them. We also ended up taking care of the air conditioning, pressurization, and liquid oxygen systems, of which I trained my troops to take care of. We ended up also having to learn how to refuel the aircraft, which we did and it took too long because we were refueling from trucks. Bruce and I scavenged some manifolds from a C124 TO and some receptacles that the trucks could plug into, and we made a big Y duct and we could plug two trucks into there and adjust the pressures to be the same, and we could refuel the airplanes in about one-half of the time it normally took. This was for the C130 Hercules, the C133 and the C141 Stratolifter. We also had the C124 Globemasters coming in that we would have to refuel. They were the old recip engine jobs that I used to ride from Africa and back. Now, the C133s had four big T234 Turbo props, of 5,000 shaft horsepower apiece. Now, we had a short runway of about 8,000 feet on Midway. It took everything they had to get off the ground. If they ingested a couple of goony birds into the engines it really got critical. They said they would start mixing water/alcohol and since there was hydraulics and fluids and all that other stuff, old Sgt. Kaye got stuck with the deal. We would have to have a water/alcohol trailer, and we would take 450 gallons of distilled water in plastic containers inside of five-gallon cans that were flown in by the 124 and we would open them up and dump them into this 600-

gallon truck, of which a picture will be shown to you. We then mixed six quarts of fish oil into the water, since fish oil would mix with the water. We would mix the six quarts of fish oil in there and we would agitate it and it turned the water a milky white. Then we would suck in a little less than 150 gallons of methanol alcohol and we would blend that in. We had to have a perfect mix of 78/28 plus or minus 1 percent. If you were off one way with too much water, which would put the fire out in the engine, or too much alcohol the other way the engine would run too hot. These people here were really tight about that so I had a hydrometer in the truck with me, and I would pull up to the 133, I would agitate the water/alcohol for a half hour prior to installing about 120 gallons into the aircraft, and I would have to show the flight crew exactly with the hydrometer that the reading was perfect. I kept a logbook and I made them sign that they verified that the amount of mixture was right. This aircraft was a beautiful, giant aircraft, but the engines really weren't worth a damn at the time. They carried two spare engines at the time. Now, you've got to realize that this aircraft is about 125 feet long and most of the time when they came into Midway they would have to have an engine change because they couldn't get but about 150 to 200 hours on the engines. Consequently, when you would lose an engine you would need more power to keep the aircraft up in the air if you had a high fuel load and a high volume of cargo. One day I got a call from airlift command post and Major Pete called me up and said, "Sgt. Kaye, we've got a 133 coming in with two engines out, coming from Naha, Okinawa. Get it all set up so we can be set to change the two engines." So he told me which engines they were and we pre-positioned all our gear so that he could taxi right up to the hanger, we could pull him into the hanger, we had the cranes ready, we could snatch the props off and then the engines off and then hang the new ones and send him on his way. As the aircraft commander landed and taxied in with the two dead engines, and he parked the aircraft where we wanted it, I said, "Sir, with your gross weight at the time you called us, how were you able to make it to Midway because according to your gross weight you couldn't maintain an altitude of about 50 foot below sea level?" He said, "Oh Sgt. Kaye, I'm an old timer and when I leave Okinawa, when we take off, we go off the end of a big hill about 200 or 300 feet high, so I never us my water/alcohol, I save my water/alcohol. Therefore, when I was flying and I lost my two engines, I let it get down to about 400 feet off the ground and then I'd shoot the water/alcohol to the engines, which would give me another 4,000 horse power and it would kite me up to about 15,000 and then I would shut the water/alcohol off and keep struggling along. Of course, as the fuel was burning it would take longer to go down so that water/alcohol that I didn't use kept kiting me back up into the air and got me here to Midway." I said, "Well you are one sharp cookie, you must have been a SAC trained killer." He said, "Yes Sgt. Kaye, I was in SAC for many years." That is how critical the water/alcohol was. Also, being water/alcohol king, I got tired using those five-gallon containers of water. That's a hell of a lot of cutting and opening and dumping, plus the airplane had to fly that in. I was talking to my one friend, Fritzi Gerber, and he was in charge of Project Seaweed, which was where all the emergency war stuff was. He took me through the hanger where the emergency war stuff was and here was a demineralization unit, used for de-mineralizing water so 105s could use it for take off, so I read the book on it and it had a little putt-putt engine on it that I could hook into the water main of the island, and pump from the water main of the island through these two big filters, capped on and on filters (?) and de-mineralize the water and verify it through a gauge and just use the little putt-putt engine to draw the water in. I tried this one time with the Colonel's approval and he said, "Well Sgt. Kaye, this will save a lot of flights on the 124s, a lot of petrol, plus a lot of labor," so I started mixing water/alcohol this way. Well, that little putt-putt engine didn't last very long so I turned around and plumbed past it and I used the water pressure of the island water system to run it right through the filters and it made the job a piece of cake. Now you've also got to remember that I was building flying model airplanes. In fact, First Class AD Roble and I were in charge of the model airplane hobby shop and we used methanol alcohol and castor oil for the engines on our model airplanes. Well, in order to get model airplane fuel you had to bring it back from Honolulu and the people didn't like to bring it on the airplane because they thought that was very, very dangerous. I got to be friends with a guy in the medics and he gave me just about every bit of castor oil on the island. When the guys wanted to fly the airplanes they'd come and see old T. Kaye and he'd always have some methanol left over and we'd mix it to get the proper mix with the castor oil and everybody flew airplanes and didn't have any more problems after that. Now, I had so much that when one wife wanted to try to have a baby early, before the first of the year, she came up to see Sgt. Kaye and said, "Sgt. Kaye, I need a cup full of castor oil. I'm going to try to bring this baby on early." I said, "Well sweetheart, I've used about all of it up but I've got about a half a cup here and it's full of sawdust from my model airplanes." So she took that and tried to use that to bring her baby on early, but it didn't work. During this time a built a B36 model airplane with 11-foot wingspan and six engines. I had to hand carve the propellers for it since they were pusher propellers. It worked and I got notoriety in the model airplane magazine and in the MATS news and everything. When we weren't working we would be building model airplanes; in fact, we had a great time in a portion of the shop, which was set aside for the people. When the airplanes weren't there we would work on our model airplanes. It kept people busy and kept their hands busy because there was no place to get into mischief on the island. There were no girls and all there was was booze and I didn't want my boys getting drunk and getting into fights with a bunch of sailors, because we were a class above the sailors, we thought. We were there about four or five months when somebody broke into the PX and stole a bunch of wristwatches and rings. Now, let me explain one thing to you; if you wanted to send anything back from the island you had to show it to an officer, seal it, and then he would sign his name across the seal and then you could ship it off. He was literally the Customs man. So these guys had stolen all these rings and wrist watches now what are they going to do with them? They can't sell them on the island. The Navy said they'd checked all their sailor's lockers and everything, now we're going to have to check your airmen. Well, my Colonel got quite hostile and said, "Well, my airmen don't do anything like that. But you can come up there." Well, I being one of the senior noncoms I had one bay, and there was a senior noncom in each bay, we had eight bays all-total. So, the Navy ONI Officers of Navy Intelligence came in. As I walked them through each place they checked the wall lockers and checked the area and checked the beds, etc., etc., etc. We got into this one place where three guys from the Aerial Port squadron were playing cards on a cardboard box with a blanket across it. They said, "What's going on Sgt. Kaye?" I told them and they said, "There's our lockers, go ahead and look in there and there's our bunks there" and they kept playing cards. Nobody could find the stolen items; they searched everything and couldn't find them. The three guys who were playing cards were the three guys that broke into the PX and stole everything, and everything was in that cardboard box that they were playing cards on. One guy got scared and he ratted on the other two. The ONI investigators found out that these three GI's woke up the Seabee that was in charge of the equipment on the base. At two o'clock in the morning they told him they needed it for a job on the flight line and they checked out a crowbar. They used this crowbar to go break into the PX, then they turned around and woke him up at five o'clock and turned the crowbar back in. They all ended up going to Hawaii and they were court martialed there and they got six months of making gravel out of big boulders for Grand Larceny.

SEVERAL FUNNY STORIES OF MIDWAY

The day I arrived was Thanksgiving Day. Of course, there I was late for dinner but the good old USN, after finding out I was ex navy, whipped us up a meal.

I got the troops together and said, "Let's check in the barracks, get blankets, etc., then let's check in with the Dispensary as we only had to places to check in. We could start work the next day. We were ready as we had all be on 30-day leave and transit time and we were bored. When we checked in with the medics, there was a big poster on the wall showing all the bad fish, snakes, crabs, and turtles so big they could bite half your foot off. Mind you, it was a beautiful beach with lovely, pure white sand, beautiful clear water, a beautiful turquoise background, but full of deadly fish, barracuda and sharks. Two sailors had tried to swim from Sand (our island) to Eastern Island at night and got eaten by sharks. They never found their bodies. Eastern was the radio center of the world and they had missed the last boat and it was just 50 yards but they never made it.

Well, the sun was still up so I thought I might as well pull a reconnaissance of the area. I went to the dock area and noticed a young lad in shorts and sneakers fishing. He was a propellor tech from Pease, so I started talking while he was fishing. Soon something was on his hook and he pulled it out of the water. It was a deadly sea snake; one bite and you're dead – like a cobra, only worse. The poison works on the nervous system. I told him to cut the string and give him back to his ocean. The kid said, "No, it's my only hook. I'm bringing him out and I will stomp him to death." He started hauling him in. I moved down the dock 50' to 75' and hollered to him to turn him loose (he wasn't going to get me). The kid snatched him out of the water onto the dock and stomped him to death WITH SNEAKERS while the snake was fighting and twisting, trying to get him, but the kid killed him. I observed this denizen of the deep and said to myself, "If he ever meets me again it'll be in an aquarium.

We received another warning that if we caught any fish inside the reef we couldn't eat them, as they had ingested poisonous microorganisms while eating off the bottom. If you at them you would get "step and a half" – it would act like a stroke and one side of your body would be paralyzed. Damn scary "but" we had two 40' launches you could pay $10.00 and go deep sea fishing about 10 miles out for Tarpon, Wahoo, etc. They were wonderful on a grill after soaked in a washtub full of soy sauce, steak sauce, etc. We ate them at our picnics.

However, we had an SMS Bigelow who went deep-sea fishing and caught several large barracuda. He cut them up, soaked them and barbecued them. In an hour he and his wife were deathly ill. Remember – Pearl Harbor is 1,100 miles away. They were blistering in the esophagus and blocking air passages, virtually strangling. Medics did what they could and the good old USN cranked up a SA16 (Grumman Albatross Amphibian) and flew them to Pearl Harbor in a six-hour journey. It saved their lives. Evidently the barracuda had been living inside of the reef and feeding off those fishes and ingesting the microorganisms. Damn near killed them.

Now I have a very funny story to tell you. I told you about that kid Hills that I was training up at Pease. He just seemed to draw trouble like flies. He was a 2-striper so that meant that he would have to pull KP on the island. All 2-stripers had to pull KP or do our share because we had 180 people who were regularly getting fed. They had a guy named Lt. Sauer who was in charge of the chow hall. He was a village idiot and he was also a dork with ears. He had his wife on the island and she was a very beautiful woman and he had a picture of her on his desk. When the sailors would come in there to talk to him, they would look at the picture. He caught one of them licking his lips and he tried to charge him with mental rape because he was looking at the picture of his old lady and was licking his lips. Of course, by that time the base commander knew he had all his marbles but his shooter was chipped. One of the people went in to talk to him, now this is an actual regulation in the USMJ, he tried to charge him with silent insolence because they guy was looking at him smirking. They threw that charge out also. Anyhow, he was in charge of the chow hall and Hills was working KP so Hills went in at night and they would give them white hats to wear so that their hair wouldn't get into the food. They were special little cooks hats. Well that night they didn't have any white hats so they told them to just wear their regular baseball hats on backwards. Lt. Sauer came down to inspect the chow hall during the time almost for the midnight meal. Here was Hills feeding the troops with his hat on backwards and not a white hat. He pointed to the three GI's and he told them, "You, you and you, you've got 10 hours EMI (Extra Military Instruction) of marching on Saturday morning." Hills said, "What for?" "Because you don't have your white hats on." Hills said, "We don't have any white hats because you don't have any of them, and it's not our fault that you don't have them. The chief in charge told us to wear the hats this way." He said, "I don't care, you've got EMI." Well, the chief in charge, actually he was a First Class in charge, he ran out the back door because he didn't want to mess with Sauer. I had always told Hills that if he ever got in trouble be nice about it and call me. I was lying in bed and Hills called me and said, "Sgt. Kaye, Sgt. Kaye, Lt. Sauer's up here picking on us." He told Lt. Sauer "I'm calling my supervisor because this is unfair and we didn't do anything wrong." I told Hills, "Okay Hills, keep your mouth shut, do what they say, and I'll go see the Colonel in the morning and take care of it all." Well, unbeknownst to me or Hills or anybody else, a navy Admiral landed at the same time to get his aircraft refueled, he was on a C118. Protocol being what it was, the navy Captain of the base was there, and our Colonel was there because we were in charge of all refueling. They decided to go down and have midnight chow at the chow hall. About 10 minutes after Hills called me, Sauer was standing there looking very smug, thinking he'd clued these Air Force people in. He looks in the doorway and here comes our Colonel in the door, along with the base commander and a Full Admiral. Well, Sauer didn't think reasonably, he just saw them coming in the door and he hauled ass out the back door and he was running at full tilt and they had a 40 inch high loading platform in the back where they could offload the trucks in there, and they say that he literally ran for 50 feet in the air like you see in the cartoons before he hit the ground running and he disappeared. Well, Hills being as he was, walked up to our Colonel, and said, "Colonel, they are picking on us GI's again." The Colonel said, "Look, I'll be back later on. Just keep your mouth shut and go back to work." So they fed the navy Captain, our Colonel and the Admiral, took them back down, put them on the airplane, and then they left. Well, about that time the Colonel started spinning wheels leaving the flight line, then blazed on up to the chow hall, slapped on the brakes, skidded to a halt, and came through the chow hall and like to tore the doors off the hinges. He said, "Hills, come over here. What's going on, you embarrassed me there." Hills said, "Well Sir, I thought Sgt. Kaye had called you and you came up here." So he told the Colonel everything and the Colonel said, "I want to see that Lt. Sauer." They called his home and his wife was there, and he was probably hiding out. They couldn't get a hold of Sauer for two days; he just kept hiding on the base. When they finally got a hold of him they ripped him a new tail. He was an absolute idiot but Hills was enough to drive somebody to drink.

Now, on the island we had for entertainment, the Japanese used these big fish balls with nets around them to hold their nets in the water as they went fishing. Now, these fish balls, big giant green balls blown out of Coke glass, would come drifting in and the wives were usually out there 3 or 4 or 5 o'clock in the morning watching them, they would get them and bring them home and leave the ropes around them and then they'd hang them. That's what they did for some entertainment. We also had three SA16s for air/sea rescue there and we also had a chopper. The chopper pilots were flying out there, and about 90 miles away was a reef called Pearl Hermes Reef. They flew out there, they checked their fuel, flew out there and they had enough fuel to get back, so they went out to Pearl Hermes Reef, which was just a little spit of land, and they looked and it was covered with fish balls. They landed and they filled up their chopper full of fish balls. Not thinking, they loaded the chopper up, took off, and were using a higher power setting to stay up in the air when the wind changed, so they could not get back to the base. They had to go back to Pearl Hermes Reef and land. Now, they didn't have fuel and they were in deep doo doo so they had to call for help. The next thing I found out, they came to me and said, "Sgt. Kaye, those 5 gallon boxes and cans you had full of water, we need enough to make 200 gallons." I said, "What do you need them for?" He said, "Well, we're going to have to dump the water out, put aviation fuel in them, then fly over the island close to the water and dump these boxes out with the fuel in them, then they are going to have to put that fuel in the chopper so they can fly the chopper back to the island. So, the first load that we took, we took the ten 5-gallon cans, dumped the water out of them, flushed them, and filled them full of gasoline, put the plastic lid back on, and then we filled the SA16 with them. The SA16 tucked in real close to the water, just about skimming the water, and started kicking them out. Well, if you are flying about 120 miles an hour, and you hit that water, of course thank God Pete wasn't around then, they would rupture and the gasoline would go into the water. They came back to see me again and said, "Sgt. Kaye, don't you have any of this water in 5 gallon containers in a cardboard box inside of a plastic liner?" I said, "Yeah." So we turned around and emptied out 200 gallons of them, flushed them and put them in there and the same identical thing happened. The next thing they did was ask me, "What can we do?" I said, "Well, the only thing you can do in my estimate is take a 55 gallon drum and fill it half full of gasoline." Being half full of gasoline gave it a dead area where when it hit the water it would compress and it would aid in helping it stay afloat. That's how they finally got it there. They took about 10 drums of it and they dropped them in that way and the flight crew had to drag them to the chopper and then hand pump it into the chopper. Of course, when they came back it was "Katie bar the door," they were in deep doo doo with the base commander. First, because they were trying to do something illegal by getting all of those fish balls, which would piss off everybody on the island. Second, that wasn't part of their mission. Third, it embarrassed the Navy because the Air Force had to help them pull it out. About two months later, Capt. MacIntyre, who was my OIC, came to me and said, "We're going to have a big Officer's Club party here, and we're supposed to make things like it is on the island, so what he said is, "What I'd like you to do for me is make a fake island, make fake fish balls on there, and we'll get a plastic model of the chopper and a plastic model of the SA16, and we'll fake it out and make a model of it." Well, that's all you had to tell me, so I got a big giant piece of plasterboard, about 4x4, and made a nice frame around it. I painted water the same color blue, as it is on Midway, absolutely gorgeous, then I took white glue and glued the shape of an island, got sand and poured it into the glue so I had a little island. Then I built the model of the chopper and glued it down there with the guys sitting there and I had little balls of plastic that I put around there to make it look like fish balls, then I took erasers off of pencils and cut them and made them like the 5 gallon cans strewed around there, then I took a little plastic, like visqueen, and glued it around there so it would look like gas was spilling out of them. Then I made the same thing, put little cardboard boxes and then the 55 gallon drums, then I made the SA16 flying over there dropping them. It was absolutely beautiful. The Colonel thought it was gorgeous and so did Capt. MacIntyre. However, when they took that to the Officer's Club and the Officers saw that, they got HOT. They were so hot that they made Capt. MacIntyre call us to come and get it and take it out of there because it was a terrible embarrassment to the Navy.

Now, upon arrival at Midway, since I was a Tech Sergeant now, I put in for base housing and I had a good chance of getting base housing right off the bat. I had sent Lorna and the two children to London to stay with her Aunt and Uncle. Now, they were on the Greenwich Meridian line, they were exactly one-half way around the world. They were on 0 degrees Longitude and I was on 180 degrees Longitude, so I was exactly half way around the world. When I got housing I immediately called and they shipped my household goods to the base housing coming in by ship, so when it was near to getting there I sent money to Lorna and told her to get an airplane ticket from London, England to New York, New York to San Francisco, San Francisco to Honolulu, and at Honolulu I was going to have a friend of mine from Pease meet her and put her on what was called a Log Flight to get her to Midway Island. Now, I want to remind you that this wife weighed 95 pounds, she had two children, one of them was one year old and the other one was three years old. The one year old was still in diapers. Now, she was going to have to travel 12,000 miles. This was before the days of Pampers, so she would have to be rinsing the diapers out and cycling them and putting them back on the child with the plastic pants. As long as they were clean, they would be damp. She would have to travel one half of the way around the world. What really gets to me is Dave Barry, the writer in our Jacksonville paper, told this tragic story about him and his wife and their one child and how they had to travel from San Francisco to New York City and what a terribly trying time it was with Pampers and everything. Here's this little foreign wife, she gets on the airplane in London, England and flies BOAC to New York City, makes a change with these two little children and then gets on an airplane and flies to San Francisco, makes another change and gets on Pan Am and flies to Honolulu, then makes another change and gets on a LOG flight, a Logistics flight, and comes to Midway. She had come exactly half way around the world with no problems. I can remember it to this day that when they got off the airplane here was Bianca and Carla in beautiful little plaid skirts with little Saddle shoes on and little white sweaters, and they came off of there looking absolutely gorgeous and they had just traveled half way around the world. These children were just like me. I could make friends with anybody in just five minutes. They had BOAC little pilot's wings on them, they had a little log book for BOAC, they had Pan Am pilot's wings, and they had entered into the log book (the pilot had logged their flight in there), and they had National Airlines little wings from them. I mean it was really something. This family had traveled half way around the world with no problems. I moved them into the apartment and she and the children were with me for the rest of the time that I was over there.

As we were working and doing our work on the airplanes and building the model airplanes we were constantly improving our work place. In order to fill up our MD3's and our trucks, we had to drag them down to the Navy fuel farm. This was a 45-minute deal to drag an MD3 down there because they were three-wheeled and not very stable. They would not give us a truck to refuel these things with, and we were looking around the island and on the backside of the island we found these giant submarine net buoys. They were probably six foot in diameter and twelve foot tall. Jonesy and I got the idea of why don't we stack them one on top of the other and get inside and make sure there's no rust inside, and blow some holes with the torch and make a stand pipe and a drain pipe, then put a hole in the top side, so we could fill them from a big fuel truck. That way we could refuel our power units off one and we could refuel our regular trucks off of the other. We made two of these and it took us about two weeks, and we had to sell it to the Navy, then they started coming about once a month to refuel our tanks for us. We would save that entire extra running around and all that trouble. Of course, anything they wanted done easier they would come to see good old T. Kaye to figure out a way to do it easier, just the water/alcohol deal.

Midway was an island built up during WWII, and the island's electricity came from (as I remember) six giant 30' long diesel engines driving generators. They were big and slow and turned about 500 RPMs. Well, the USN got a new engineering officer in and he said he was going to shut them down one at a time and perform periodic maintenance on them. The old chief in charge said, "don't do it. They have been running for 20 years without a shutdown, and if they ever cool down and parts shrink, they will never start again." Needless to say, the officer shut two of them down and they wouldn't start again. He called for some help from Pearl Harbor. This other officer and engineer said they would pour a big concrete pad and install a new generator – no problem. The Seabees did what they were told, warning that this wouldn't work. They pressed on anyhow, got new gen-sets put in place and started up. In a month the pads started titling from the vibration and hammering of the cylinders. I left the Island. I don't know how they finally fixed it.

Now the Navy, as antique and ancient as they were, had one thing left over from the days of old. They had a beer ration where everybody on the island was allocated one can of beer per day. Unbelievable as it was, the Air Force did not know about that. I found out about it and went to see the Colonel and said, " Colonel, it's time for us to have a picnic." They had two fishing boats that would go out about 20 miles from the island and they would fish for Wahoo and Grouper and all those big fishes. We got volunteers to go out there and go fishing and catch big fish to have on our barbecue trough. I said, "I will be your dog robber." I started off, cause I knew everybody on the base, and I went to the chow hall and they needed some paint. I went to our supply and got about 25 gallons of white paint, took it back to the chow hall and swapped it for 180 steaks and a ton of hamburger and a bunch of hot dogs. I then went to the bakery and got bread from the bakery. I had to swap them for something. I got bread from the bakery and hot dog buns and hamburger buns. I went to the Commissary and swapped something and got mayonnaise and mustard from there. We now had everything that we needed. They had pits down there so we found somebody in the squadron who could do all the barbecuing.   The troops came back with these big fish and the cut them and filleted them. We went to Sgt. Neil's house and he had a big number 3 wash tub, he mixed up his own sauce, so we put all the steaks in one big number 3 washtub with soy sauce, Worstershire sauce and everything else, then we put all the fish in another one and did the same thing with it. It was protocol, and up to me, and I went to see the Naval base commander, Captain Sabacoul, and I told him that I was representing my Colonel and I was there to invite him and that we were going to have a squadron picnic. I asked him if he would please come and bring the Exec with him and the Chaplain and the Air Boss. He said he would contact them and they would be there. Now, you have to understand that the Captain of a Navy base is like the Captain on a ship, nobody talks to him, nobody looks at him, nobody says anything to him; they were deathly afraid of the Captain. That didn't bother old T. Kaye any. So, I told him when to be there and I got everything organized and the day of the picnic we had everything set up. We had baseballs and mitts and everything and we were going to play baseball and have teams and choose up sides. Everything went off like clockwork. We had the Navy Chaplain there, Capt. Fitzgerald, to give the blessing and to thank God for looking after all of us. We started barbecuing the hamburgers and the steaks and the hot dogs and the fish. There was a greater call for the fish than there was for the steaks and the hamburgers. It was absolutely amazing and they tasted wonderful. Of course, we ate all of that and while everybody was eating they chose up sides and were playing baseball. The base commander, Capt. Sabacoul, said, "I like to play baseball and so does my Exec. Can we play?" I said, "Now lookee here Sir, they are going to hooha you just like everybody else cause if you miss a ball or you don't pitch good or anything they are going really to stay on your butt. You have to understand that we aren't like the Navy." He said, "I can take it, I'm tough." So, we chose up and got him on one team and he was the pitcher and the Exec was out in the field, and when he was pitching, oh my God, those corporals and sergeants of ours were really riding him ragged and when he went up to bat they'd give him hell. He was enjoying it and having a good time and he said he really enjoyed it. So by the end of the picnic everything had gone fine.

About a month later they had a big earthquake up in Alaska and we were supposed to get ready because we might get a ten-foot tall tidal wave. Needless to say, who lived at the highest point of the island but good old T. Kaye? I had all the power units and all the heavy equipment and everything up in my front yard, side yard, and back yard. However, the tidal wave never hit us.

Bianca was about 2 years old at the time this incident happened. She was out playing with Carla and the kids on the block. She came in crying, very subdued. We asked her what was wrong but she couldn't tell us. She started getting physically cold, her body was cold and she was moving very slowly. I put her on the back seat of my bike and went down to the dispensary. Lucky for us Dr. Leng was there. He checked her over and said she was going into shock. He noticed her lower lip was swollen. He rolled it around and found a bee stinger there. He removed it and immediately gave her a shot of adrenalin. Then we bundled her up and treated her for shock. She was allergic to bee stings. She had to carry a hypo package until we got her back to the states. She was treated later and supposedly was cured, but it kept her out of the U. S. Air Force.

It was coming time for the Fourth of July and Captain Sabacoul was riding around the island inspecting it. I had my little daughters on my bicycle, one was riding on the back fender on a little seat back there and Bianca was riding in the basket on the front off of the handlebars. As I was pedaling down the street I looked and saw Capt. Sabacoul; he would drive about 20 feet and look to the left and look to the right and then he'd drive up some more. I got about 50 feet away from him and I stopped and as he drove up I threw him a high ball, a salute. I said, "Capt. Sabacoul, I don't know if you remember me but I'm Sgt. Kaye." He said, "Yeah Sgt. Kaye, I really enjoyed that party. It really made us feel good and made us feel like we are part of a team." I said, "Well Capt. Sabacoul, people in your position sometimes can't see the forest for the trees. I noticed you riding around and looking to see what has been done. I've got to tell you that from the time you came aboard there has been a tremendous change on the island for the better and you have really made one's tour much better with all your ideas and the golf course and the hobby shops that you allowed us to have, and our picnics and everything. Sir, from one old Sergeant to a Navy Captain, you are doing a mighty fine job." I threw him a salute and rode on down the street. That had never happened before. In fact, as I was leaving about a year or two later, he was still there. As I was saluting him, he was the last in line and shaking everbody's hand, he held on to my hand and said, "Sgt. Kaye, I must thank you for that time you stopped me on the street. You really made my day because I really couldn't see where I had done that much and accomplished that much." He really enjoyed my complements to him. He said, "You're really something. Never seen nothing like you before." I said, "Yeah, you'll probably never see nothing like me again." Now, we didn't have the greatest supply in the world for spare parts for the aircraft, so they had certain things that they told them they could fly without. One of them you could fly without was a modulating valve in the air conditioning system. That's what they said. But you wouldn't be able to trim the heat up or down. Now, let me explain to you pressurization on a C130. It takes a tremendous volume of air to fill that aircraft and pressurize it so you could go up to cruising altitude of 33,000 feet. Also, ambient air temperature at 33,000 feet is probably about 30 degrees below 0, so you have to have heat. Also, if the air conditioner is stuck in the cold position, you do not get the volume of air necessary to pressurize the aircraft so you can go to altitude. You have to go to altitude because the higher the altitude the less fuel you burn because of less wind resistance and you can really stroke on and get up into a jet stream. This aircraft came in and he had a write up and he wrote it up on a red cross and he said, "I don't have any warm air and I'm having difficulty pressurizing the aircraft due to the low flow of air." I went to see him and I said, "Sir, that's not a go or no go item. But, I'll be able to fix it for you and it will be hot on the ground but when you get up into the air your temperature will be all right and you'll be able to pressurize all right and you'll be able to make it back to the states all right." He said, "Well, do what you can, Sgt. Kaye, because we have got to get the aircraft back and get this stuff back and then turn around and come back." So we pulled off the side panel off of the right wheel well and went into where the air conditioning unit was and the modulating valve. Jonesy and I took the modulating valve out and it left a serrated shaft sticking out so we had one of the guys on the crew fire up one of the outboard engines and turn the air conditioner on. I took a pair of vise grips and got on this shaft that operated the modulating valve and said, "Now you guys tell me when you've got a lot of hot air in there, almost so hot that you can't stand it. I kept moving the modulating valve and they said, "Well, it's hotter than hell in here right now Sgt. Kaye." I said, "Okay, go ahead and shut down the engines." I told Jonesy to get the safety wire and we safety wired those vise grips holding that valve in that position with this safety wire. It was holding it and looked like a spider web of stainless steel wire holding it in the proper position. We put the cover back on and I put a note on the aircraft telling the flight crew to call me and I would meet them when it was time for them to leave. The aircraft commander showed up and I said, "Sir, now when you taxi out don't pressurize until you get to about 5,000 feet then go ahead and put it on for pressurization. Now, it's going to be hot but when you get to altitude it will be all right." He said, "Well, what did you do, Sgt. Kaye?" I said, "Well, I fixed it with a pair of vise grips but I'll want my vise grips back when you come back through the next time because I can't get any tools out here." He said, "Show me what you did." We went over and pulled the panel off and he looked and he saw that and he said, "Oh my God, cover it up, cover it up. Put the panel back on. Put the panel back on." He said, "Are you sure this will work?" I said, "Yes sir, it will. I'll stay in the airlift command post and I'll call you every ten minutes and I'll want to know how your pressurization is doing." I went up to the command post and he fired up and he took off and when he got to about 10,000 feet he turned on the pressurization and he said, "Pressurization is just fine, Sgt. Kaye, but still a little bit warm." I said, "All right, go up to cruising altitude." So he went to cruising altitude and he said, "It is perfect. I will bring your vise grips back." About two months later he came back by and gave me the vise grips back. God Bless him.

I had a C130 come back for an emergency landing for a large Hydraulic leak at the flap pack. It was a #8 bulkhead fitting with a jam & seal that had broken due to repeated shock of fast stopping of flap movement. After removing it I checked bench stock, none; went to Navy supply, none. It was one of the new kind of M/S fittings (Military Standard), not the old AN Flared fitting. This was a flareless fitting but it came out of the flap control down to a shuttle valve "T" fitting. Now, I was not going to hold up a mission for one fitting so I decided to improvise. As I was looking at a drain valve on an oil Bowesen, I noted a #8 AN bulkhead fitting. I swiped it and stuck a plug in its place, took this to the airplane, installed it and op checked it. It worked fine. I signed the red cross off with a temp repair. A no no – I showed flight crew what I had done and told them to write it up when they got home. Boy, did I hear from the States about that. It worked fine but Quality Control got into it because I made an unauthorized change. My C.O. told them to get bent and we went on working.

During this time on Midway Island I met a Navy First Class Petty Officer named Tom Rowell and we were the ones who got together and we were building and flying the model airplanes and we started a model airplane club and he was instrumental in flying all the way to Japan to get the models at the dirt cheap prices and we would go to Okinawa to buy more models over there for the island. We had everything you could desire; we had a better model airplane shop than anybody in the United States did, and at about one-tenth the price. That B-36 model that I built, of which you'll see the picture in there, cost me $16.00 for the kit. The same kit in the United States is about $400.00. I started building the fuselage, fin and rudder and stabilizer and elevator. It was a giant. It was 9' long. There was a young flight line crew chief. He built and flew models with me. His name was Dan Fergenson. He said he would build wing & engine and nacelles while I would build the fuselage and we will finish it together. Our squadron commander said he could set up a 10' plywood bench to build the wing on, in the barracks. Everyone was interested. No one had every build a flying B36 before, anywhere in the world, mainly because of pusher propellers. No one manufactured them. Well, one of my navy friends was a carpenter in the SeaBee's. He could do anything. He said, "I will make and balance them." He did make them. We finished the plane and flew it twelve times on the island and the chief made me a big box, with forklift pockets. I was to send my plane home to the states in it, which I did.

The young Buck Sergeant, Dan Fergenson's, tour of duty was up and he was up for discharge. I tried to talk him into reenlisting but he said no. He was going to Emory Riddle in Daytona Beach and would get his pilot's license there. We communicated for a while. He got a private, commercial, instrument, and multi-engine license and went on to fly in DC8's. That was the last I heard; he was a copilot on a DC8. It's wonderful when your troops do well. A lot of my boys became pilots. It's very rewarding emotionally to see your men progress like that.

So anyhow, Tom Rowell and I became fast friends and we're friends to this very day, and we see each other probably every two or three years at the Midway Island reunion.

As my tour of duty was coming to an end I put in to go back and they said, "Where do you want to go, forecast for?" and I said, "Well, forecast for Pease Air Force Base in New Hampshire because I'm known there, and Westover Air Force Base because I'm known there and know the area." About that time, Capt. McIntyre, who was my OIC Officer in charge of my area, came in and he says, "I got my orders, Sgt. Kaye." I said, "Yeah, where are you going?" He says, "I'm going to McGuire Air Force Base." I said, "My God, Captain, if I got a set of orders like that I'd cut my wrists." So he laughed and said, "Aw, it isn't going to be too bad." So, I forecasted for those two Yankee bases because I knew nobody would be asking for them. So, my orders came in and guess where I was going – I was going to

McGuire Air Force Base. So when they came in, he took the TWX and he brought it down to my office and he sat on the corner of my desk and he said, "Here's where you're going, Sgt. Kaye." And, he took his knife out and made like he was cleaning his fingernails. So I said, "My God, I'm going to McGuire Air Force Base. I'll be damned." So he said, "Here," and he handed me the knife. I said, "Well, what are you handing me the knife for?" He said, "I want to see you cut your wrists cause you told me you'd cut your wrists if you landed a set of orders going to McGuire." So, anyhow, we had a big going away party at the Acey-Duecy Club and, as we were leaving, as protocol would have it, they had like side boys, and they were standing on both sides of the line; the enlisted senior non-coms that I was affiliated with on the bases on one side and the officers on the other. It started off with my Colonel and the Air Boss who was in charge of the flight line, the Executive Officer who flew us to Japan to get all the model airplanes, and Capt. Sabacool, who was my Captain all during the time. So, as I said goodbye to each person, I said to our Colonel, "Thank you, Sir, for the help," because I was leaving under pressure because Mother had broken her hip and I had to leave early or I would have been there for another six months. I said, "Thank you for all the help in getting with the Red Cross to get me home early. I'm going to reenlist in Hawaii and thank you for getting that all set up." Then I went to the Air Boss and said, "I want to thank you for allowing me to fly my model airplanes on the flight line." Then I went to the Exec and said, "Thank you for all the help with the model airplane shop." Then, I went to the Captain and I said, "Captain Sabacool, I want to thank you for making my two years on Midway Island the best tour of duty of ever had in my whole life." Then I climbed up on the airplane and we sat down and we looked out there and they were all looking back and forth at each other, laughing and pointing to where I was sitting, like I was really something and they were really going to miss me.

Before the last part is typed I'd like to interject one more story in that we had a C133 that was coming in, you'll see a picture in the book, and as he landed he was coming in with one wing up real high and the other wing was down real low and it was out of kilter and something was causing that. So, as they pulled in there I met the flight engineer and said, "You've got a problem here, don't you?" He said, " Yeah, I need to get my struts serviced." Now, these had four shock struts on the aircraft, two on each side of the aircraft It was a very wide aircraft, and they were serviced with air pressure versus the extension, the amount of shiny surface on the struts. What you did was you found out how much the total weight was on the aircraft and you put the air in the struts and aired it up till the pressure was reading right for the extension. What I did is I made a manifold so we could service all four at the same time so they would all be perfect and it was an easier job. So we went in there and we serviced all four landing gear to the proper pressure versus extension and, when we got done, after they refueled it, the airplane still had one wing low. So the flight engineer told me, he said, "Hey Sarge, how about airing these struts up some more on the left hand side." I said, "No, the struts are aired properly, pressure versus extension." I said, "You've got a problem someplace." He said, "No I don't, everything's all right." I said, "Have you got fuel in it, all the way across the board even, all the wings are full?" He said, "Yeah." I said, "Well, let's go look at the gauge at the instrument panel." We went and looked at the panel and when we got to the number two tank, which is on the left hand side, it was showing a green light but it wasn't showing anything on the fuel gauge. I said, "Well, this is the wing that's sitting too high. How do you know that that thing is full of fuel?" He said, "Well, the green light comes on when the fuel shut off valve closes, showing that that's full of fuel." I said, "What I want you to do is go up on top of that wing, pull that cap, and dip that tank to see that it's full." He said, "No, it's full Sarge, just air the strut up." I said, "No, just do what I say cause I'm not going to service it against the TO." So he went up and he pulled the cap off, and lo and behold, that fuel tank was dry and he was getting a false reading. If he would have gone and flown across the pond he would have been 2,000 gallons short. He would have still made it to the States, but he would not have had the prescribed amount of extra fuel to change from one base to the other. So, he said, "I can't get any more fuel in here through the manifold, I'm going to have to service over the wing." So, what you do is you lower a rope down from the wing and you pull the fuel hose up there and then you put it directly into the wing tank. But he put it directly into the wing tank and as he filled that wing tank up what do you think happened to that wing that was high? It went right on down and the aircraft was perfectly level. And then he closed it off and he said, "You know you were right, Sarge. You might have saved our lives." And I said, "Well, if you do it by the book everything is going to come out alright and we came out alright." I said, "Now, you're going to have to figure out how to transfer that fuel out of there while you're flying or you're liable to end up with it stuck in there." He said, "Well, I'll figure out how to route it out, but I've got an extra 2,000 gallons that I didn't have coming in here."

Bruce Reichenbach came in on a transfer about halfway through my career and he was a young Buck Sergeant at the time and said he'd come from Tampa. I said, "Oh yeah, I used to be stationed in Tampa." So he says, "Yeah, my daddy was down there. He's a Sergeant in the Air Force and he's in Vietnam right now." I said, "Yeah, that's nice." Then we started talking motorcycles. He said, "You were in the Golden Eagles." I said, "Yes." He said, "Well, you might have known my father." I said, "Who's your father?" He said, "Chrome Dome Reichenbach. He used to ride that Matchless and that big Harley." I say, "Yeah, Yeah, Yeah," and he says, "Well, I was that little five year-old kid riding on the back of the motorcycle." I said, "Oh my God, and now you're grown up and you're a Buck Sergeant." That's when I started feeling my age. Now, Bruce stayed with me for his tour on the island and when I went back to McGuire he followed me to McGuire. There's more about Bruce to be told when I get to the McGuire Air Force Base parts. Bruce was an excellent worker, had a good attitude and was real sharp, and he and I would work on the long jobs while everybody else would be falling by the wayside from being tired or exhausted. We would turn around and do the jobs, the really hard jobs.

While I was on Midway another really interesting thing happened to me. There was one young Airman 3rd Class who would go to the Airman's Club on base and get a snoot full of liquor and he'd get rowdy and get in fights and punch ups and everything, so one night he got rowdy and they threw him out of the club and they took him back to the barracks and he got in a fight in the barracks, so they call the Shore Patrol. The Shore Patrol came and got him and took him down to see the Officer of the Day and he was threatening to beat up on everybody, and like I say, he was kind of squirrelly and he grabbed the two Shore Patrol guys around the head and ran with them, bulldogging them, and dove through the big pane glass window, and carried the two of them with him right out the front of the building. Well, needless to say they beat the hell out of him, everybody got sewn up, and they put him in the brig. The Colonel came to me and he said, "Sgt. Kaye, you need a new blue hat." I said, "Yeah. I've been trying to get you to let me go to Honolulu go get one." He said, "Well, I'm going to give you a four day pass to go to Honolulu and get a new blue hat. But," I said, "But what?" and he said, "You're going to have to take that crazy Lewynn in there and turn him over to Tripler and send him to see the Psychiatrist over there." I said, "What are you talking about?" He said, "You're going to be responsible for him." I said, "Then I want him handcuffed, I want him brought to the airplane last, and I want him to be sitting all the way in the after section of the aircraft, and he and I will sit back there." Then I said, "And I want a gun, and if he makes one wrong move I'm going to shoot him because there's a whole bunch of people on that airplane and families with children. I don't want to get anybody hurt." He said, "Well, I'm not going to let you have the gun but I'll see if I can't do the rest of it." The day came for the long flight, I'm down there and I'm waiting, and I'm calling the medics and asking, "Have you got him yet? Have you got him yet? Because I want to sit all the way in the back." Meanwhile, I told the Crew Chief on the airplane that I wanted to sit all the way in the back, but what happened was that some other people went back there who had a bunch of children. By the time they finally brought Lewynn (I'll have to delete his name there) he was in uniform and was giggling and he wasn't in handcuffs. I said, "Oh, I can see this is going to be a good flight." They handed me his records and said, "You've got him Sarge." By now everybody is on the airplane so we climbed up on the airplane and I looked and saw there were only two seats left. He ran and jumped in the seat by the window so I sat down next to him, and I looked and noticed this fool had decided to sit right next to the emergency escape hatch. As we took off I didn't want to try to move the people around him because they might get excited and he might get excited. I just looked at him and grabbed my seat belt and cinched it down real tight and thought, well, if he's going to pull that hatch he's going out but I'm not going out with him. He wanted to read his records so I let him read them, and when we landed we were the last people off the airplane. I got off the airplane and I looked, because there was supposed to be an ambulance with a couple of guards from Tripler to pick him up. Tripler was a hospital in Honolulu. So, I took him with me. I didn't have any handcuffs or anything and he was jumping up and down on tables, laughing and giggling, so I went and found the closest telephone and called Tripler and said, "A couple of people from Psychiatry are supposed to be down here to pick up this crazy guy from Midway Island." They said, "Aw, we'll be down there in about an hour." I said, "Look here, he's running around, I've got no control over him and if he runs out onto the runway it's not my fault, it's your fault." So they came on down and they took him off of my hands, and I went and got me a new blue hat for inspection and went on back to the island. And wouldn't you know it, about three weeks later, they sent him back to the island and said he was perfectly all right. So, what the Colonel did, I says "There's a regulation that says 'unadaptable'," I think it was 3916 or 3917, I says, "just ship him back to the states and get rid of him as an unadaptable person to the island." So that's how we finally got rid of him.

160

When I got to Honolulu, after I left with Capt. Sabacool and all, we went in to the base and got some quarters there, and then I went to see about reenlisting, because it was about time to reenlist for my final reenlistment. Doing it either on Midway or Honolulu was real good because my base of original enlistment was Jacksonville, Florida. They had to pay me six cents a mile from California all the way to Tampa, Florida. So I made a good chunk of change there. I reenlisted and then we flew Pan Am to California, from California we flew to New Orleans, and from New Orleans we flew home to Jacksonville. While we were enroute Lorna was pregnant with the third child but she miscarried so we lost the third child in Jacksonville. From there we transferred to McGuire Air Force Base, so I took the Studebaker off the blocks and put a new battery in it, changed the oil again, aired up the tires, and fired it off. Then I put Lorna and the two children, and the dogs, back into the Studebaker Golden Hawk and we drove off to McGuire Air Force Base for my last tour of duty.

CHAPTER 10
MCGUIRE AFB, NJ

Upon arriving at McGuire I was already in for quarters but it was going to be three weeks, so we had to rent a trailer until I could get onto the base. After three weeks I got quarters and we moved onto the base. We got very nice quarters. It was a very nice base; a gigantic base. We had C130s, 131s, and 141s. We were just getting the 141s, as they were just new off of the line. I was familiar with the 130s from Midway Island so I was over the hump. Now, this was a gigantic shop, another 140-man shop, and half of them were civilians and half were GI's. Well, the GI's were the ones who did all the work; the civilians were a lazy bunch of bums. They were making about $6.00 an hour at the time, and the GI was making probably $150 to $200 a month. These civilians, if it was cold, they would go and drag a job; I've seen them take 8 hours to let the air out of two struts. I could put two GI's on that and they could reservice the struts in about an hour and a half. I saw them take 8 hours, two men, to change an engine driven pump on a 130. I got letters of recommendation where Victor Fisher and I went out and changed one in 8 minutes on a flying aircraft. I had absolutely no use for the civilians in the shop, and as fast as I could, I found justification to get rid of them because they wouldn't work at night, they wouldn't work on the mid-shift, they just wouldn't work, period. I had one, I won't mention his name, who was allergic to hydraulic fluid and had been working as a hydraulic man in the shop for years. I had another one that came to me from the butcher shop, because they had a Union there and they had an opening in hydraulics, so he ended up coming to the Hydraulics Shop. But he was still a butcher; he would bend lines, he would cross-thread fittings, he would screw the job up, and finally I wrote enough letters and showed where he was detrimental to our job, so they pushed him out of our shop. He was another one of them who couldn't work on the second shift or the third shift because he couldn't see at night. That was another reason why I got rid of him. I knew he was faking it. So, he went back to the butcher shop and he bumped one guy in the butcher shop, and the guy in the butcher shop was on the second shift. So he had to drive nights and work in the butcher shop at nighttime. So, I went to see the NCOIC over there and I said, "You know, "B" over there, I threw him out of my shop because he couldn't work second shift or third shift." He said, "Well, he's working nights over here." I said, "Yeah, and he bumped a good guy out, didn't he?" He said, "Yeah!" I said, "Well, if you look in his personnel records he states that he can't work at night, and if he can't work at night, you need to get rid of him and get him out of the shop." He did, he got rid of him and got him out of the shop, and he lost his job completely. And I was very happy because he was a detriment to the Air Force, with no practical value to the Air Force. But we had a magnificent shop in size, and of course, the first thing I did there (I like to clean up everything), I turned around and saw the NCOIC and I was going to end up being the assistant NCOIC, so I told him "I want to start off on the third shift and that way I can get the lay of the land and find out how supply works and how this works and how that works and everything. It was cold and we had two trucks, which resembled bread trucks, in our shop, and they were used to take the people out to drop them off on their jobs. Well, these people, the NCOs that were there at the time, they would take that bread truck and take the guy out and drop him off at the airplane and then when he got done they'd leave him to find his own way back in or bum a ride or something, and they would just sit in the shop and play cards. I put a stop to that real quick. I took my assistant shift leader and I put him in that truck and he would take the people to the jobs on the flight line and he would just go from job, to job, to job, to job checking on the people. Now, these people, I've got to describe to you; they looked like unmade beds and smelled like Billy goats. They had long hair, they hadn't shined their shoes in God knows how long, and they just had a piss-poor attitude. So the first thing I did, I braced them at roll call, and I said, "Now, there's a shoebox over there that I bought myself and you will have shined shoes. You don't have to have spit-shined shoes like I do but you will have shined shoes." Of course, this one guy, Kenny P., put up his hand and said, "Well, Sgt. Kaye, we change struts around here and we get oil all over them." I said, "Airman, I've changed probably 20 strut seals in these shoes and they still shine good. You will shine your shoes." I said, "Furthermore, you will have creases in your pants. Now, if you can't afford to send them to the laundry, what you do is you put a board underneath your bed, and you lay them folded and you sleep with the mattress on top of them, and you'll have nice creases in the morning." Then I said, "You will get haircuts. If you don't get haircuts I will carry you up there, and I will get ten pounds of hair cut off and I will have it cut just like the regulations. So I suggest you go get a haircut." Well, in about a week they were starting to shape up. So then I make a habit of going out with each one on the job. When we got out to the flight line, I would let him start the job, then I would tell him, "Now, sit down over there on your toolbox, and you watch." And I would go ahead and change the valve, or reseal the valve, or change the hoses, and I would do the job. So, he knew right away that I knew how to do the job, and he knew that if he had a problem he could call me. He also knew that I knew how long it took to do the job, so it wouldn't be very good for him to featherbed. So, now he knew what a leader was. I went with everybody in the shop on the third shift, until they all knew that I knew what was going on. It was amazing how fast they shaped up and started looking real sharp, especially compared to the day shift that was relieving them. Now, a lot of people used to pass the work off to the next shift; that's called AWP; and they'd order a part at the last minute. Well, when we came on we'd have all these leftover jobs from second shift and first shift. I had friends in supply and I would go and get all the supplies that we needed. In the morning, at 7:00 o'clock when we turned over the shift, they'd say, "What have you got left over, T. Kaye?" I said, "We've got a clean board. Everything's done. You just start off with the day." These guys starting taking great pride in this fact. They would stay over if it took an engine run or something to clear the write-up; they'd stay over until their job was done. Now, we had these two trucks; if you needed a part you had to come all the way back to the shop. Now, I had the one guy reconnoitering the flight line all the time checking on my people. So, what I did was I set up a forward supply point with many used items in that truck, under lock and key. If anybody needed anything, when the truck came around, the just walked out to the truck and the shift leader opened it up and took what he needed out, and while that guy was changing that part he was filling out the yellow tag to get that thing repaired and when it came back we turned it into supply. For the other truck we had, we went and commandeered the paint and we repainted it, by hand of course, and we repainted the inside gray, and we stole rubber to put on the floor, and what we couldn't put on the floor we painted black and put sand in it for nonskid, and we had us a first class launch truck. So, when we were launching the aircraft, we'd take our two launch people and we'd pick up two pairs from aero-repair, two engine men, and we'd have that truck full of people and we'd be sitting right next to the aircraft that was getting ready to leave, so if they had any problems we were there. Our availability and on-time takeoffs just went through the overhead because we were right there, we were doing great. We had a wonderful camaraderie. Then we turned around and did the other flight line truck that the assistant NCOIC of the ship would drive around just like it. We cleaned it up and we painted it. Now, I would go out there about half way through the shift, especially when it was cold, and I'd go down to the flight line snack bar. If I had ten people out I'd buy ten cups of coffee and put them in a box, and I'd get Scalzi, who was my assistant, to drive me to each guy so I went to where each guy was working, gave them a hot cup of coffee, told them to drink their coffee; I'd jump in there and start doing his job and when he'd finish his coffee he'd finish the job and I'd go on to the next guy. I'd go around until I'd given everybody out there a warm cup of coffee. It's amazing how quickly you can build a bond between the men because the men knew that I wasn't sitting in a warm office. The men knew that I was with them, I could do the job, I would bring them coffee, I would look after them, I would protect them, and like I told them, "If you screw up, run, don't walk, run and tell me and I'll fight for you." I said, "But when I get done I'll probably rip a good piece off of your hide, but you're my men and nobody's gonna mess with you." So, I had very good camaraderie among the troops. Now, they had another silly deal; we needed new tires on our one truck; the way the Air Force figured it if you expended one-third of the value of the cost of the truck, it was time to junk the truck. You couldn't put any more money into it. We had that truck all shaped up and we even went so far as to buy our own spark plugs and points to make it run better; but we needed four new tires. I mean these were some slick tires. So, one night I said, "You just run around and you see if you can see another truck parked like out truck, the same model and same make." Well, behind the docks we found another truck like ours so we went out there with car jacks, jacked it up, and stole their four wheels and tires and put our four wheels and tires on there; the rubber on ours was so thin that you could look in and see what the air looked like and how dirty the air was in the tires. That's how we kept our truck for a long time. When the people saw that, w you just couldn't stop them. I had a habit now, after three months on a shift, the NCOs on a shift would rotate;

the NCOs would rotate to the day shift and the airmen would rotate to the swing shift. That way you didn't build a clique. NCOs rotates one way and the airmen rotated the other way, so you never had a clique built into there where somebody would be freeloading and not doing his share of the work. Now, I had mighty fine people there. Billy Boat showed up, coming back from Vietnam, who had been with me down at McCoy. Eddie DeSells, who had been with me at Westover and Honolulu, showed up with me. And, Dirty Bruce Reichenbach came from Midway up there with me. We had a fantastic shop in as much as eighteen of the men in the first six months we were there received commendation medals and awards from their previous service overseas. I had some other people that were fantastic; another one who won the commendation medal was Sgt. Engle, he came from Tactical Air Command. He ended up being my assistant once I went on day shift. I kept him with me all the time. He went on to leave later on and went to Holland, and after Holland he came back and went to SAC. I had another fine NCO named Victor Fisher. He was a very quiet guy but he taught me a lot. He was a Tech Sergeant. I had a habit of going and sticking my hands in a job when that job was a hard job. An illustration of that was; we had the flap packs on a C141, and they had a set of brakes in them; two sets, one on each side. Now, to change a flap pack was quite a deal when somebody had burnt out one set of the brakes. You could burn out the brakes by running the flaps down with the interconnect valve open. A hydraulic man will understand that. Your pressure drops off and your brakes on one side drag. When I found out that this would happen I would take the old flap packs as they came through, where other people would change them, steal the good brakes out of them and keep them in a packet. Now, when you had to change a flap pack to do that, you had to crank the flaps all the way down to the stop and then run them up a little bit and put a little block in there so they wouldn't go all the way down and cause tension. So, you wanted it to stop before it got all the way. You also had to disconnect the torque tubes, the asymmetry devices which would stop it automatically if one led the other, and you would have to reset them, you had to disconnect all the lines, and in general, you had to take the position transmitter out and you had to reset and readjust the metering valves. It was quite a job. I didn't like us doing that but I found that all I had to do after taking one of the flap packs apart, was that we would pull the motor off the right hand side, pull four screws out, remove the plate, take the old brakes out that were burnt up, and put a new set in, put everything back together, and operational check it properly. So, I would always go out on that job and sit there and watch them, after doing about the first ten jobs by myself, and Victor kept telling me, "T. Kaye, just leave the boys alone. They're all right. They're all right. They can do it and then we'll just go out there and operational check it and sign off the Red Cross." Well, I would just march back and forth while they were out on there because this was not the way that was sanctioned by the DEPPA, the DEPPA wanted us to take the whole thing out and send it back. We could do this job in a half hour in just our shop, but if you did it the other day we involved three or four other shops and it took about eight or ten or twelve hours. So, our way was better. Finally, one night Victor turned around and Timmy had gone out there to replace the disks and after about 20 minutes I said, "I'm going out there. I'm going out, Vic, I'm going out. Call the truck in. I'm going out." He said, "No your not." I said, "Well, I need to go out there. I need to check on Timmy." He said, "Just sit down and light up a cigarette." Finally, I sat down and lit up a cigarette and about 10 minutes later Timmy came back in and the job was all done, checked out all right, and then we went out there and signed off the Red Cross. That was really the first time that I had turned loose my people. Like I said, Victor Fisher was the one who did it and he was a wonderful technician. I had another little wonderful technician named Kermit Boyer. He was about 5 foot 6, 5 foot 7, and was a young Buck Sergeant, and he was like a sponge. He was just like me, only 20 years younger and I was trying to instill all my knowledge into this young man. He just ate up everything on that airplane and there was nothing he couldn't do. He was a young tiger. Well, we had the horizontal stabilizer in the elevator of a 141, which was 45 feet up in the air, and the elevator boost pack, with three shutoff motors, and three pressure switches, was right up on the top. The way you would have to get up there is to climb up through vertical fin, take the roof off, and take the strap and harness and put it around you and tie the harness to a special place so if you fell of it would catch you before you hit the ground. This was in the middle of the winter and the snow was out there and it was cold and when you were doing this work you had to take your parka off, and you couldn't get the safety harness on with your parka on, so he had to work out there in this 10 degree weather in just his plain fatigues and he would throw his parka over the top of himself. Well, he was absolutely a wonderful young lad so I went out to check on him and there was a crane type bucket truck next door, so I said, "Well, I'm going to save my little airman." So I got him a cup of coffee and Sgt. Engle and I took a BT400 heater and safety wired it to the bucket. Now, I'm standing in the bucket and I've got the BT400 running (now Boyer doesn't see this) and we pull up behind the aircraft, we put the stabilizing jacks down, and I go up with the bucket and the heater running and, all he knows is, all of a sudden he's got warmth flowing over his body so he comes out from underneath the parka and here he sees his leader there with the heater to keep him warm and a cup of coffee. Now, once you do something like that for your troops they're yours for life, and Kermit and I stayed friends for probably 35 years. He went on in the service, became a Master Sergeant, ended up in Alaska, got a private pilot's ticket, a commercial pilot's ticket, instrument rated, became a bush pilot, and God was not good to him; he crashed into the side of a mountain while he was quite young, and died. But he was also with me on a couple of other jobs. Our Colonel Graham, who just adored our shop and adored us; he had come off of B36's in the olden days; and he was our squadron commander and I had brought my B36 model back from Hawaii and I had it hanging up in the shop. The first time he came in there and he saw the model airplane sitting up there, 11 foot of wingspread and oil dripping from the engine bays and everything, he was just awestruck. He would come by every day just to go by and look at it and when I flew the model airplane in the back line I would call him and he would come out with Colonel Auger just to watch the airplane fly. Now, he came to us one night (now there's something I didn't put in the front – there's a red diagonal that goes in a 781A, which is your flight handbook, and that tells you that you have an existing problem but you can fly the airplane like that; we have a red cross that tells you that this has got to be fixed before it can fly; then we had what's called a circled red cross, which is an urgent action change, that had to be done to the aircraft before it would ever fly again). Now, we were sending airplanes by the tons to Vietnam carrying all of their goodies. So he came to Sgt. Engle and I one night when I think we were on the 3 to 11 shift, and he said, "Sgt. Kaye, I've got a problem. I need to have an aircraft to fly about 8 o'clock in the morning and the only aircraft we have that's in fairly good shape has got an urgent action TCTO to be pulled, which is a replacement of the old seals in the landing gear struts with the new green tweet type seals." He says, "Well, how long does that normally take?" I said, "Well, if we got aero repair tied in there, and once we get the aircraft jacked, if you can keep all the quality control people away, and all the officers and the NCOs in the hangar away, and let us do it my way and not by the book, we'll have it ready for you in the morning." So, little Kermit Boyer, Sgt. Engle and I went and got our tool boxes and we went out there and we helped them jack the airplane and we told everybody to get away. We went in there and took the scissors apart on the landing gear and did several other things on the strut that helped us not have to go through it again, and we let all the air out of the struts and all the fluid out of the struts, we dropped them both at the same time and we rolled them forward a special way and left the air in the strut leveling cylinders to help us so we wouldn't have to have more people and more machinery to do the work, pulled the old seals off, put the new green tweets on, lubed everything up so everything would slide together, pushed them back up in there and ran the gland nut back up, and tied the scissors back together, and very gently lowered the aircraft down off the jacks, and then we went ahead and serviced it in a special way. In a period of about six hours we had the aircraft ready to go. I called the Colonel at about 2 or 3 o'clock in the morning and he was just overwhelmed. Normally what would have taken about 24 or 36 hours we had done in 6 hours. But, we hadn't done it by the book. Another story about little Boyer; he had to go up and work on a pitch trim actuator one night and it was cold, must have been about 900 degrees below 0; actually it was probably down around 0. He was up working inside the vertical fin and of course, in order to climb up the vertical fin you had to strip down. So, he had changed an arming control valve and it took a cotter pin in there, so I asked him when he got done with it, I says, "Boyer, did you put the cotter pin in there?" and he says, "Yeah, Sgt. Kaye, I put the Cotter pin in there." I said, "Well, I'm going to sign it off. I'm going to trust you." So I signed it off. So we got about half way back to the shop and he said, "You know, Sgt. Kaye, I didn't have a cotter pin but I made one out of a stainless steel piece of safety wire." I went bananas and we turned around and drove back there and I got another cotter pin and made him run all the way up there and change that cotter pin. But normally he didn't do anything like that but that probably would have lasted for a hundred years.

The Colonel, anytime we went to squadron roll call, if he was up there, all he could say was, "My hydraulic shop, this. My hydraulic shop, that. My hydraulic shop, this." He really doted on us and come promotion time, out of the 70 some guys, we got about 20 promotions. In fact, I made Master at that time, Victor made Tech, and we got a couple of other Techs, a bunch of Staffs, and a bunch of Bucks. We really did well, and it was all because we had set a precedent and made everything look good. One day we had a call on a flying airplane that we had to go out and check something very quick because it was fixing to leave in about an hour and they had a bad leak back in the after section by the control valves for the doors. Eddie DeSelles was in the launch truck and he called me and he said, "T. Kaye, I've got a valve leaking. Bring me this certain size control valve that we have rat holed in our own little private stock and I'll have the old one out by the you get here." So he was removing the valve, I grabbed the valve and got in our other truck and drove on out, came flying in and there was about 2 or 3 Colonel's standing right there watching him work. Now, these were special fittings in there, they were called MS fittings; you didn't just tighten them down real tight, you took them all the way till they bottomed out, then you turned them 1/6th of a turn one flat. So, he and I were working and laughing and the people were looking at us like we were a couple of crazies, here's a Master Sergeant and a Tech Sergeant laughing and joking and carrying on and pulling wrenches so when he got it all the way in I said, "Okay, Eddie, you ready to torque them fittings? He said, "Yeah, Sgt. Kaye." So, I pulled his collar down and I said, "go ahead" and he would tense up his neck when he had it tight, and I'd say "that's okay on that one, go on to the next one." This one Colonel came over and he said, "Sgt. Kaye, what are you two doing there?" I said, "Sir, this is a very complicated job, you have to have a certain torque on these fittings and I use the muscles in his neck for a torque wrench." Well, needless to say, about three Colonels and the rest of the people around there scampered off the airplane and didn't want to have nothing to do with us.

By now, my two daughters Carla and Bianca were getting a little bigger. They were probably 5 and 3 or maybe 6 and 4 by this time and Saturday mornings we'd all get up early, go down and make them a big breakfast, then comb their hair for them, and then I'd open the back door and they'd go out and they'd play in the court with the other 100s of children that were out there. And I looked out there, and somebody had put up a tent, a beautiful tent with all external aluminum tubing bracing. It had like three bedrooms on it and a patio and the children were playing in there. I said, "Aw, that's nice. That Sergeant's out there and he did that for his children." So, they scampered on off and they went up there to play by the tent. So about two hours later I decided I'd better look out there, and the tent was down and Carla and all the children were running around and jumping up and down. I thought he must have decided to take it down because he got sick and tired of the noise. So they came back in, we had lunch, then later we had dinner, and we were sitting there watching television when I hear this knocking on the door. I went over to the door and opened the door and there were two AP's standing there and they said, "Does Carla Kaye live here?" I said, "Yeah." So I said, "Carla, come over here." Now remember, this little child's got no front teeth, she's about 7 years old, and looks like she swapped legs and ass with a sparrow and the sparrow got the worst end of the deal. So she comes up there and she's looking at these two AP's and they said, "Are you Carla Kaye?" She said, "Yes, sir." So they whipped out Article 32 and start reading Article 32 to her "You have the right to remain silent, you don't have to say anything, (like the 5th amendment)" and I said, "Whoa, Whoa, you're talking to a seven year old kid, what's going on here?" And I looked at Carla and said, "I feel something coming on, you've done something wrong today." And he said, "What happened was this guy had a tent out there and when these children were playing, and your daughter was the ringleader, they tore the tent down and the aluminum bracing for the tent they bent into macaroni sticks. It looked like macaroni when they got done and he wants $180 for the new bracing for that tent." I said, "Well, you go out there and tell that guy to take a hike. He put it out amongst 100 children. He bought that farm himself."

We had another tough job that Boyer and I were working on all the time, because we could do everything real quick if it was a flyer. It was what's called a spoiler pack in the wing, and it was about 12 inches wide and about 2 foot long and the actuators when extended made it about 4 and ½ foot long, so it was kind of hard to slip it down into the hole in the wing and get it all hooked up. What happened was there were shuttle valves built into the unit so when you took off on the ground you used just ½ of the cylinders, they were dual tandem cylinders, but when you were in flight where you had to use it for air brakes, they needed all the pressure they could get, so then you would energize the in flight control valve, which allowed fluid to go through these shuttle valves and position them and allow fluid to go to the other side of the tandem cylinder so they would have more force to put the spoilers up into the air stream and slow the aircraft down. Well, these had a bad habit of leaking. They had some very strange little thin seals in there, and after we'd changed about 5 or 6 of them, I said there had to be a different way. "We're going to find out where they are leaking from." They had little weep holes and what we did was slowly and meticulously tore the hydraulic pack apart and we found these little sleeves in the shuttle valves by shoving a piece of soft copper wire up there to find out where they were venting and to find out where the fluid was coming from. So I looked at them and said, "We can fix these on the airplane." So I ordered a bunch of seals for them so the next time they came in we had made two special aluminum rods and what you would do is you would go in and pull the cap off the end and very carefully, with a pair of pliers, pull the slide out of one side and then put this aluminum dowel through to the other side, pull the cap off of that end, and then you would knock the whole sleeve and everything out through the other side, come back in and knock the other one out, replace the seals, put everything back together, close everything up, and then you would go ahead and pressurize the ground system, and then you would go and tie down a squat switch, and then pressurize the in flight system and thereby check it out. Well, we became the heroes there because these things were rebuilt in Canada, they were a bitch to change, and we could go out there and do that in about 20 minutes in what was normally a 10 or 12-hour job. So little Kermit the Hermit and I we saved a lot of time and a lot of late aircraft. We had one hose and one fitting and two swivels that were on the down lock, unlock, line. Now the only time you could get pressure on this particular line was when the gear handle was pulled to the up position. What it did was it unlocked the down lock. It pulled a mechanical linkage over center. Well, when these damned things were leaking you would have to turn around and de-fuel the aircraft, pull it into the hangar, put it up on the jacks (which took a jacking crew and six jacks and a couple of jacks on the wing) and we would go in there and in five minutes we'd change that stupid little swivel or the hose, and then would have to open the interconnect to start up the hydraulic system, and then retract the landing gear and lower it a couple or three or four times to pressure check it, and then sign the job off that it's been done, then they would have to down jack the airplane, drag it out, refuel it, get it ready for the flight, and I kept looking at that and saying, "There's got to be a better way to do that." So I was looking at the down lock mechanism on the landing gear itself, on the main landing gear, and I figured that I could take and cut an aluminum block that was about 2 inches square, cut a groove down it, drill a couple of holes going across it, and I could put this in around this cylinder and trap it in there with the two pins, and then we could put the landing gear handle up, so momentarily you would put pressure on that down-lock, unlock line. So, I went and I did this a couple of times with the aircraft on the jacks. So then I went and got Colonel Graham one night and I showed him what I wanted to do, and then, when the aircraft came back down on the ground we left the jacks in place, and I went ahead and did the same thing with my blocks in place and I said, " Well, you see how we can do this? We can save all these retraction tests." He was enthused so I wrote it up as a change and I sent it to Lockheed and I got a Golden Screwdriver Award from that.

Well, I had submitted the paperwork in but we had a guy named Sergeant Sexton in the shop, I think he's passed away now God Bless him, but there was a tremendous amount of documentation that had to go along with it and he turned around and did all the documentation and looked up everything that went along with it so when it came time for me to get the award the Colonel 's got me up there in front of all the troops in the squadron and he's says "I want to give you this award, Sgt. Kaye" so I said

"Well Sir, I thought of the idea and I filled out the paperwork but I'd like to have Sgt. Sexton up here with me while I receive this check because he was the one who did all the analysis and everything else for it, and he deserves even more credit than I did." So, I held the whole thing up, the Wing Commander's Call, as Sgt. Sexton came on up there and I received that award and the check and then we shook hands with the Colonel and then I went and cashed the check and I gave Sexton $200 of the $1,400 that I got. I was a pretty nice guy.

As I told you previously, my boy Dirty Bruce had come in from Midway Island and he was stationed with me now. Dirty Bruce had five children and he was a young Staff Sergeant, and he says "T. Kaye" he says "I don't know how I'm going to get through, it's just too hard being in the service," he says "I'm coming up on discharge and I have a chance to go work for the Royal Saudi Air Force on C130s, which we're familiar with. So," he says, "I'm going to get out." I said "Well look, before you get out completely, you go and see about joining the Reserves and see if you can't make your Reserve meetings in Germany once a month and get the Saudis to let you fly back on the flights into Weisbaden". Well, he did get into the Reserves and when he got over there he informed the Saudis that he had to make a monthly deal for one weekend up in Germany because he was a member of the Reserves. They figured they were making money because he would stay proficient in everything that's going on. Well, he went over there for, I think, two years and he came back and he hadn't really saved any money. They had got along and had lived good but he hadn't saved any money so now he was looking for a job and I had a friend, a chicken colonel and a general who was in one of my special operations that I had teaching them about 141s so I called them up and said "he'd been flying on a 130 as a Flight Engineer. Can't you see about getting him into the active Reserves over here?" So, what they did is they got him in the McGuire Air Force Base active Reserves but they didn't have 130s, they had 141s, so they sent him to C141 school to become a Flight Engineer on 141s. Well, needless to say he came out top of the class and went on to fly with them. He became the Stand Board inspector for C141s and he was then transferred into C5s out of Altus, Oklahoma. He got proficient on them and became the Stand Board inspector on them. Now it was time for him to either do it or get off the pot so he had to join the regulars. Now, he was a MSgt in the Reserves but when he went to join the regulars they wouldn't let him back in as a Flight Engineer or as a MSgt so he lost his rank down to a Staff Sergeant and went into the SR71 outfit. He stayed with Blackbirds for about 2 or 3 years and then he came back to C5s, upgraded again to Stand Board, and then he was the first Flight Engineer on the KC10s and the first Stand Board on the KC10s. He retired and all during this time he became a private pilot single engine, instrument rated, commercially rated, multiengine rated, and he became rated as a Flight Engineer on many aircraft. So he got to fly as a Flight Engineer on Northwest Airlines and then he upgraded to a copilots position, and then he left Northwest and went and flew for the DOD (Department of Defense) flying on a DC8, a special DC8 that was playing the part of an intruder on the fleet and while he was there he upgraded from a copilot to a pilot and ended up being a pilot on a DC8. He also came on back after about 2 or 3 years with them, and went to work for another airline, which I believe was American, and he became proficient in DC9s, he became proficient in a 707, 727, 737, 747, 757, and 767, also DC10s and MD11s. He covered everything. He was so good that they wanted him to become a teacher out there in Dallas and they wanted him to work the DC9 and the MD80 flight simulator. So while he was out there working, of course we stayed in contact and we saw each other as the years went by, one day Bruce had a heart attack and as he fell to the floor his wife called 911, and him being a good old grumpy sergeant, he said just put me in a car and take me downtown and they said well we've got the ambulance coming and he said "I ain't dying in no damn ambulance on the way to the hospital, just put me in the car and drive me on down to the hospital." So she put him in the car and drove him to the hospital and he sat in line till they finally got to him and then they put him in the hospital but by this time his heart was wrecked. It was gone. He had fantastic insurance with American Airlines so what they did was they flew a plastic heart which worked by an air compressor and put that inside his chest cavity for about 3, 4 or 5 months until they could find a heart big enough for him. He was about 5'9" but he had a big structure and he had to have a pretty big heart so he laid in the hospital with that thing going kachug, kachug, kachug kachug for months on end, and when one of them wore out they had to fly another one in, and as it just so happened a young, ex marine was driving an ambulance and he got killed and he came up for his heart and it just happened to be the right size, so they put that marine's heart inside of him and it works good, lasts a long time, but just don't mess with it. So the last time I saw him, which was probably about a year ago, I asked "So how's that heart working?" He said, "Well, it's working fine T. Kaye except that three times a day I run up to the wall and smack my head against the wall and say 'Semper Fi, Semper Fi, Semper Fi' for the Marine Corps but I guess that goes with the heart."

Now, I was always great in instilling pride in my shops and in my men in my workforce and in my shop on the one wall I had a picture of every airplane that was in the Air Force at the time, and then I had the history of the 438th Military Airlift Transport Command Wing where it was started of in World War II flying C47's for Dday. I made sure that the people knew all about that kind of history and then I had the history of all the Generals that we had and that we had to work for, and then the history of McGuire Air Force Base. McGuire Air Force Base was named after Thomas Buchanan McGuire, who was a Major in World War II and he had shot down 38 Japanese airplanes. He was two underneath Richard Ira Bong. He had inadvertently gotten killed; he was exhausted; he'd been out there fighting for 3 years from the beginning and Bong just came in there and rode the gravy train and got more than he did but Tommy McGuire, had come in as a Lieutenant in the South Pacific, had malaria God knows how many times, and dinky fever and everything that went with it, he was a tough guy but was depleted in strength and he inadvertently got killed, but his top number was 38 and McGuire Air Force Base was named after him. I would stop airmen on the base and ask them who McGuire was named after and nobody knew. Of course, I would berate them severely and say, "Obviously you're not in my shop. You come by my shop and you can read his history on my wall". We were also having a little problem with the other people from morale in the wing. Now, my people we didn't have any problem with. I had them all psyched up and they were working well. But the rest of the wing, to them, the C141 was not an airplane, it was just a tin shed that appeared, and you had to work your heart out on it for about 3 days, get everything fixed, and then it would disappear for 7 to 10 days while it went to Vietnam and came back. They had no concept of what the mission was. Well, what happened one night is we were having what's called a dining in and an Order of the Sword. It's a formal dinner for a Colonel who is leaving, and they give him a big engraved sword engraved. I believe it was Colonel Goings who was leaving, and of course, we had a One Star General, General Herring, who was in charge of our wing, since we had such a giant wing, we had 80 C141s and then we had the 21st Air Force Commander, General Brandon, who was in charge of the 21st Air Force, they were going to be there. This was going to be a big deal. So, anyhow, we also had a big program on the base, and everywhere you could paint PRIDE you would paint PRIDE on it, which stood for Professional Results In Daily Effort. And they thought that that would help instill pride into the people. Well, after the dinner, we were drinking drinks and I had about 4 or 5 drinks in me and I was feeling pretty good and one of the guys said "Sgt Kaye, why don't you go over there and trap General Herring and General Brandon in the corner and give them a moral of leadership lecture on Pride." I said, "I just think I will do that." So they were in the back so I walk up to them and threw a salute and I says "I'm MSgt. Thomas Kaye, the best hydraulic man in SAC, MAC and TAC," and I said "I'd like to talk to you gentlemen about PRIDE". And they looked and said "Well, we've got to humor this old drunken sergeant." So I said, "Well Sirs, I'm quite upset emotionally because people here have very little pride in their work and the first reason is, they don't understand who the base is named after." They looked at each other, and I said, "It's named after Thomas Buchanan McGuire, the second greatest fighter pilot in World War II who shot down 38 Japanese airplanes and who was killed trying to save the life of his wingman. He was a wonderful guy and yet none of these airmen know the story of him and I know the historical section could make up a movie of him and it could be shown to the people. Now, there's another movie out called MAC AND IT'S MANY MISSIONS," and I said "it covers the airlift, air/sea rescue, it covers transportation, it covers everything, and we need to show this to the people because what they really think is that this is an aluminum shed that disappears for 10 or 12 days and comes back and they have to work like a dog on it, and then it will leave again. They have no concept of where it's going. What they need to do is take one man off the ground crew on each flight, and carry them as flight crew and take them all the way to Vietnam and back. That would also give him one month where he wouldn't have to pay income tax because if he flies in country he's eased up from having to pay income taxes for that month. That would be a great motivational factor for the troops." I went on and on and on and on and finally I said, "Well, thank you very much sirs. Sorry to have taken your time." And I saluted them and I left and I looked back over my shoulder and I saw the two of them talking together. Well, the next morning I had to go to 21st Air Force Safety to talk to this Colonel who had been my Colonel out on Midway Island; he was in charge of Safety; about these inadvertently burning out their brakes on the flap packs by not using the interconnect valve and the flap shutoff valve properly. As I went into the Colonel's office I eyeballed him and my eyeballs were laying on the cheeks, and I looked in pretty bad shape cause I'd gotten pretty drunk. He said, "Well, Sgt. Kaye, did you make that Dining In last night?" I said "Yup." He said, "Well, what sort of mischief have you been into lately?" I say, "Well, I gave General Herring and General Brandon a moral of leadership lecture about Pride last night." And he smacked his hand on the desk and he said, "I'll be damned, I should have known it was you." I said "Well, what happened, sir? What are you talking about, sir?" He said that when he came back last night he had everybody in maintenance and every chicken colonel on the base up at 7:00 AM in the base theatre and he was going to give them a moral of leadership lecture. So he went up there and called them all in there and he told them he had had a moral of leadership lecture from an old sergeant last night about Pride. And he covered everything that I said and he said that when people check into the base, for one week, the families and them will go to an orientation; they will see movies about Thomas Buchanan McGuire, they will know who he was, they will know his history, they will see this movie MAC AND ITS MANY MISSIONS, and they will go on a tour to see all of the shops and see what is done and they will be taken out in a bus and watch an aircraft leave for Vietnam. So everything that I had told them came into play so I felt very good because you can make a change. Another thing that I did while I was there; when you change a hydraulic pump on the aircraft the intake line, the inlet line had a big giant fitting, about a size 20 or 24 fitting which is about a 2" fitting. Now, you've got this pump out on the deck by the airplane and you're trying to get this big fitting out so you can change it over and put it into the new pump that you are putting on. Well, after having to do that just one time I says "When we overhaul these pumps in the shop, and we send them back, we will send them back with the fittings already in there, so that when the guy goes out to change the pump he will merely have to remove the pressure line, the case drain line, the supply line, and the vent line and four bolts, take the old pump out, put the new pump in, and the engine driven pump change will be cut down to about eight or ten minutes". And of course this happened one time on a launch and the pump was changed in about 8 minutes and the Colonel was amazed and he wanted to know what happened so the guys told him that Sgt. Kaye was putting the fittings in the pumps when they were coming out of overhaul. And, of course, Supply got in on this and Supply said, "You can't do that because you're using up our fittings and you'll deplete our supply of fittings". I said, "Well, how many pumps do you have in there?" He says "20" and I said "Well, I don't think the Air Force is going to go broke for 20, now do you want to go see the Colonel with me and tell him that you don't want to do it my way." Needless to say they chicken-shitted out. Normally every year we had what was called "Project Reforger" where we would go to some fighter base with F-4s and we would move everybody on the base lock, stock and barrel and all the aircraft in flyaway kits to Germany in a matter of about 90 flights. So, we would do this in 10 days. We would move one fighter wing from Texas to Spangdollum, Germany and the existing fighter wing would be ready to go back, and as the aircraft went back we would take them back to their base and drop them off and cycle back through and bring more back over there. So, it was going to be a 30 deal so I turned around and said "Well, I'm gonna go". I put myself on that TDY. I said "This will be my last big TDY and then I'll take a ten day leave in London coming back to see the big L one more time. I figured it was getting close to the end of the hunt; it was almost 20 years in the service. I said, "It's about time." So we went over there and we were in Spangdollum, we had no late takeoffs; we had no problems over there at all. Everything we did just went perfect. We had one hard job where we had to change a pitch trim actuator up on top of the T-tail but we got that done in a minimum amount of time. So I jumped on the last airplane that was going to Mildenhall, England and I flew with it to Mildenhall, England. I got off there and got on the road with my uniform and my B4 bag and I hitchhiked into London and went to the Douglas House and got a room for the night, rested up, and then I went out and started partying in the old places. I met a few of the old girls, Margo and Murial were still hanging around. Of course it had been about 10 or 11 years, but the same clubs were there. I ran into Lolita, the Spanish girl I had been with before and she was working in another club up by the 55 Club. I ended up meeting two ladies, one Indian and one English girl so I spent the night with the little Indian girl one time. She was from Bombay. Cause after she got off work we went downtown to the Golden Star and had breakfast, and then we went out to an after hours club called Paul's up in Soho and crawled underneath this big desk and through a hole in the wall to the club behind there. After that we went back to her flat, made the beast with two backs for the rest of the night and then the next morning I got up and I left and I went on down to the Douglas House, took a shower and shaved and cleaned up and laid down and went to sleep until about 7 or 8 o'clock, and then I went out and went drinking and dancing and screaming and hollering and carrying on again. I met a beautiful little English girl, stayed with her for about 3 or 4 nights and made out like I was a young lad again. It really makes one feel pretty good when you're 39 years old and can still do things like that. When we came on back from that we had a big, what was called and ORI. If you look it up in the front of the book it's the same thing as in the Strategic Air Command, where the General sends a team in there and they check everything that goes on in the Wing, and they check the Supply Systems, and they check your Maintenance Systems, and they check that you are doing the maintenance correctly and that your scheduling boards are done right and everything. Well, being as how they didn't want me around in the daytime because I have a tendency to mouth off too much, the inspectors put me on the swing shift as a Master Sergeant running the swing shift because, by rights, it should be a Master running each sift. So, while I was running it Sgt. Ingle was with me again as my assistant and Boyer was on the shift with me. Well, we had a lot of work and all the troops were out on the line and Sgt. Ingle was going crazy out there running around from one to another with getting parts for them and taking them parts and getting them coffee and everything, and our other truck was launching and I think Timmy was in there driving the launch truck and taking care of that. I was sitting in the shop, keeping everything on the board right, and I had little Boyer there, in case we had an extra hot job that had to have the best man. Kermit Boyer was an excellent airman that I had the privilege of mentoring for a couple of years. He soaked up knowledge about these aircraft just like a sponge. Well, I was filling out the paperwork and I looked, and Boyer had been sitting back on the picnic table reading some books, so I turned around and I said "now don't you go nowhere," I says, "cause if the inspectors come in here they're going to want to know where everybody is at, and I can say where everybody is at and that you are sitting over there." So, I went back to my paperwork and I looked up in about 10 minutes and he was gone. So, I stuck my head out the door and I hollered one time with my 1st Sergeants voice and I could here this call coming where he was over there talking to some people with an aircraft on jacks. So I brought him back and I said "now you stay over there, and you read these TO's." So about 15 minutes went by and I looked and there he was, gone again. So I went out into the hanger and I hollered for him one time and here he was up on the third tier, which is a blockhouse within the hanger, and I said "Get back on down here, Boyer." So he came on back down and I brought him back into the shop, I sat him down there and I took safety wire, and I safety wired his left foot to the bench so he couldn't leave. He said "how are you going to explain that to the Colonels if they come in and they see me safety wired." I said, "I'll just tell them how hard you are to keep up with." Needless to say, they didn't come in and bother us, but I got my point across.

CHAPTER 11
ATC, MCGUIRE

Now, I was in the twilight of my military career and I had all this knowledge and I say, "Well, what I'd like to do is go to Air Training Command and teach 141's and 130's on the base." So I went up there to see them and the guy that was currently teaching was about to retire so I told them that I would like to volunteer. So they said, "we'll submit this paperwork and you'll be transferred to the field training detachment here and then we'll send you off to Instructor's School in Shepherdfield, Texas and then you'll come back and you can fall right into the slot." So I said, "okay." So, I filled out all the paperwork and everything went through and I came back up and as I checked in they said that the other instructor had already gotten sick and he would be in the hospital for about a month, so I would have to teach the 130's. I said, "Well, I haven't been to school" so he said "well, you already know the 130's, right;" he says, "well, here's a lesson plan and here's how you do it." So I jumped in there cold and taught the C130 for about a month, and really got into the swing of things and really got to really love teaching. So then it was time for us to go to Shepherdfield, Texas to go to instructor school. So, we flew on out there to Texas and was bunking with this other Master Sergeant and we were going through the school together and we would go up to the NCO Club in the evenings and have a couple of drinks and a couple of dances and come on back to the barracks. Well, as things would progress one night, we got pretty drunk and we bumped into a few ladies and I swear to this day the one I had was a beautiful blond, she had a brown sweater on, and a brown skirt, and nice stockings, and she had gold loafers on too, and the other girl was dressed pretty nice too, and this girl could dance. So, we were there drinking and dancing and hollering and carrying on and having a good time until the club closed, so, as the club closed I said, "well, I hate to put an end to the good night but everything is closing up." She says, "Well, no, we don't have to stop, there's a place in Lawton, Oklahoma. They call Lawton, Oklahoma 'Sin City'; it stays open till 7 in the morning and then they shut the bar down and swamp it out, clean it out, and open up again at 7:30. They only have a half an hour for cleanup." I said, "Well, we don't have any cars." They said, "Well, we've got the cars." So, we jumped into this one Chevy and we flipped coins and the other guy, who was my roomie, he was going to drive up there and he was going to have that girl in the front seat, and I'd be in the back seat with the little blond. So I was in the back seat, and we were fooling around, and locking tongues and swabbing tonsils and just having a good time like a couple of teenagers, and I was trying to have her sit on it and she wouldn't do it because her girlfriend was in the car with her and because we were in the car going down the road. So, anyhow, we got to Lawton, Oklahoma, which was about 90 miles away and we went in there and we partied till dawn, till light was coming up. So at 7:00 they turned around and said we'd have to leave because they had to clean up and swab it out. I said "okay" cause we were about out of money anyhow. So, we jumped into the car and he was going to get into the back seat with his girl and I was going to be sitting up front with my girlfriend. As we're driving down the road and we're taking our time, the sun is coming up, and I'm looking up at this young tender blond that I'd been dancing with all night and swapping spit and locking tongues swabbing tonsils and I look and I see gray in her hair. And then I drive another 5 minutes and I look and I see more gray in her hair and I look at her face and I see wrinkles there. I drive for another half hour and I see her hair is all gray and, them ain't wrinkles in her face, them's crevasses; big giant crevasses!! I said, "Lord, have mercy, this woman was a wine waitress at the Last Supper." Booze made her look good, and if you've ever seen that cartoon with a picture of a girl where she looks beautiful with 8 drinks in you, and then you turn it upside down and it shows you what she looks like when you're sober, that is the truth, that is what happened to me!! And when we got back to the base, we got on the base and I didn't want them to know where we were living at so I drove us over into the students area and we got out over there and he said, "Well, we don't live right here, T. Kaye," and I said, "just cool it, just cool it." So, we kissed them goodbye and told them we'd see them at the Club that night, and they're probably still waiting for us to show back up again. Then we took off and went into the barracks and I explained to him that I didn't want them coming by our barracks there trying to get us, or knowing who the hell we were, because again we had used Chuck Jones and Paul West for our names instead of telling them our true names. We went scampering back to the barracks laughing like a couple of teenage corporals coming back from an all night stand somewhere; but we had a good time. Well, needless to say we didn't go back to the club for about a week or two, and when we went back again we saw them one night and they wouldn't even talk to us. When we finished up the school, it was the first time I did not come in first place in a military school that I had attended. I had a big argument with a guy in about the seventh week about teaching and I had aced all the tests in all the other weeks but he gave me a "C" minus which brought me down so I wasn't at the top of the class. Anyhow, we went back to McGuire and I started teaching the C141, and I really loved my teaching. I taught the people the proper way. I told them, "I'll not teach you to test; I'll give you workbooks. You do the workbooks and you take notes and you learn how to use these TO's. You can use the TO's during the tests, but I will not teach you the test, I will not stomp my foot like some instructors do when you come to a question, and probably 10 or 15 percent of you are going to fail because you think it is just a piece-of-cake course. And I actually had about a 20 percent failure rate and I was very disheartened in as much as most of the guys that went to school went to school to get out of the cold in the winter and get out of the heat in the summer. This really upsets you emotionally. So I taught for about a year and all my boys were still down at the line so I went and I saw Sgt. DeCelles and I told Eddie, I said, "Look Eddie, I'm going to retire in another six or eight months. How about coming up here and replacing me?" And he says, " Okay." So we put it in there and we got him up there as my replacement.

Seeing I was in the twilight of my carrier, I was bound and determined to replace myself with another person who ate, slept and breathed the Lockheed C141A aircraft. I knew that removing him from the Flight Line would hurt the 438th hydraulic shop, but I thought he could teach the people the tricks of the trade better in a classroom with 7 million dollars of trainers.

I decided on T/Sgt. Edouard DeCelles, who I had mentioned since he came to me as an Airman 3rd class at Westover. I managed to get him off to Instructor school and as he returned he took over teaching. I was also NCOIC of the school so it eased my burden, and I could devote my time to insuring the classes, manning, scheduling, and all other problems were taken care of.

We would periodically be called out on problems that couldn't be solved by the shop personnel. First let me describe the epennage (tail) of the C141 – the vertical fin and rudder stuck straight up and on top was the horizontal stabilizer and elevator. The elevator was 45' above the ground. It was operated by 3 hydraulic cylinders (sys 1, 2, 3 in emerg.) when pulling the yoke (steering wheel) back it would cause the elevator to go up 25° above neutral. Pushing it forward would cause the elevator to go down 15° below neutral. To prevent over-controlling at great speeds, a spring was attached in the mechanism. This was called a Q-spring. The pivot point would be adjusted by the central air data computer (CADC) so that at slow speed it took 51-lbs. of force to pull it all the way back. At mid Q (305 knots), it was 68-lbs of force and at Max Q it was 100-lbs.

Now, to work on this equipment a large stand (60' tall) would be moved into place. It had a walkway extending forward over the hydraulic pack and one underneath the stabilizer, so with removal of panels you could see and work on the Q-spring, linkage and electric motor that repositioned the Q-spring by signal from the CADC.

We were called in because the shops had been working for two days and found that, when pulling back, everything was normal, until 15° up movement, when everything would stop moving. We went down to the hangar and checked it out. Sure enough, it wouldn't come back for full travel. Eddie went and climbed to the top of the stand to observe the hydraulic pack etc. and had me operate the yoke with fish spring scale, checking force needed to move it. Yes, there was a problem. Suddenly Eddie started laughing. He found the problem. The aircraft was empty of fuel so it was sitting high on the struts. This brought the elevator too close to the stand. Therefore, the elevator was hitting the stand, limiting the movement. We met at the rear and carefully moved the stand back a foot or so. This gave the elevator clearance and everything was fine. We were the heroes for a while.

When we started teaching, we told them to keep adequate clearance and told how the shops had screwed up. Aero repair was quite upset. We were persona non grata for a while as we made them look bad.

One last story and this will be the end of the book. Now, if the book sells good, or it sells enough to pay for the printing of the book, I will come back with another one and tell you about the next 20 years of my life working as a civilian; I worked for Fairchild-Hiller, I worked for Grummond, I worked for the Port Authority, I worked for the ship yard, and Consolidated Rigging and I had another wonderful, exciting 20 years. This one last story is about a little young airman named Hart. I always was a stickler for haircuts. This was when they started having Afros and when they started having sideburns. Well, I wouldn't tolerate any of that because I was the NCOIC of the detachment and when you come there, I give you a half hour lecture in the morning of the first day and I say, "You will have shined boots, shined shoes (there's a shoebox over there for you to do it), you will have pressed pants, and your hair will be cut like AFR35-10 (I believe it was 35-10). Now, if your hair is not cut right I will take you up there and get it cut for you. Mind you, if I have to pay $1.10 for your haircut, I'm going to get ten pounds worth of hair." And I said as I was walking amongst them, "Now, the good fairy if passing amongst you with the magic wand," which was my pointer, and I says, "If the good fairy's magic wand touches your shoulder that means you need a haircut and you'd better have one by tomorrow." So, I told about five or six of them to get a haircut. One of them was this kid named Airman Hart, a good-looking young corporal. The next morning I went there and I looked and Hart had gone up there and he sat in the chair and told them to give him a trim. The rest of them had good haircuts. So, I went over to him and I said, "Hart, go get in that Studebaker out there, we're going to get you a haircut." He said, "Well, I got a haircut, Sgt. Kaye." I said, "Don't argue with me, you got a trim, you did not get a haircut." He said, "I ain't going." I said, "you had better get in there. I am giving you a lawful order to get in that car. I am going to take you up there and buy you a haircut." I said, "If you don't get in that car you may rest assured that I am going to court martial you and I will have you over in Ft. Dix in the brig over there for 30 days, now get in the car." So we got in the car. We went up there to the PX and I marched him right up to the front of the line and I told them, "Now, you cut this guys hair just like that picture shows over there." So he sat in the seat and he started to get out of the seat and he says, "I want to go see my supervisor." I said, "You sit in that seat. If you get out of there I have 15 witnesses that you are violating a lawful order and I will put you in the crossbar hotel." So, he got his haircut and I paid the $1.15, I took him back and he went through class and he did very good in the class, but he was always mumbling when he went by me. So I said, "Well, that's just part of the game."

So, after I had retired and had gotten married again; of course, as any good sergeant would do I brought my new young wife up to show her where I had been before and where my airplanes were, and what was happening. She was a lovely looking blonde girl, and she was in a pair of red shorts with a red and white striped blouse and white sandals. I can remember it to this day. We were climbing around the airplanes and everybody's trying to look up her shorts and as we were coming out this young Staff Sergeant came up to me with a spit-shined hat bill and spit-shined shoes and he looked immaculate. He says, "Sgt. Kaye, Sgt. Kaye" and I says, "Yesss?" and he said, "I'd like to talk to you for a minute." I said, "Sure." I said, "What's up?" He says, "Well, do you remember me?" I said, "No. I don't remember you, son." He said, "Well, I'm Sgt. Hart." I said, "Oh, son, there's been a lot of water under the bridge, I don't remember you." He said, "I'm that young airman that you took up and got a haircut back when you were an instructor on the C141s." I said, "Oh, I remember. I remember. Boy, you look fine, young sergeant." He said, "Well, I'm a lifer now. You got me on the right track and I reenlisted and I'm on my way to Greece now for a three year tour and I wanted to thank you for changing my life and giving my life some direction." It was a wonderful way to finish up the twenty years in the service.

This is about SMS Bruce Reichenbach (USAF, Ret), who as a civilian acquired a Private, Multi. Engine (4), commercial license allowing him to fly just about every US plane built. He also worked for the DOD with the USN on a one of a kind DC8. He was the only USAF enlisted person who was upgraded from Flight Engineer to Pilot by the US Navy.

Below is a story that took place while waiting for another mission while in Puerto Rico. The aircraft was a special test plane to evade radar and using ECM to simulate an attack by unfriendly forces.

Author

Story as follows:

This is the last vignette, as the book is now finished. It's about my lifetime friend, SMS Bruce Reichenbach, on one of his trips as a Flight Engineer. They had flown to Puerto Rico and it was a place to party, because they had a 24-hour layover. They went into town and had gotten pretty well boozed up. Now they were in their rented van coming back. Louie was driving and Larry was copilot and navigator. The rest were in the van (which seats seven). The following story takes place on the way back.

After eating gigantic meals and quaffing enormous quantities of the nectar of the Gods, we board the mini bus for the journey back to the hotel. Louie was driving and Larry was riding shotgun as copilot and navigator. The rest were in the van, which seated seven, and they decided to stop at Burger King for a late snack. Bruce had about 2-dozen chicken nuggets with that sweet and sour sauce (we could smell that stuff for months, for some reason), and a half-gallon of Coke. The nuggets got mostly eaten, and the sauce got mostly stomped into the carpet, and all the Coke joined an already ample amount of brew in Brucie's tum-tum. We were screaming down Highway One enroute to the Mafia Manor (remember that place). Louie was disregarding red traffic lights, as is the custom in Puerto Rico after 2200. Brucie says, kinda low, "I gotta take a piss…" Louie ignores him, really bent over the wheel, switching lanes back & forth, shakin us in the back two seats up pretty good; Larry's remembering how much beer Louie's had and he's not feelin warm & fuzzy about ninety, and Bruce says a little louder, "I gotta piss…" and Louie drives faster. So, Bruce announces to the whole van in a voice no one can ignore, "I GOTTA TAKE A PISS!" and everybody laughs and continues on with what they're doing until Bruce stands up in the van and opens the side door. Now, we're going lickety-split down this four lane "highway", with some of the usual late-night unlit (well, some of them probably ARE lit, but not reflective) foot and horse and bicycle traffic along the edges of and occasionally veering into the roadway, and Bruce unzips and takes a piss. Larry looks back in absolute horror at Bruce sort of steadying himself with one hand on the doorframe draining his lizard mostly outside the van, and says "Good lord, Louie, don't swerve, Bruce is in the door!" About that time I notice a rather fine mist coming into the back seat of the van with the rush of air from the open door, and tell Brucie, not in a mean way but just by way of an announcement, "Hey Bruce, we're getting wet back here…". He looks back and explains the phenomenon to us with his usual flight engineer brevity: "Aerodynamics". Well, the story gets better with retelling of course, and I've embellished it over the years with the detail that some of the bike riders and walkers along the road put their hands out and looked up for rain clouds after we passed; dunno whether that's true or not, but you can imagine the possibilities of sudden evening showers in rainy Puerto Rico.

It all turned out all right. I thing Bruce was asleep before we got to the hotel…he just needed to take a piss.

This is the ending of the book. I hope there will be a volume II to follow from my life as a civilian because I did go on and worked for Fairchild-Hiller, and built T28s for the Royal Laotian Air Force. I worked for the Port Authority. I worked with Consolidated Rigging; and I worked for Grummond building A4M Skyhawks for the Royal Malaysian Air Force and lord knows, I had many, many adventures as a feather merchant. A feather merchant is another name, a good old GI name from back in my day, for a civilian who is working and doing duty for the military. Now, the reason that that name was hung upon the civilians was, during the time when Alexander the Great was marching all over the world conquering the known world, they had farmers following the armies for logistics for food with ducks and chickens. And what they would do when the ducks or chickens wouldn't produce eggs, they would kill them and of course, sell the meat to the supply men of Alexander the Great and the feathers were taken out and pillows were made from them for the men so they could rest their weary heads as they were on their march. Hence, anybody who follows the military and lives off the military is then known to be a feather merchant. Now, my address will be in the front of the book. If you enjoyed this book and you want me to go ahead and write the second volume for the next twenty-some years, in which I had even more exciting things happen to me than you read in these, the adventures I was in for the following twenty years, most of them were death-defying deals that I got myself into on the docks. I worked on the docks for almost 20 years, besides working for Fairchild-Hiller and Grummond. During my time with Fairchild-Hiller I fought the unions as they were trying to slow the project down to make it go longer. I got in a big lot of trouble with that. But, if you are interested, just drop me a line or a card saying, "Go ahead and write the second volume, T. Kaye."

LETTER FROM ONE OF TK'S TROOPS

I first met TK when I arrived at Midway Island in 1966 on Northwest Airline DC-6. (I never realized then I would one day instruct and fly for NWA). He was the sharpest one there and stood out. It was obvious he came out of SAC. In fact, this was the first assignment to MAC for both of us.

Working with TK, I soon discovered he had traits a soldier admires. True to the many professional enlisted men, he never acquired the high recognition he deserved, but the people working with him or for him will never forget he is the best SAC, MAC, and TAC ever had.

At Midway we were a support squadron, which means we did everything that was not in our usual job description. TK had been in the Navy in his younger days and I soon learned the Navy training is better-rounded and more intense.

Many years later, flying for the Navy, I learned the Navy term TACMO (take charge and move them out). TK was the right NCO for the time. He soon had us under his arm learning and doing everything. What impressed me were his common sense, know-how and the fact that he never sugarcoated anything. If you were a hockey-puck, look out, and heaven forbid if your appearance was lacking.

It was on Midway I was inspired by TK with the knowledge allowing me to make MSgt in eight years, learn all I could and always do the right thing. I never forgot the word can't is an unknown word to TK and pity the fool looking for sympathy, as he was happy to refer you to the dictionary and said it was somewhere between SHIT and SYPHILIS. TK loved airplanes and you better treat them with respect. He always took care of his people.

186

TK's military career was short circuited due to family needs, but before he retired I had the privilege to attend his class on the C-141 when I was a Flight Engineer. I still employ the principles today that I learned from a great Air Force hero and Patriot.

Bruce Reichenbach

I thought this might show you what well-rounded training in other career fields will do for you. Bruce clearly saved this plane and crew – Alaska's waters are very cold.

This is to record the averted ditching of a C5 after two missed approaches to Shemya, Alaska on June 28, 1980.

We were a basic crew with me, J. Waldron and B. Reichenbach as the Flight Engineers. We had a discussion with the Aircraft Commander concerning the fuel load he wanted to fly to this distant island and Bruce tried explaining his experience with the weather there, but the Colonel said his mind was made up. Bruce said, "Colonel, Sir, you're not thinking straight with your head in your ass."

The flight enroute was quiet and after the first missed approach Bruce advised we should head back, but the Aircraft Commander elected to fly another approach. After the second miss we headed back, but the slats decoupled when the flaps were retracted. Bruce and I independently checked the performance charts and determined there was insufficient fuel to reach Anchorage.

Radio calls were initiated but the nearest air sea rescue units were many hours away and we quickly calculated we would run out of fuel before they arrived. Bruce advised we could recouple the slats, but the AC said this was forbidden in flight. Bruce felt the emergency in progress warranted ignoring the manual.

Once the slats decouple the brakes fire and even if they are recoupled they will not work without releasing the brakes.

I wasn't sure how to do this maintenance function. Bruce is a recognized expert and can read and draw everything. He regularly has maintenance folks requesting training from him and he has amazing troubleshooting skills. I saw him troubleshoot problems in the gear, ramp and door systems the maintenance folks couldn't fix, using two paper clips.

He showed me which circuit breakers to open. He told the AC he was going to the troop compartment to inspect the flap drive and slat decoupler. The AC said, "DO NOT recouple the slats". Bruce said, "Yes, sir", winked at me, took his ford wrench and headed aft. He was on interphone but I didn't see what he was doing.

He told me later he inspected the drive system, and then asked for the flaps to be extended. This was the cue for me to open the brake circuit breakers. He re-coupled the slats and screwed the decouple nut all the way in so they could not de-couple, reset the switches in the rear, and called for flaps up. Total retraction was completed. When he came forward the AC didn't say anything.

I talked to him for quite a while and hinted to the AC about recognition and to Bruce because I thought he should get the DFC. He thought the AC would be too embarrassed to make an official report, and Bruce never said any more about it.

One last vignette from 1953. Sorry about that, but I just remembered this. One Saturday night I was riding down Main St. between 8th & 5th St. I, with my fantastic eyesight, perceived a good looking chick walking down the street. I never forget them; what they looked like, what they wore or what they were wearing. She was about 5'6", wearing loafers, white socks, maroon plaid pants and a white sweater. I swooped over and started talking. I got her on the bike and went to a 5th & Main coffee shop and we talked for a while. I said, "Let's go for a ride to St. Augustine and get coffee and come back. We had a nice ride down and back and I took her home. She lived on Silver St. When we got there we kissed and fooled around for a while and she invited me up. After we had indulged a couple times she told me she was married to a truck driver, but not to worry, he wouldn't be back until the next day. Needless to say I evacuated the area promptly. We used to see each other occasionally but I never endangered my body again.

Printed in the United States
By Bookmasters